Underground Urbanism
Elizabeth Reynolds

Have you ever wondered what lies beneath the streets of your city? Do you picture, in isolation, a series of train tunnels and pipes? Or perhaps the foundations of tall buildings that lie scattered, like icebergs, beneath the surface? As our cities grow up, out and down, it is time we better understood how the different layers of these complex urban environments relate to one another. Underground Urbanism seeks to provide a new perspective on our cities, and consider how this might be used to engage more positively with them. So, tip your cities upside down to have a closer look, and let us rethink them from (below) the ground, up.

Author Biography
Elizabeth Reynolds is a Chartered Urban Planner and Director of Urben, an east London studio focused on planning, design and problem solving for urban environments. Over the past 20 years Elizabeth has worked in multidisciplinary teams on major infrastructure and regeneration projects including the Queen Elizabeth Olympic Park and Crossrail. Urben works from macro scale strategic city plans to detailed street design, with a common theme of making cities creative, productive and resilient places. She is a co-founder of Think Deep UK and has undertaken extensive research into the overlooked but important places beneath our cities.

Under-ground Urbanism

Elizabeth Reynolds

Routledge
Taylor & Francis Group

NEW YORK AND LONDON

First published 2020 by Routledge
52 Vanderbilt Avenue, New York, NY 10017

and by Routledge
2 Park Square, Milton Park, Abingdon, Oxon, OX14 4RN

Routledge is an imprint of the Taylor & Francis Group, an informa business

Library of Congress Cataloging-in-Publication Data
A catalog record for this title has been requested

ISBN: 978-1-138-69678-5 (hbk)
ISBN: 978-1-138-69679-2 (pbk)
ISBN: 978-1-315-52333-0 (ebk)

Design by BOB Design
Typeset in Terrazzo by Luke Archer

Visit www.undergroundurbanism.com

Publisher's Note
This book has been prepared from camera-ready copy provided by the author.

1. Urban Growth — Up, Out & Down

2. Understanding the Underground

3. Planning in 3D

4. Adapting Underground Spaces

5. Architectural Responses to the Underground

6. Creating Quality Underground Places

7. As Above, So Below

8. References

1. Urban Growth

Up,

Out &

Down

Underground Urbanism

Urbanism is the study of the way of life, and physical needs of urban societies, however, urbanists are failing to see the whole picture. Our cities don't just comprise the streetscape and skyline, but also the subsurface. To better understand and resolve the challenges faced by growing cities, it is vital that we begin to look beneath the surface of our city streets. As urban populations grow so does the pressure on land, and for some cities, growing up and out is no longer enough to meet their development needs. Resourceful, design led solutions are necessary to better manage urban growth, and must include a fundamental rethink of our relationship with the ground beneath us. Underground urbanism advocates a vertical stitching together of our urban environments. This book brings together geology, urban planning, engineering, architecture and design, to explain what lies beneath our cities, and how it can be used to create great, sustainable places.

Growing Cities

Physical space is a valuable asset in cities. Housing, manufacturing, transport, utilities, waste, commercial and cultural uses all compete for space in our cities. For cities like Hong Kong, outward growth is constrained by natural barriers, forcing urban density to increase in order to accommodate population growth. In other cities, the limitations on urban growth are theoretical and policy based, using green belts to prevent urban sprawl. In London, demand for access to the centre of a global city has seen development leap over the green belt and stretch into the catchment of a far bigger area. Therefore, whether the constraints to urban growth are physical or policy based, competition for land in our cities is fierce and values are high.

Although it is possible to condense a population into a smaller urban footprint through the construction of tall buildings, spatial challenges remain at ground level where access is needed to and from buildings, particularly during peak hours. Taken cumulatively, the clustering of tall buildings in dense urban areas can lead to insufficient space at street level to safely and conveniently move goods and people.

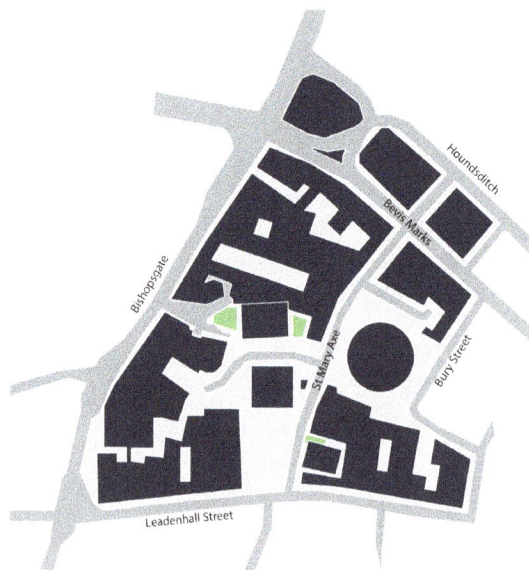

Fig. 1.1
Density and Urban Realm
Capacity, London

> 700,000 sqm, Gross Floor Area
> 12,000 sqm, Public Realm

Urban Connectivity

In growing cities, the connectivity of people and goods is key. From complex rail networks, to purpose designed freight facilities and pedestrian linkages, growing cities rely on transport infrastructure both above and below ground.

Underground passenger rail networks enable high speed travel over long distances without conflicting with vehicle movements at ground level. But as cities grow, so too the networks of infrastructure beneath them. In London, the iconic underground network has expanded to incorporate 400km of track and 270 stations, much of which is underground and integrates with additional stations and tracks on the London Overground and Network Rail. Construction of the latest addition to the London Underground is almost completed, with the Crossrail project (to be known as the Elizabeth Line) due to open late 2018. One of Europe's largest construction projects, Crossrail will add an estimated 10% to central London rail capacity, with 40 stations, 10 of which will be entirely new. Population growth and decreased car ownership mean however, that further transport capacity is urgently needed, and as such Crossrail 2 is already planned.

Fig. 1.2
Connected London

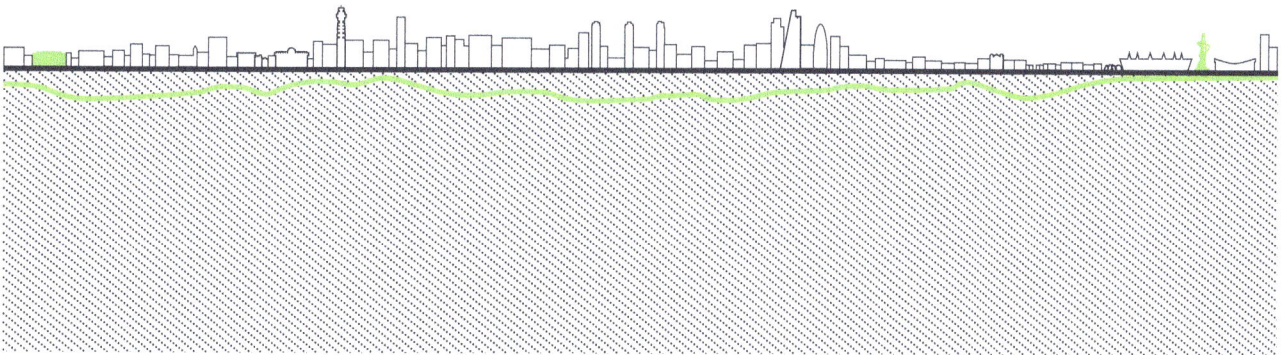

It is not just people but goods that regularly need to make long distance journeys to the centre of a city. Predicting a 45% increase in road freight traffic between 2010 and 2030, the Cargo Sous Terrain is an innovative solution to improve commercial efficiency, reduce traffic congestion and lower CO_2 emission in Swiss cities. Cargo Sous Terrain (CST) was conceived by Swiss company Loglay AG in response to their client's concerns about inefficiencies in the delivery of their goods to market. To achieve maximum efficiency in the delivery of goods by freight and avoid increasing levels of traffic congestion, it was decided that a new, dedicated freight network was needed underground. The CST network would comprise a 66.7 km long tunnel, 6m in width, located 50m below the existing road network, connecting 10 integrated freight hubs at ground level (Cargo Sous Terrain, 2016). At the purpose designed, integrated hubs freight pallets and containers can be collected from or added to the underground transport system, 24 hours per day, 7 days per week. The hubs and freight network would use 100% renewable energy, mostly sourced from solar panels mounted on the roof of the hubs. The tunnels would be divided horizontally, with the upper section used to move goods, and the lower section used as a conduit for cables and pipes. Larger items or pallets in wagons would move through the tunnel on conveyor belt "tracks" powered by electromagnetic induction and above them, smaller packages would move on tracks suspended from the ceiling. As the system is automated and driverless, the wagons would move at a constant speed of 30km/h and the overhead packages at 60km/h. For the CST to be effective, intelligent city-wide logistics are also required. A key role of the system is to collate freight from different destinations, allowing delivery routes to be scheduled and optimised. Furthermore, the smaller, constantly moving wagons reduce the need for large trucks to wait to be filled before making a commercially viable delivery. The first stage of CST for Harkingen to Niederbipp and Zurich is planned to be operational in 2030 and is estimated to cost $USD 3.5bn. Despite the significant financial investment needed, the project has widespread support from industry and the Swiss Government. Recently, US based technology and transport company Hyperloop One also joined the CST consortium, and there has been interest from other cities hoping this innovative model could also resolve congestion on their roads.

Fig. 1.3
Cargo Sous Terrain, Switzerland

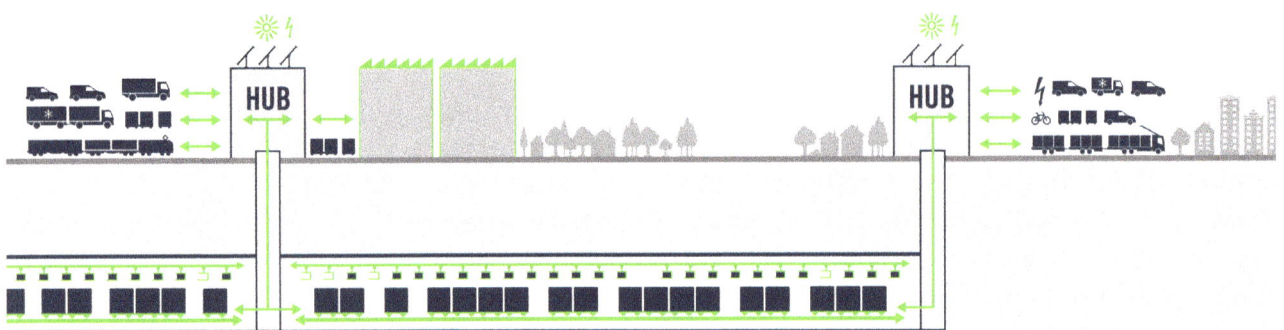

Underground Urbanism

Land Values

Sometimes, regardless of how far out a city expands, or how many layers of transport connectivity it creates, sheer demand for access to the centre of a city can increase land values to a point at which underground development becomes viable. For cities with the world's highest property values such as London, Hong Kong and Singapore, their unique economic context can even mean that the development of underground space is not just viable, but also profitable.

Iceberg Mansions

In recent years London has seen the emergence of a new building typology known as the iceberg mansion. Iceberg mansions feature predominantly in "super prime" parts of London, and are typified by multi-level basements even greater in area than the original houses to which they are attached. In order to accommodate home cinemas; bowling alleys; swimming pools; spa facilities; or garages, private basements (Wainwright, 2012) have been known to extend as deep as 15m below surface level.

The motivations for developing such large basements are partly lifestyle, but also financial. In the United Kingdom, the rights of a Freeholder extend to an unlimited depth below the surface of a property (except for any gold, silver, treasure, oil, petroleum, coal or gas found beneath the surface, which becomes property of the Crown). Should the subsurface below a private property be compulsorily acquired for an infrastructure project, a nominal fee of £50 is paid to the land owner. Yet, in the case of residential properties in prime areas of London, land values can average £4,779 per square foot (Wetherell, 2015). Given that in 2014 the average cost of a residential basement extension was estimated at £500 per square foot, the financial incentive is clear.

The Iceberg Mansion reflects a broader trend in the property market with many households in central London opting to extend down rather than move out of their house as their family grows. Statistics compiled by Glenigan demonstrate that in 2015 there were 887 applications to develop basements on residential properties in London, up a quarter on the previous year (Croft, 2016). Regardless of scale, excavation to create basements can generate significant construction traffic, alter ground conditions, and undermine the structural integrity of adjacent buildings. Although the introduction of planning policies in some boroughs has led to a decrease in basement planning applications and a reduced scale of development proposals, the small cost to obtain planning consent means that the value of a property is able to increase significantly before the diggers even begin their work. Basement planning policies and the design principles within them are discussed further in chapters three and six.

The Primacy of City Centres

In stark contrast to the mega basements of London, in Beijing an increasing number of people are seeking affordable accommodation in basements beneath the city. A study undertaken by Dr Annette Kim of the University of Southern California titled 'The extreme primacy of location: Beijing's underground rental housing market', found that approximately one million people live in underground apartments in Beijing (Kim, 2016). Beijing has a large amount of subsurface space due to laws requiring the construction of basements as places of refuge during conflict, but able to be used for domestic and economic purposes during peacetime. For many years housing was an allowable use of basement space, however in 2010 regulations were passed to prevent the use of underground space for housing and to evict existing residents within 3 years. Although residential occupancy of basements is now unlawful, and many bunkers and basements are in terrible condition, they remain in high demand. The research identifies basements as providing a housing product at a price not offered by other private rented accommodation, nor available through the public sector. The majority of basement units (some of which are two storeys below ground with no natural light, limited utilities, and measuring just 10 sqm) are occupied by rural residents without the correct Hokou (local birth registration) to benefit from the social services provided by city governments. By undertaking a detailed analysis of classified advertisements, the researchers were able to map the location and price of underground units. The research found that demand for underground accommodation was similar to normal housing, with a premium paid for accommodation closest to the city centre. Indeed, spatial proximity to employment was found to be paramount, allowing residents to save money by walking or cycling to work. Ultimately, the 'overriding demand for being located in the central city rather than the periphery is the impetus behind this underground housing market' (Kim, 2016 p.155).

Fig. 1.4
Iceberg Mansion, London

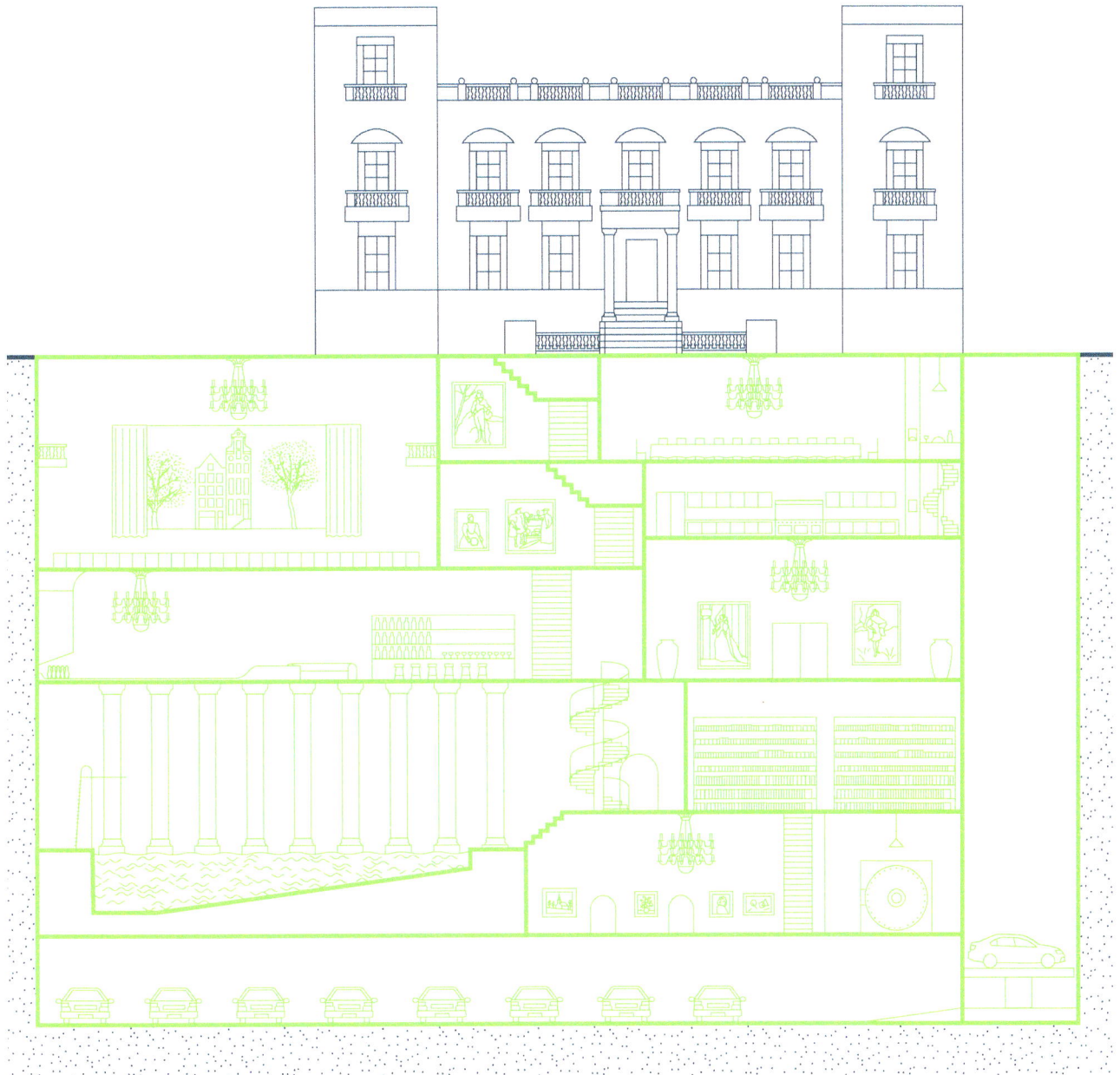

Valuing Land

It is not just the financial value of land that influences the development of space beneath cities, but also the value of land in qualitative terms. For example, where the finance, geology and physical space permits, it can be preferable to relocate transport infrastructure below ground, in order to improve quality of life at street level. From Le Corbusier's vision of the Radiant City in the 1920s to the American Federal Highway Bill in 1956, the desire to create fast flowing elevated roads has scarred many cities, yet this once popular trend is now being reversed by many cities.

In Seoul, the Cheonggyecheon Restoration Project was transformative in not only removing an elevated roadway constructed in the 1970s, but also restoring a natural stream that had been concreted over years earlier. The project took three years and cost $900 million, an undertaking difficult to justify when it opened in 2005, however, the landscaped pedestrian walk has subsequently proved popular with residents and tourists. For Boston, the Big Dig project was a costly and embarrassing project, blighted by accidents and delays, but ultimately successful. From its construction in 1959, an elevated section of the Interstate 93 highway had divided downtown Boston from its waterfront, with significant impacts on the quality of the urban environment. The elevated roadway became steadily more congested, until it was decided in 1982 to redirect the traffic through a 5.6km tunnel. The Central Artery / Tunnel Project was estimated to be completed by 1998 and cost $2.8 billion, but was not in-fact opened until 2006, by which stage the estimated cost of the project was $15 billion (perhaps up to $24 million with interest). Reasons for the costly delays varied, but included the recall of unsafe materials such as guard rails, lighting fixtures and ceiling panels that had been affixed with a glue unable to safely bond the ceiling panels it was used on (and tragically resulted in a fatality to a road user). The tunnel itself was found to have "hundreds" of leaks, which resulted in primal charges against the concrete supplier for the project. Basic excavation for the project was also difficult, using a slurry wall method in soft, saline, and partly made ground, with no tunnel boring technology available at the time the project was commissioned. Despite all of the money and time invested in the project, it has at least managed to create a positive legacy through the creation of the Rose Kennedy Greenway. Of the 27 acres of land above the tunnel, 75 per cent is dedicated to public open space and facilities, and the remainder for residential and commercial development. The series of five interconnected parks stretch across 2.4km and are maintained by the Rose Kennedy Greenway Conservancy who describe the space as 'a roof garden atop a highway tunnel' (RFKGC, 2017). The parks have transformed the character of this part of Boston, and opened up new opportunities for the surrounding communities.

Fig. 1.5
Big Dig Project, Boston

Where it is not possible to remove elevated roadways and rail lines, efforts can still be made to repair the damage caused by these structures to urban streetscapes. In Under the Elevated, Susan Chin, Executive Director, Design Trust for Public Space New York says 'Have you ever walked underneath an elevated highway, rail, or subway line, such as the Brooklyn Queens Expressway or the 2/5 subway line in the Bronx, and observed how dark, noisy and forbidding these places can be? Or ever thought about how the tracts of parking or storage beneath these structures divide neighbourhoods and serve as barriers to economic vitality?' (Bauer and Fletcher, 2015). Although land beneath elevated roads and rail lines is not underground per se, people often have similar reservations about the safety and desirability of these dark spaces. In New York, the Design Trust for Public Space has spent considerable time studying what happens beneath the 700 miles of elevated structures. Several of the Trust's design and community engagement projects provide useful examples of how to address the challenges associated with underutilised, underground spaces. In the Gowanus Expressway between 32nd and 57th Streets they identified potential to use the overhead structure as a frame to create enclosed workshops, studios and exhibition spaces. On Hamilton Avenue in Red Hook, the space beneath the F/G rail line was identified as having the potential to be converted into a dedicated bike and pedestrian corridor. Although these projects have not yet been fully implemented, they show that clear community led design strategies could improve these (often neglected) spaces, and with relatively limited investment.

Heritage & Height Constraints

The need to avoid harm to the setting of historic buildings can sometimes lead to the development of low and deep, rather than tall buildings. On the perimeter of London's famous Leicester Square, the design of a new Edwardian Hotel needed to consider its position within the landmark viewing corridor and protected vistas contained within local planning policy. The resulting design was for a 10-storey building, five of which are located below ground level in order to provide a 360-bedroom hotel with function rooms, spa, restaurants, bars, cinema and auditorium. The depth of the hotel building has enabled the floor area ratio and property value to be maximised, without creating an overly tall building that would otherwise impede protected views.

> In modern Singapore, another 10-storey building with a five-storey basement is also being constructed, but for a very different reason. The Jewel will be nestled between the existing Terminals 1, 2 and 3 of Changi Airport, on the site of a former car park. The under-utilised space will be transformed to provide 134,000 sqm of airline; entertainment; recreation; food and beverage; accommodation; and transport facilities (Winston, 2014). Although the building is over 60 metres in height, by placing half of the storeys below ground there is no conflict with aircraft flight paths. Basement levels 1–5 will accommodate a cinema, restaurants, taxi station and parking for 2,500 cars. Travellators and a monorail will allow the Jewel to act as a transfer hub between the three existing terminals, amplifying their total passenger handling capacity to an estimated 85 million people per year (including Terminal 4). The centrepiece of the striking, ovoid shaped building by Safdie Architects will be a 40m high waterfall, surrounded by a five-storey garden with over 100,000 plants. The waterfall (known as The Rain Vortex) by WET Design, will be the world's tallest indoor waterfall and run primarily on rainwater collected on the building's roof (Zhang, 2016). The building looks and functions unlike any designed before and is sure to enable Changi to remain its title as World's Best Airport for many years to come.

Fig. 1.6
The Jewel, Changi Airport,
Singapore

Shelter

Though for many people the notion of underground living conjures up the fictional works of J. R. R. Tolkien or Jules Verne, the reality is that for centuries people have sought shelter underground. Settled in 1800 BC, the Cappadocia region of Turkey has a surreal landscape with tall volcanic mounds created by years of erosion into a plateau. To protect themselves from hot dry summers and cold snowy winters, the residents of Cappadocia have carved their homes, churches and entire underground networks deep into the rocks for over 1600 years (Erdem, 2008). In China, a different geology found in the Loess Plateau once enabled almost 40 million residents to live in Yaodong or "house caves". Residents of Yaodongs were able to excavate the earth to create sunken courtyards, around which rooms of the house were positioned, saving the cost of constructing external walls and making the most of scarce building materials. These very basic forms of housing recognised that the high thermal mass of the earth is able to regulate fluctuations in temperature, improving comfort in locations where temperatures are extreme. Toronto and Montreal in Canada have extensive networks of underground malls to protect shoppers and commuters from harsh winter weather. In Toronto, the PATH network connects over 50 buildings across a 30km underground retail arcade with 125 ground level access points. In Montreal, the RESO has 32km of tunnels linking 80% of all office space and 35% of all retail space located within central Montreal, and is used by an estimated 500,000 people per day. Although the pedestrian networks are not without their faults, they offer refuge from harsh Canadian winters and have become an accepted part of their cities.

Fig. 1.7
SMART, Kuala
Lumpur

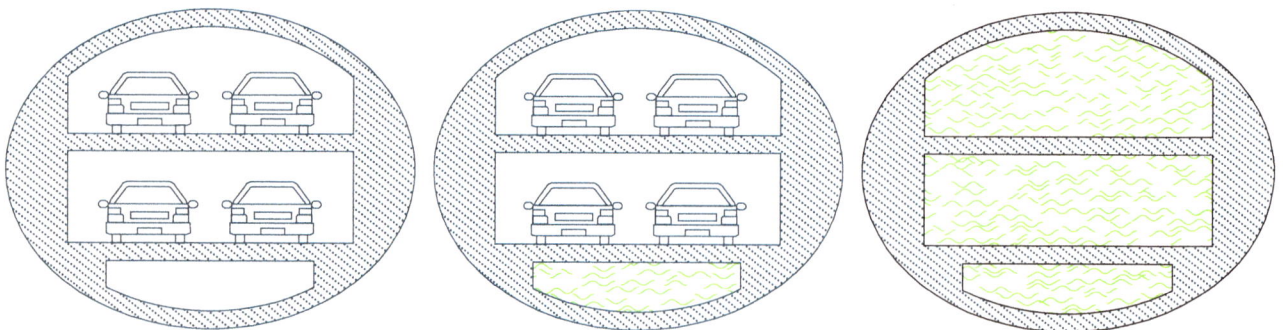

Underground Urbanism

Resilience

The land beneath cities can also have an important role to play in their resilience to natural disasters. For many years seasonal typhoons have wreaked havoc on Hong Kong, and although modern buildings are built to withstand the high winds, managing significant rainfalls in a dense urban area remains a challenge. The Mongkok area of West Kowloon suffered particularly bad floods in 1997 and 1998 due to local stormwater drains being inundated by water from expanding urban settlements further upstream. Rather than undertake a lengthy programme of upgrades to the existing drains and constructing new box culverts in densely populated areas, in 2001 the Hong Kong Government commissioned the construction of a vast underground flood water storage tank. Constructed beneath a recreation ground, the Tai Hang Tung Storage Scheme (THTSS) is 136m long, 130m wide and 9.5m deep, with a 100,000cbm capacity. During flood events, it is able to intercept 70cbm of water per second from the surrounding drainage network. The THTSS was Hong Kong's first large underground flood storage tank and has succeeded in reducing the risk of typhoon related flood damage in the city. In 2007 The SMART (Stormwater Management and Road Tunnel) infrastructure project in Kuala Lumpur introduced a 9.7km long, underground roadway and stormwater retention tunnel that is divided into three sections that can be collated to absorb urban flood waters (Broere, 2013).

> For those cities, prone to earthquakes rather than floods, underground spaces can also support emergency resilience measures. The various consequences of seismic activity are typically felt less below ground than above. In Santiago, the metro system experienced relatively minor levels of damage after an 8.8. magnitude earthquake in 2010 (Broere, 2013), and in Japan the devastating earthquake and tsunami of 2011 resulted in negligible damage to underground infrastructure (Cornaro & Admiraal, 2012).

By using scenarios to test the ability of a city to cope with potential threats, mitigation measures can be implemented to make a city as robust as possible. As demonstrated by the Bahnhof data centre in Sweden and similar facility built by Academica in Helsinki, underground spaces might have a role to play in accommodating the information technology infrastructure needs of modern cities. The risk of sea levels rising in many cities could potentially be ameliorated with undergroundwater storage facilities by adapting underutilised spaces such as pedestrian underpasses. Where population is expected to grow, pedestrian streetscapes could be narrowed and offer an improved pedestrian experience by separating out vehicles, refuse and utilities to below the primary surface level, similar to the approach being trialled at the experimental Masdar City in Abu Dhabi.

Theory

The drivers explained above have led to researchers from a range of disciplines investigating the urban subsurface. This book is not the first to use the term 'Underground Urbanism', but it endeavours to provide a different lens through which to frame the subject. There is now a growing body of literature on the importance of these natural resources and ecosystem services in urban areas. In 2004 Parriaux et al. asked engineers and architects to consider underground space, water, geo-material and heritage resources as an important part of urban environments. Admiraal (2006) states that a "bottom-up approach" is needed to recognise the value of underground space as a vital resource for sustaining life on the surface, rather than just an unlimited resource to be exploited for development. Huan-Qing et al. (2013) reference the 'underground urbanism' research undertaken by Utudjian (1972), Barles and Guillerme (1995) and Belanger (2016), and also suggest that a holistic approach should be taken to managing underground resources (geothermal energy, groundwater, geomaterials and underground space), which they refer to as the 'deep city method'. Eduardo et al. (2015) also supports the use of full life cycle analysis including societal gain when considering the cost viability of underground construction.

Despite very good research by geologists, hydrogeologists and structural engineers, there are other disciplines who seem to have overlooked the underground. In his excellent book Vertical (2016), Stephen Graham comments that 'Flat perspectives seen from the 'God's Eye' view of the cartographic or satellite imager inevitably fail to support understanding of such three-dimensional geographies. This problem is especially acute when we try to understand contemporary cities. Though vast libraries and many disciplines of the social sciences are devoted to exploring the structuring of the horizontal aspects of cities stretched across the world's surface, the attention to the vertical structuring of cities and urban life remains patchy and limited. This is especially within Anglophone geography and urban studies traditions' (Graham, 2016, p. 6). In the urban design and urbanism fields, there is what urban design scholars Barrie Shelton and his colleagues call '"flat earth" viewpoints of urbanism' that are remarkably dominant. Despite a proliferation of literature on the architecture of individual tall buildings, such perspectives remain wedded to the traditional idea of the urban ground, with its atgrade street networks and public encounters on sidewalks and in traditional urban spaces (Graham, 2016, p. 8). In Vertical, the value of looking at our cities from a sectional rather than bird's eye perspective is explained through a quote by Pierre Belanger, who says: 'processes that are often isolated in plans, or divided in conventional categories from above, can be better understood and revealed. From the side, as being associative and integrate — often overlapping, intertwined and entangled. Opening a lease on the complex urbanisation of the underground and of the atmosphere, this association of the quanti-tative with the qualitative made possible by seeing sideways offers three important observations on the once and future hinterlands of the underground, the ocean and the atmosphere' (Belanger, 2016).

> Like all good cities, this book brings together a diverse range of ideas — from writers and academics, city governments, urban planners, property developers, architects, urban and interior designers. In taking an international look at the competing demands on resources beneath our cities, it is hoped that we can rethink them from (below) the ground up, and create better urban environments for future generations in the process.

2.

Understanding

the

Underground

Underground Urbanism

Spatially the underground, or subsurface, is considered to be anything below ground level, with the ground level varying based on terrain. Geologically, the subsurface continues down through four primary layers of crust, mantle, outer core and inner core, before reaching the centre of the earth. It is within this initial earth crust of up to 60km below ground level that the book is focused, indeed urban underground developments rarely extend further than 100m below ground level. So what is meant by underground and what might we find there?

Underground?

Undercroft

Undercroft spaces are partially open to the air, but located at or slightly below street level. Storage cellars located in the spaces between structural supports underneath buildings were traditionally described as being undercroft. Contemporary undercroft spaces are typically found within the residual spaces beneath structures such as bridges, elevated roadways, or multi-storey car parks. These spaces might not be entirely underground, but share many of the same characteristics.

Fig. 2.1
Undercroft

Earth covered

Partly hidden within a grass hillside, Villa Vals in Switzerland by architects Bjarne Mastenbroek of SeARCH and Christian Muller of CMA is a form not typically found in cities. However, the Asian Crossroads Over the Sea (ACROS) office building in Fukuoka, Japan by Emilio Ambasz is a good example of an earth covered building in a dense urban environment. Buildings constructed either partly below ground or later covered with earth can offer improved energy performance, blend discretely into the surrounding landscape and retain space at surface level for other uses such as recreation.

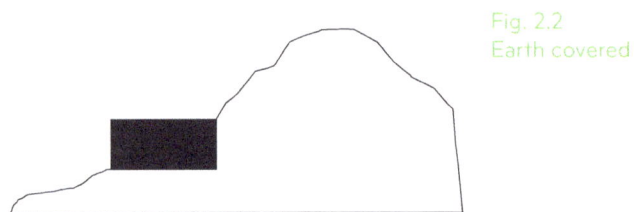

Fig. 2.2
Earth covered

Sunken

Sunken buildings are carved into the ground but retain access to natural light. In China, Yaodong or "house cave" dwellings are excavated horizontally from a central sunken courtyard. Rooms around the courtyard benefit from a central source of natural light and ventilation, plus the thermal benefits of the outer perimeter of the building being formed from earth. Modern interpretations can be found in dense urban areas where homes extended below ground to maximise floor space without overlooking neighbours, or having a detrimental impact on the streetscape.

Underground
Spaces located below ground level without walls, windows or a roof exposed to daylight are considered underground. These can include the basement of a larger building, a bunker or underground car park where only the access is visible at street level. These buildings typically need artificial lighting, but have low operational and maintenance costs as there are no external walls to decorate and the surrounding earth provides insulation.

Fig. 2.4
Underground

Tunnelled
Located deep below ground and formed either by cutting and covering soil, or mechanised tunnel excavation accessed by a shaft, this is a form typical of underground road or railway systems. Tunnelled construction is costly but sometimes necessary to avoid obstructions or poor geology closer to the surface.

Fig. 2.5
Tunnelled

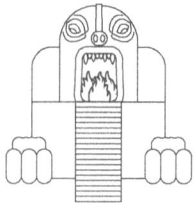

Mythology

From the myths of the ancient Greeks to the writings of Jules Verne, and representations of the underground in contemporary cinema, it is not just a case of understanding what physically exists beneath the ground, but also what we perceive could exist.

In Greek mythology, earth holds the entrance to an underworld for the kingdom of the dead. For the Mayan civilisation, the mythical underground city of Xibalba was overseen by demonic rulers who set fearsome traps for intruders. In almost all corners of the ancient world, there were myths concerning what lay deep below the ground. In Dante's 14th Century Divine Comedy Inferno, the illustration Overview of Hell imagines the layers of the subsurface, not as the shown in figure 2.01, but rather as nine circles of hell. Thankfully, by the late 19th Century in a world of exciting scientific advances, the underground began to imbue a sense of adventure rather than fear. For French author Jules Verne, the underground was a constant source of inspiration, writing Journey to the Centre of the Earth (1864), Twenty Thousand Leagues Under the Sea (1870), and The Child of the Cavern (also known as The Underground City) in 1877. Similarly, J.R.R. Tolkein often found mystery and adventure in the underground, using it as the setting for The Book of Lost Tales (1914), The Hobbit (1937), and the Lord of the Rings trilogy (1954 – 1955). The 1926 film Metropolis, directed by Fritz Lang, was one of the first films to portray the perceived contrast between society above and below ground. The film imagines a positive light filled Metropolis of sky scrapers where its highest echelons play in a heavenly "Club of the Sons", whilst beneath a dark and foreboding ground, workers toil to support the beauty above. These fictional depictions of the underground tap into some of our deepest psychological fears.

In their book Underground Infrastructures Planning, Design and Construction, Goel et al. (2012 p.23 - 24) assert that 'For common people, the idea of working or living underground elicits a negative (emotional) reaction. Negative associations with underground space generally include darkness combined with humid, stale air, and no sunlight. Among the most powerful associations (emotions) are those related to death and burial or fear of entrapment from structural collapse. Other negative associations (fears) arise in relation to feeling lost or disoriented, as normal reference points such as the ground, sky, sun, and adjacent objects and spaces cannot be seen'. Although society evolves in response to its habitat (life without the underground is almost unimaginable for Londoners), our relationship with the underground is complex. Societies have long feared the literal and metaphorical darkness of the underground, creating stories of the evil we imagine residing there. Yet we also seek comfort and protection from these same spaces — metaphorically going underground until it all blows over.

Fig. 2.6
Mythology

Archaeology

Most contemporary cities are built up layer upon layer from modest beginnings, with recent and ancient artefacts hidden beneath their surface. From the catacombs of Paris; to woolly mammoths in London; and Aztec temples below Mexico City, it is important to acknowledge the layers of history that exist underground. Most of London's archaeological heritage is found in the first nine metres below ground, with Modern, Early Modern, Medieval, Roman and Prehistoric layers sitting above the city's natural geology. During construction of the Crossrail project a comprehensive archae-ological strategy was used to locate; identify; record and protect items of archaeological merit. Working with the Museum of London, project archaeologists found a tremendous range of artefacts and ecofacts including the remnants of buildings; a piece of 55-million-year-old Amber; coins; pewter mugs; jewellery; household pottery; leather shoes from the 15th Century; and even 25 skeletons buried in a 14th Century plague pit. Tens of thousands of objects have been excavated from sites across the 118km Crossrail route, with many now donated to the Natural History Museum and Museum of London's Archaeological Archive, contributing to the understanding of how London evolved from the Roman settlement of Londinium in AD43 to a metropolis of 8.5 million people today.

In Rotterdam, architects MVRDV led the creation of a spectacular new market hall near to where the original city was founded in 1270, and although the hall is best known for its kaleidoscopic ceiling (covered with a one-hectare mural by artists Arno Coenen and Iris Roskam), credit should also be given to design of the basement levels of the building. As the site was excavated to create a four-level basement car park beneath the market hall, various archaeological discoveries were made. These artefacts are now showcased within the 'Time Stairs', a permanent display designed by Kossmann.dejong exhibition architects. Each level is colour coded and on the side of the escalators leading up from the car park a timeline is provided, summarising the history of the city from 900AD to 1940. Glass display cabinets showcase artefacts found on the site including pottery and tools, some of which might have originated in Portugal and been transported by the sailors so important to the history of the port city.

Fig. 2.7
Archaeology

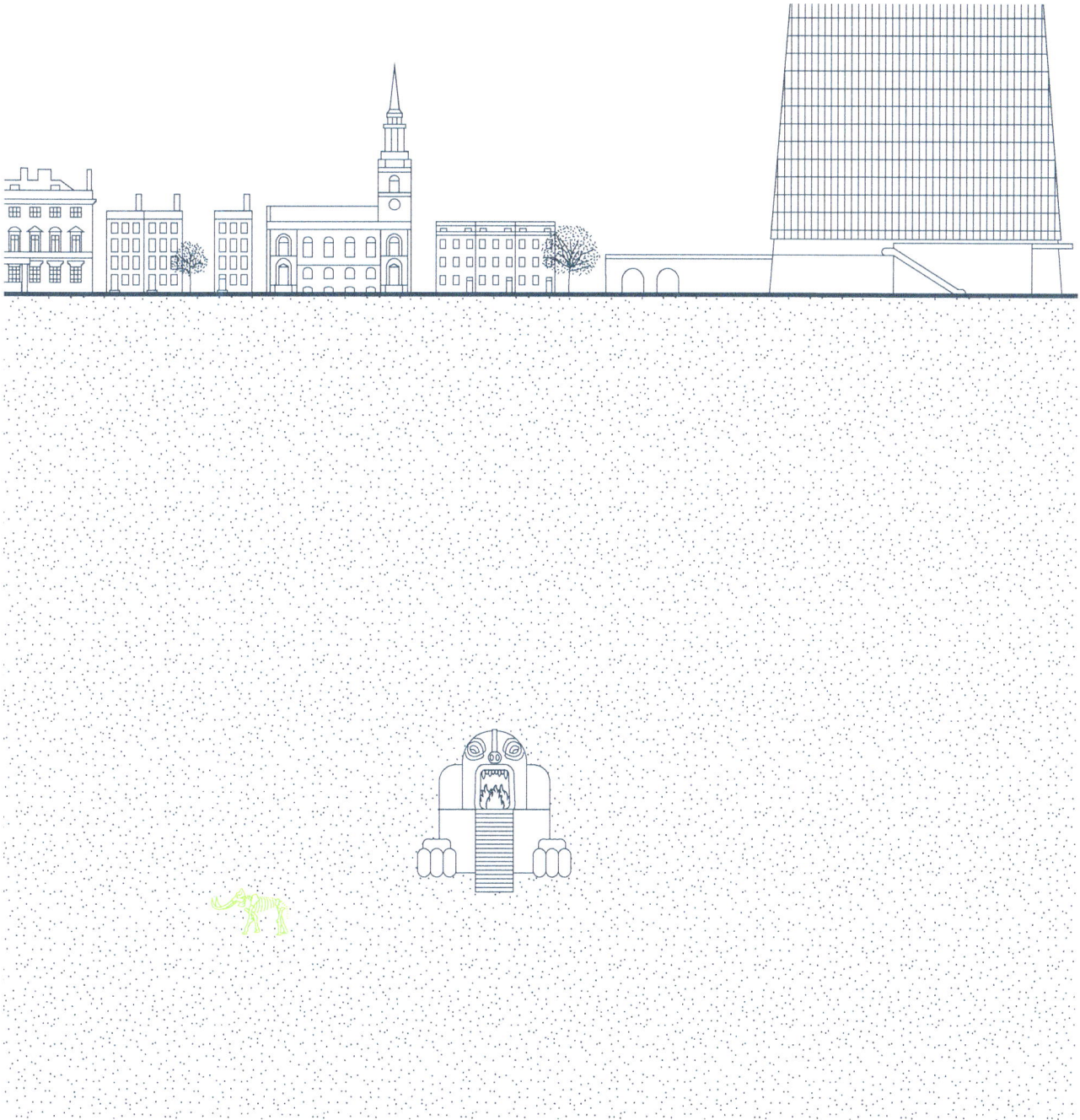

Heritage

In Rome, Italy the construction of the new metro C Line has also (unsurprisingly) uncovered a great number of archaeological treasures. Two of the new stations on the C Line will include "museums" to display the items found during construction. At San Giovanni Station, some 40,000 artefacts were discovered during construction, many of which are displayed in softly lit glass cabinets that line the station's escalators, corridors and platforms. Passengers are able to travel back in time through the layers of Rome's history as they descend down into the station, concluding in the Pleistocene age at platform level, some 30m below ground.

> In London, construction of the European Headquarters for Bloomberg led to the careful preservation and showcasing of ancient buildings and artifacts from the Temple of Mithras. Known as the London Mithraeum, a culture and education hub has been created beneath the 1.1m sqm Bloomberg office development to permanently display remnants of the mysterious cult of Mithras who worshiped in Londinium (the Roman name for London) around 300 AD.

It is not just ancient artefacts that lay hidden beneath our city streets, but also more recent built and cultural heritage that has been discarded as plans change. The Basilica Cistern that provided fresh water to Istanbul from the 6th century AD is now a tourist attraction, similarly some of the aquifers beneath Rome. In London, New York, Antwerp, and Paris disused underground train stations lie mothballed, occasionally used as film sets. During the Cold War, many cities including Beijing, London, Prague, Paris and Berlin also constructed underground bunkers or fallout shelters. Near Stockholm one former nuclear bunker has been converted to a data centre for the internet services provider Bahnhof, with Albert France-Lanord Architects using the bunker's history to inspire an interior fit for a James Bond villain. In Barcelona plans to construct an entire underground city only progressed as far as creating the Avenida de la Luz mall, which began construction in 1929 but was abandoned in a decayed state in 1990 — with some parts subsequently integrated into a shopping centre. Although some of the historic places beneath our cities are sacred or secret, others have the potential to be rediscovered and repurposed to find new life in today's cities.

Fig. 2.8
Heritage

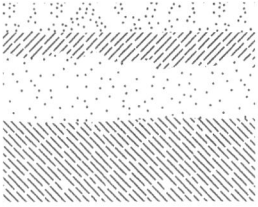

Geology

Geology is a key factor in the shape of our cities. The island of Manhattan is part of a landscape sculpted from an ice sheet formed in the Pleistocene Era approximately 1.5 million years ago). It is built on three strata known as Manhattan Schist, Inwood Marble, and Fordham Gneiss. The Schist forms the island's spine, running from the Henry Hudson Bridge at its north end to the Battery on its southern tip; it dips abruptly several hundred feet below ground at Washington Square, and makes a gradual ascent beginning at Chambers Street. These dips and rises account for the gap between "midtown" and "downtown" in the Manhattan skyline as the tall buildings had to be anchored on solid bedrock, and not on the glacial till that forms the valleys. A large portion of central London comprises London Clay which is considered an ideal medium for excavating and tunnelling and this has been a key factor in the development of London's underground rail network. In Singapore and Helsinki, the presence of bedrock can increase the costs and safety risk associated with constructing underground spaces, because blasting rather than tunnelling can be required to break through or expand natural formations. In these and almost all cities, what is considered ground level is often not geological, but rather artificial ground, created through successive waves of human settlement. The Archaeosphere is a term used by Professor Edgeworth of Leicester University to describe the hybrid of natural geology and urban archaeology, gathered over hundreds of years to form layers of ground (Graham, 2016 p.290).

The earth, water, energy and minerals below our cities can provide valuable natural resources, as well as ecological services. Although it is uncommon to find large scale minerals extraction occurring in densely populated cities, groundwater and energy resources are often exploited. Reykjavik in Iceland derives all of its energy from geothermal sources, with 750MW of power from steam, and 63mn cbm of hot water extracted from as deep as 1,000m below the surface. In Glasgow, Scotland research is being undertaken to estimate the feasibility of extracting heat energy from the water within disused mine shafts across the city. The combined study between the British Geological Survey and Glasgow City Council has so far identified that 40% of Glasgow's energy needs could be met by pumping waste heat from the mine shafts into buildings for warmth in winter, then reversing the process during summer to restore the excess heat below ground. However, the resources beneath our cities can also be of great benefit when left in situ to perform ecosystem services such as the decomposition of waste and filtration of water. In urban areas where hard surfaces make the ground impermeable, aquifers

are deprived of the rainfall needed to recharge fresh water supplies. Where waste disposal is not adequately managed, and there are intrusions into the earth's surface, contamination of aquifers can also occur.

Fig. 2.9
Geology

～～～～～～～ Water

The geological and hydrogeological conditions beneath our cities can be a risk as well as a resource. Mexico City is sinking at over 30cm per annum due to a combination of its position on a former lake bed; the presence below ground of abandoned gravel and sand mines; leaking water pipes; the extraction of groundwater; and the sheer weight of urban development associated with a city of 20mn people. Similar to Mexico City, the capital of Thailand, Bangkok, is also experiencing rates of subsidence that could fundamentally change large parts of the city. Located close to the equator, Bangkok has a challenging context — with a tropical monsoon climate; tidal river basin location; a geology of marine clay above natural aquifers; and low-lying topography, with most of the city built just 1.5m above sea level. Subsidence caused by fresh water extraction from the aquifers and ground disturbance caused by the weight of buildings has led to parts of the city now being located below sea level and suffering from increased flooding. For some cities, gradual subsidence is less of a concern than the rapid and unpredictable creation of sinkholes. In 2013 a sinkhole 10m deep subsumed buildings in Guangzhou, China and in 2010 a significantly larger sink hole of 90m deep and 20m wide caused fatalities and building collapses in Guatemala City, Guatemala. Sink holes are influenced by a variety of factors, primarily the erosion and eventual collapse of soft limestone or chalk earth when dissolved by acidic water, with the water sometimes originating from leaking pipes.

Other seemingly natural disasters can also be caused or exacerbated by the exploitation of the subsurface. In the small Dutch city of Groningen, despite not being located on any natural fault line, earthquakes of up to 3.6 on the Richter scale have been recorded, causing damage to an estimated 36,000 homes. The Groningen field is a 900-square km area used for gas extraction by companies including Shell and Exxon Mobil since the 1960s. It is believed that the process of extracting the natural gases has exposed the city, along with the surrounding towns and villages, to a significantly increased risk of personal injury and damage to property. Although the seismic activity seems relatively low on a Richter scale of up to 8, the shallow level at which the earthquakes occur leaves less ground in which primary shocks can be absorbed. The clay soil found in Groningen also has a resonating effect. With almost 1,000 manmade earthquakes recorded since the 1990s, this small city and its surrounds have the unfortunate reputation as being a test case for the potentially harmful effects of fracking and other forms of gas extraction.

Ultimately, for our cities to develop more sustainably, it is important that Urban Planners collaborate with their peers in the Earth Sciences. Indeed, urban plan making should begin from below the ground up, with knowledge of the earth's subsurface used to inform the first of many layers within city spatial development plans.

Fig. 2.10
Water

Hidden and Buried

The subsurface is often used as a repository for the things that society no longer needs or wants to see. Centuries of formal and informal waste disposal make up the ground level of modern cities. Dedicated landfill facilities for noxious industrial, or general household waste on the periphery of cities, are sometimes encroached on by cities as they spread outwards, constraining the potential uses at ground level both functionally and financially. In countries with high environmental health standards, landfill sites are fortunately reducing in number, as efforts are made to divert waste through campaigns to reduce / reuse and recycle. However, for many cities, there is a mismatch between the large volumes of waste produced by residents, and the limited number of waste disposal and recycling facilities. Whether the continual accumulation of waste in cities will one day see urban mining as a viable exercise remains to be seen (Balch, 2017), until then, the burial of household and industrial waste is a short sighted, singular use that risks sterilising valuable land in cities.

> For most cities, it is secrets as well as waste that are buried beneath the ground. The Tower of London was built in 1066, expanding and fortifying under successive monarchs, many of whom relied on its network of secret tunnels to ferry goods, prisoners and even forbidden lovers. Throughout history, tunnelled passages have serviced governments, royalty and resistance movements. With the passage of time, these spaces are sometimes declassified and become open to the public, and others are discovered accidentally during the construction of new projects. Yet in many cities, infrastructure of national significance and access to secure places remains hidden below ground.

Perhaps an uncomfortable subject, but there is no denying that in many cultures, earth is also needed for human burials. Here too, population growth is leading to an acute shortage of space in urban cemeteries, and conflicts with adjacent land uses that risk encroaching on cemeteries built on (historic) city limits. In particularly dense, geographically constrained cities such as Hong Kong, Singapore, and Venice, burial space is in particularly short supply. The environmental health standards for developing land near to burial grounds, or above former waste disposal sites, can constrain cities' potential to grow, and add significantly to the cost of development, through ground remediation costs. Allocating land for things that need to be buried or hidden for long periods of time, needs to occur as part of the overall strategic urban planning of our cities.

Fig. 2.11
Hidden and Buried

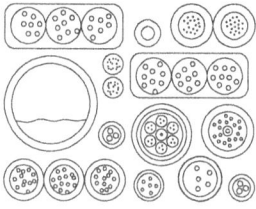

Utilities

Beneath many city streets lay a complex web of utilities, with most people only aware of their presence when they fail and are dug up for repair. So, what utilities are down there? For most cities, it is a combination of pipes and cables for gas, electricity, steam, water, waste water, telephone, TV, broadband (optical fibre), street lighting and stormwater drainage. Each utility is often the responsibility of a dedicated provider, with a statutory responsibility to supply their customers. Most utilities are placed within the first metre below street level, however, some waste water tunnels are constructed at depths of up to 70m. Although utility companies have maps of their known assets, these are not always accurate, and pipes or cables can sometimes be struck unexpectedly during construction works. In the UK ground risks including the discovery of unexpected utilities is one of main causes of delay in construction projects. There are various techniques for locating and identifying subsurface utilities, however, where records have been lost; repair or installation work has been undertaken differently to approved plans; or services are critical (and confidential), then it can be difficult to gain a clear understanding of what utilities are located where.

The distribution of utilities below ground can significantly influence the appearance of cities above ground. Not only can major gas mains and waste water tunnels constrain the location of building foundations, but the distribution of shallow level services can increase street widths and constrain potential landscaping. In 2016 the Abu Dhabi Urban Planning Council (UPC) in the United Arab Emirates released an updated version of their Street Design Tool. The tool is the product of over 10 years' work with stakeholders including 12 local utility providers, with whom they had already worked to produce the Abu Dhabi Utility Corridors Design Manual (UCDM) in 2014 and the Abu Dhabi Urban Street Design Manual (USDM) in 2010 (with a revised edition in 2015). Significantly, the UCDM was driven by an aspiration for more enjoyable and sustainable streets within the city. By rethinking street design, utility providers were challenged to consolidate their assets into narrower corridors. Through these combined efforts, the width of utility corridors (and consequently the streets above them) is being reduced, creating more comfortable street environments for pedestrians.

In other cities, the distribution of utilities has been further rationalised with the creation of dedicated utility tunnels, which also reduce or eliminate the need to dig up streets to repair the services below. Both Helsinki in Finland, and Prague in the Czech Republic have extensive networks of combined utility tunnels, large enough to walk or even drive through. Cables are stacked and easily accessible, reducing the amount of time and money needed to locate, access and repair utility assets. Utility tunnels can also offer the benefit of providing services with a stable temperature in which to operate, compared to when they are buried individually near surface level.

Fig. 2.12
Utilities

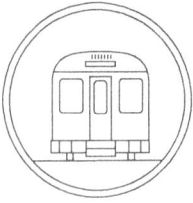

Transport

Beginning with construction of the world's first underground rail line in 1843, London's rail network has grown to include 182km of underground rail tunnels. The construction of each rail line becomes progressively more complex as the number of subsurface obstructions increase. The Crossrail project (to be known as the Elizabeth Line), is adding a further 42km of 6.2m diameter tunnels to an already complex underground railway network. One of the most challenging moments during construction was referred to as "threading the needle" and occurred when a 900-tonne tunnel boring machine constructing the east bound tunnel needed to thread through a small gap between the southern side of the new Tottenham Court Road London Underground Station; a new bank of escalators installed for the project; and an existing London Underground line. At the narrowest point, the TBM was driven 600mm above the Northern Line whilst it was in operation — a remarkable achievement given the potential risks involved. Yet, engineers and construction managers involved with future underground rail projects such as Crossrail 2 face an even greater challenge as the amount of transport infrastructure and other subsurface obstructions increase.

In New York, delivery of the Second Avenue Subway project has also been a lengthy and complex process. First mooted in 1919, the Second Avenue Subway has been delayed by recession and war, along with the usual challenges associated with financing and constructing a major transport infrastructure project. In 2005, New York State passed the Transportation Bond Act to facilitate the project and ground officially broke two years later, supported by a $1.3bn federal funding commitment for phase one of the project. The project comprises four phases, stretching 8.5 miles plus a track connection to the existing 63rd Street and Broadway Lines. In total the line would feature 16 new stations with climate control and disabled access (features not often found in New York's subway stations). Delivery of the project has been extremely challenging, taking place in a dense urban area, with little room to move construction; materials; machinery and workers, either vertically or horizontally. A tangle of shallow level utilities meant construction at a deeper level was preferred. However, geological conditions including Manhattan schist meant that excavation required mining and tunnelling as well as digging. The mining was especially problematic, with considerable noise and vibration impacts on surrounding residents, and construction accidents. An incident in 2012 occurred when a (supposedly controlled) rock blast sprayed construction debris eight storeys high- damaging surrounding buildings, but incredibly not harming anyone. Construction accidents, cost overruns and delays have blighted the project and impacted heavily on the lives of people living and working nearby. Thankfully, despite these challenges, the first phase of the Second Avenue Subway opened on 1st January 2017 (Sneider, 2017).

Fig. 2.13
Transport

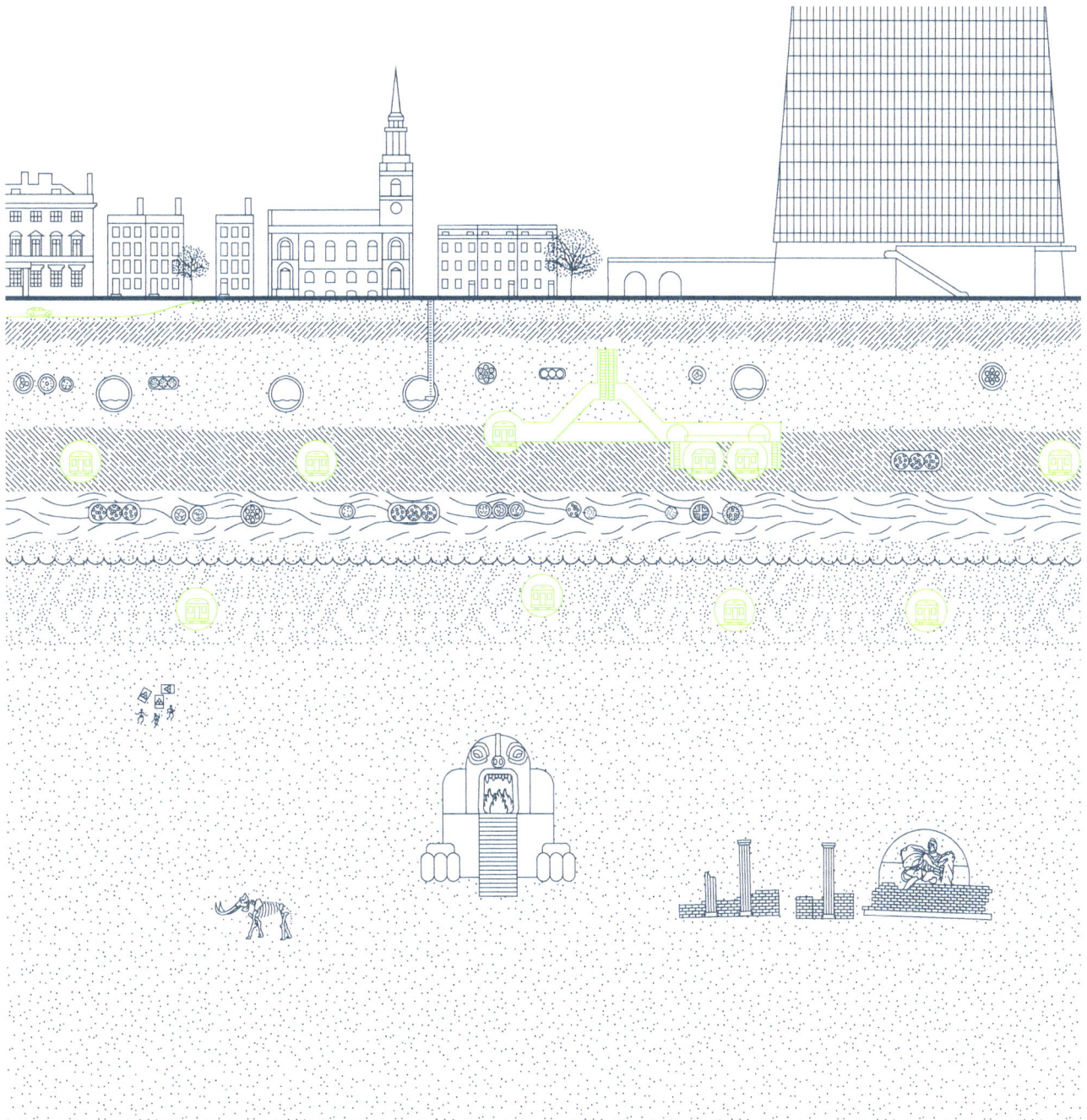

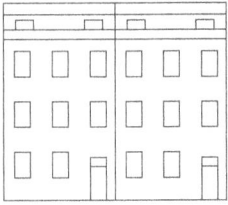

Buildings

To imagine what a city might look like, we often picture skyscrapers of glass and steel, yet this is only part of the picture. Like icebergs, many buildings extend deep below the level visible to us. Along with utilities and transport infrastructure, the basements and foundations of our buildings compete for space beneath our cities. London's tallest building known as The Shard extends not just 310m into the sky, but also 3 storeys and a further 53m into the ground. The building is stabilised by a large concrete slab up to 3m thick, pierced by concrete piles 1.5 – 1.8m in diameter, extending through the London clay to the sand beneath. Excavation and construction of the enormous building needed to navigate underground remnants of previous developments on the site, as well as utilities infrastructure, and London Underground tunnels located just 5m from the north-west corner of the basement. It is not just tall buildings with deep foundations that occupy significant space below ground, basements and the uses within them can be an impediment to the development of transport and other public infrastructure. In London, the Francis Crick Institute is a state of the art biomedical research facility that houses sensitive electromagnetic monitoring equipment within its basement. The 12-storey building includes four basement levels encased by a 1m thick reinforced concrete diaphragm wall, to reduce the risk of external vibration distorting results from specialist equipment including super-resolution microscopes. Construction of the basement was complex, with a need to avoid disruption to existing subsurface assets beneath and near the site including a 120-year-old gas main, the British Library, two underground train lines, and the St Pancras rail terminus. Land immediately to the south of the site is also safeguarded for the potential future development of Crossrail 2, a major planned north to south rail line across London. The Francis Crick Institute objected to the proposed alignment of Crossrail 2 on the basis that it could introduce additional and excessive levels of vibration. The tunnel design has now been lowered and is likely to include measures to further mitigate vibration caused by construction or operation of the rail line.

Conflicts between underground infrastructure and building basements can also occur at a much smaller scale. Although a £50 flat rate has been accepted as the nominal value payable to aquire the subsoil earth needed for tunnelling infrastructure projects, increasing property prices in London are influencing the perceived financial value of the subsurface. The High Speed 2 rail project faced challenges from 204 different objectors who claimed that £50 was an insufficient payment for acquisition of the subsoil beneath their property. With residential basement depths of up to 15m and commercial developments such as the Edwardian Hotel Leicester Square having five basement levels, there is concern that the cost of acquiring or insuring against damage to private sub-surface developments could add more to the already significant costs to delivering major infrastructure projects as residential basements.

Fig. 2.14
Buildings

The Whole Picture

The layers of objects that gradually accumulate beneath our cities paints a complex picture. Although our concept of the underground is often limited to picturing dark damp earth, our cities contain so much more beneath their surface than we often acknowledge. Gaining a better awareness of the urban subsurface is therefore critical in better planning and designing our cities. The emergence of new city data and infrastructure mapping tools offers the potential to better understand what is already located beneath our cities, however it will never be possible to build an entirely accurate picture. Urban mythology also extends to the places beneath our cities that are rumoured to exist but are not publicly accessible or acknowledged. In the Bldgblog Book (2009) Geoff Manaugh describes the mysterious tunnels that don't officially exist below London yet leave definite question marks on surface level. With the best data available, urban planning should literally be rethought from the ground up - starting with an appreciation that underground space is a complex, scarce and valuable resource. The current first come, first served approach to development of the underground jeopardises the function of environmental services and reduces the availability of land for critical future infrastructure. Strategic, three-dimensional planning that involves a broad range of relevant stakeholders is needed to find innovative solutions able to balance competing demands on the subsurface.

Fig. 2.15
The Whole Picture

3. Planning

in

3D

Why do we plan our cities, and are we doing enough to balance the complex demands placed on our urban environments, both above and below ground? From ancient China, to the Roman empire, and the town and country planning movement in England, cities have used spatial planning as a tool to improve quality of life. For most cities, their urban planning systems include a spatial development strategy; policies to direct the amount, type and location of urban growth; and a development control system to ensure that development occurs in accordance with their overarching plans. Yet why do so few cities plan for their subsurface? Perhaps it begins with the notion of "out of sight, out of mind". A sense that the appearance of a building which isn't a visible part of the landscape shouldn't matter. Underground development might also be considered an anomaly, such as an occasional new metro line enabled by specific legislation such as an Act of Parliament. These types of major projects can be seen as needing technical expertise to engage with, something that could deter a wider audience from becoming involved. Finally, planning policy seems to lack the confidence and clarity of purpose to plan for spaces that are (to an extent) ungoverned. In an attempt to resolve some of these challenges, this chapter seeks to explain why cities need to better plan for the spaces beneath them. In response to an underground gold rush of sorts, the ownership and governance of the subsurface is also discussed. Case studies are then provided of nine cities and how they engage with issues surrounding development of the subsurface.

Cities are Complex, Multi-layered Spaces

As the subsurface becomes more congested with vital infrastructure, building foundations, and miscellaneous "space junk", the options for cities become more limited. To encourage planners, architects, engineers and geologists to work together and create visions for the future of urban underground space, in 2012 the International Society of City and Regional Planners signed a Memorandum of Understanding with the International Tunnelling and Underground Space Association (ITA). Building on this initial professional collaboration, in 2014 the United Nations Human Settlement Programme (UN-HABITAT) and the Associated Research Centers for the Urban Underground Space (ACUUS) also signed a Memorandum of Understanding to raise awareness of the sustainable use of underground space for urban development. These organisations have also inspired the creation of Think Deep UK, a multidisciplinary group of professionals working to stimulate debate, and to share knowledge on a range of issues relating to the subsurface. Similarly, the COST suburban project sets out to explore, promote and improve the use of the urban subsurface, including through its knowledge sharing platform, the Urban Underground Community (COST, 2016). Despite these initiatives, the subsurface is generally an ungoverned and unplanned part of our cities. Most planning systems consider cities from a bird's eye or street level perspective, rather than a holistic and three-dimensional arrangement of interrelated parts. Consider central London, a dense city that is built upon layers of historic human settlement, and a tangle of new and old infrastructure. When the Central Line began construction in 1891, it was necessary to follow the alignment of the narrow winding streets above, in order to avoid the requirement to pay wayleave license fees to surrounding private property owners. Although advances in tunnel construction techniques have allowed new railway lines to be built deeper below London, obstacles to the creation of new infrastructure are only increasing. To ensure that Government is able to successfully deliver the types of public infrastructure needed for long term growth, strategic spatial visions are needed for the subsurface.

A Race to the Bottom

It is not just city Governments and transport or utility companies that are seeking to develop the subsurface, but also private business. London's basement boom was driven by the opportunity to profit from some of the world's highest land values by simply excavating to create new floor space. In describing the vulnerabilities in the planning system that were exploited before the introduction of local basement planning policies, one architect said: 'We analysed the planning laws and realised that they cover everything about the surface of the ground, but nothing beneath it. There was nothing whatsoever that could stop us from drilling all the way down to the south pole', continuing 'of course, the council hated it, but we had a barrister, and the policy would not cover their reasons for refusal, so they had to grant permission — and it has triggered a whole avalanche of stuff ever since' (Wainwright, 2012). Although mega basements seem like a uniquely London phenomena, their aggressive expansion should be the subject of wider debate — what are the cumulative impacts of these types of development? Should the rights of a property owner continue to extend to the centre of the earth?

In Los Angeles, and on a grander scale than even the biggest London basement, there is The Boring Company. Founded by Elon Musk in 2017 in response to frustrating traffic jams, the company aims to radically change the tunnel boring industry, in order to enable the creation of a dedicated subsurface transport network for automated vehicles to travel at depths and speeds not yet offered by traditional road tunnels. Vehicles would be able to exit busy city streets in lifts extending deep below ground and connecting to a tunnel network of multiple layers whereby vehicles could move at 124 miles per hour on automated, guided trays. The deep subsurface is envisioned as endless dirt ready for the taking, all that is needed is a faster, cheaper way of tunnelling, hence creation of The Boring Company. Aiming to reduce the cost of construction by a factor of more than 10, The Boring Company intends to increase the power of traditional Tunnel Boring Machines (TBMs) by using electricity rather than diesel fuel. The company also intends to invest in construction Research and Development, including how spoil from excavation could be used as a valuable material for construction, rather than disposed of as a waste product.

Notwithstanding the intellect, resources and creativity of the company's founder, there are considerable hurdles to this type of project being realised. Firstly, the question should be asked — is this what a city needs to improve transport, quality of life, and environmental sustainability? In describing the efforts of Uber and The Boring Company to take personalised transportation to the skies and down to middle earth, Andrew Hawkins (2017) expresses frustration at the fans of these futuristic concepts, as what 'they're missing is the subtext: our streets are in such poor shape the only innovations worth pursuing are ones that completely abandon the surface. We must become skylarks, or mole people, if we're to get around in a stress-free manner'. Emerging transport solutions also need to be workable for mass transit. As with Braess' Paradox, trying to resolve traffic congestion by building more freeways (even if they are underground), only stimulates more journeys, and more vehicles. Secondly, assuming this is a form of transport that cities decide is desirable, in order to access deep level geology, it will still be necessary to navigate surface, and shallow subsurface level obstructions, both during construction and operation. The trench at the SpaceX headquarters built to test Hyperloop is uncomplicated by an absence of existing development above it. Yet the transition zones needed at street level for motorists to enter and exit the proposed tunnel system would have a sizeable footprint needing to integrate with the surrounding streetscape. In summary, although The Boring Company holds great potential, as a private venture in the absence of a governance structure to address land ownership and to coordinate development, it also risks compounding a sub-surface gold rush. London has a legacy of disused and unmapped corridors, cables and tunnels, often only discovered when struck by equipment excavating for new projects. In the late 1800s London's streets were crowded with traffic and it was difficult to deliver important, time sensitive documents and parcels. Multiple private companies therefore began to construct pneumatic railways, including the Waterloo and Whitehall Railway project which was only partly constructed when abandoned in 1871. Once constructed, buildings below ground might be abandoned and forgotten, but they have a half-life or permanence that can be very difficult to "unbuild" — leaving a gradually accumulating legacy of underground obstructions.

Where to from Here?

There is a clear need for urban planning systems to consider land both above and below ground, so that competing resource and spatial demands can be better managed. At both plan and decision-making stages, the merits or disadvantages of development should be balanced, giving consideration to:

- The need to maintain environmental services such as water filtration.
- Cumulative impacts of individual water and energy abstraction.
- Protection of areas with good geology (i.e. clay that is suitable for tunnelling, or minerals that need to be reserved).
- Safeguarding land likely to be needed for future public infrastructure.
- Policies that identify and enable the conversion of certain types of disused underground spaces, subject to appropriate design and building standards.
- Cumulative impacts associated with private development such as the loss of mature trees and water table imbalances.

- Creation of a government framework for the subsurface to manage a common resource, drawing on the theory, debate and practice of the laws of the sea and outer space.
- Support the introduction of cycle and car parking storage solutions that reduce the amount of land required at street level.
- Undertake life cycle costing to consider the potential for combined utility corridors.
- Seek to create open data platforms of existing underground assets where security considerations allow.

The following pages compare how various international cities address the subsurface within their legislation and planning policies. The cities have been chosen either because they have begun to integrate subsurface considerations into their planning policies, or because there are compelling reasons that they should. The development context of each city is explained, along with their legislation; spatial planning policies; and development control processes. Opportunities are identified for better integration of above and below ground development.

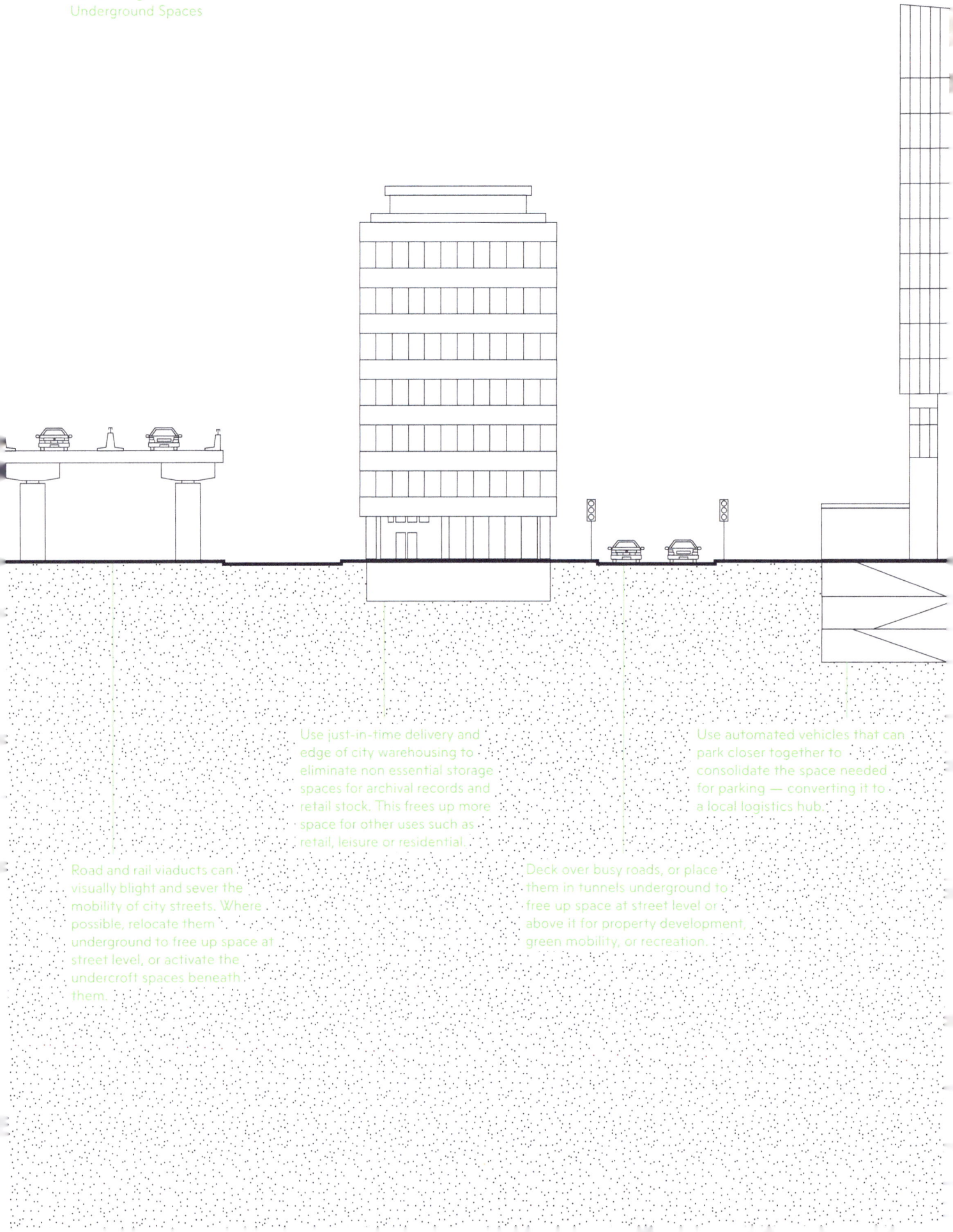

Fig. 3.1
Retrofitting Urban
Underground Spaces

Use just-in-time delivery and
edge of city warehousing to
eliminate non essential storage
spaces for archival records and
retail stock. This frees up more
space for other uses such as
retail, leisure or residential.

Use automated vehicles that can
park closer together to
consolidate the space needed
for parking — converting it to
a local logistics hub.

Road and rail viaducts can
visually blight and sever the
mobility of city streets. Where
possible, relocate them
underground to free up space at
street level, or activate the
undercroft spaces beneath
them.

Deck over busy roads, or place
them in tunnels underground to
free up space at street level or
above it for property development,
green mobility, or recreation.

As the number of private vehicles in cities reduces, convert other underutilised car parks to retail or leisure uses.

Utilise ground source heat energy or move mechanical and electrical equipment to basement level to free up rooftop space.

Consolidate utilities to narrow road widths and reduce disruption from maintenance.

Flood storage tank underground with permeable open space above.

Amsterdam

Amsterdam has a unique character and at its heart are concentric rings of canals lined with terrace houses built during their Golden Age of trading in the 17th Century. Like other Dutch cities, Amsterdam has learnt to live with water, however building remains difficult. In explaining the setbacks experienced in constructing the city's North-South Line metro project, Barbara (2017) estimates that building foundations within Amsterdam are held up by over 1 million piles, sunk between 10 – 50m deep into the clay, peat and sand beneath. In 2008 Architects Zwarts & Jansma worked with engineering company Strukton to propose the Alternative Multifunctional Underground Space Amsterdam (AMFORA) project to build almost 50 km of tunnels underneath the canals in the centre of Amsterdam (Zwartz, 2008). This radical proposal stimulated a great deal of discussion, but does not appear within the Structural Vision Amsterdam 2040.

Amsterdam is seen as a world leader in sustainable transport and development. The city was therefore an appropriate setting in which to agree an Urban Agenda for the whole of the European Union. Known as the Pact of Amsterdam, the 2016 meeting of European Ministers agreed priorities for the growth and management of European cities including the circular economy; climate adaptation (including green infrastructure solutions); sustainable use of land; and urban mobility. The city is applying these international priorities to their own development planning, as is the Netherlands government. The Spatial Planning Act (2008), and the emerging Environment and Planning Act (due to be adopted in 2019) inform national, regional and local urban planning in the Netherlands. These Acts, along with the primary policies such as the National Spatial Strategy and Spatial Vision on Infrastructure & Spatial Planning (2011) also map and reflect the legislative obligations of the European Union. The National Policy Strategy for Infrastructure and Spatial Planning aims to make the Netherlands competitive, accessible, liveable and safe. Within the goal of enhancing the Netherlands' competitiveness, the efficient use of the subsurface is recognised, saying

> 'Several national interests are at play in the subsurface. It plays an important role in energy supply today (extraction, storage and transport of oil and gas) and in the future (geothermal energy, including underground thermal energy storage) and in the storage of CO2 and nuclear waste. Other factors to take into account include the extraction of mineral resources (such as salt, coal and sand), archaeology (such as the former Roman border the Limes, which is part of our cultural heritage), national underground infrastructure (tunnels and pipelines), management of fixed soil contamination (or the remnants thereof), and protection of the supply and quality of

groundwater. The various uses of the subsurface impact on each other and on uses above ground. Without regulation, individual functions of the subsurface would soon become inefficient. Given the limited space available in the subsurface, its significance for the economy and the need to coordinate with activities above ground, efficient use of the subsurface is a matter of national importance' (Ministry of Infrastructure and the Environment, 2011, p10).

Subsurface resources are also recognised as important in a document being prepared collaboratively by the ministers of Infrastructure and Environment; and Economic Affairs titled Structural Vision for the Subsoil, A Compass for the Subsoil. The Structural Vision explains that drinking water supply and the extraction of gas, oil, geothermal heat, and the storage of substances in the subsoil are matters of national importance. The Structural Vision then maps the locations where companies can or cannot apply for permits for subsoil activities. High level Spatial Plans that support the National Spatial Strategy also address topics such as groundwater protection and provide a Multiyear Infrastructure and Transport programme (MIRT). Elsewhere in the Netherlands, the cities of Arnhem and Zwolle are employing a three-dimensional approach to spatial planning with an occupation layer (e.g. housing and offices), network layer (e.g. road and rail infrastructure), and an underground layer with subsurface functions such as storage of water (Admiraal, 2008). Amsterdam would do well to continue evolving national policies and learning from these other cities in the Netherlands. Plan Amsterdam is the key land use planning document for Amsterdam. The Structural Vision Amsterdam 2040 is produced by the Department of Physical Planning and Sustainability and contains six tasks: densify; transform; public transport on a regional scale; high quality layout of public space; invest in the recreational use of green space and water; and converting to sustainable energy. These tasks are needed to help the city provide an additional 70,000 homes by 2040. Another aspect of Amsterdam's long-term thinking is their commitment to becoming a smart city, with 75 projects currently underway. The Amsterdam Smart City initiative encourages innovation in the fields of infrastructure and technology; energy, water and waste; mobility; circular city; governance and education; and citizens and living. Resilience to the rising sea levels also associated with climate change could be one area of future subsurface planning policies.

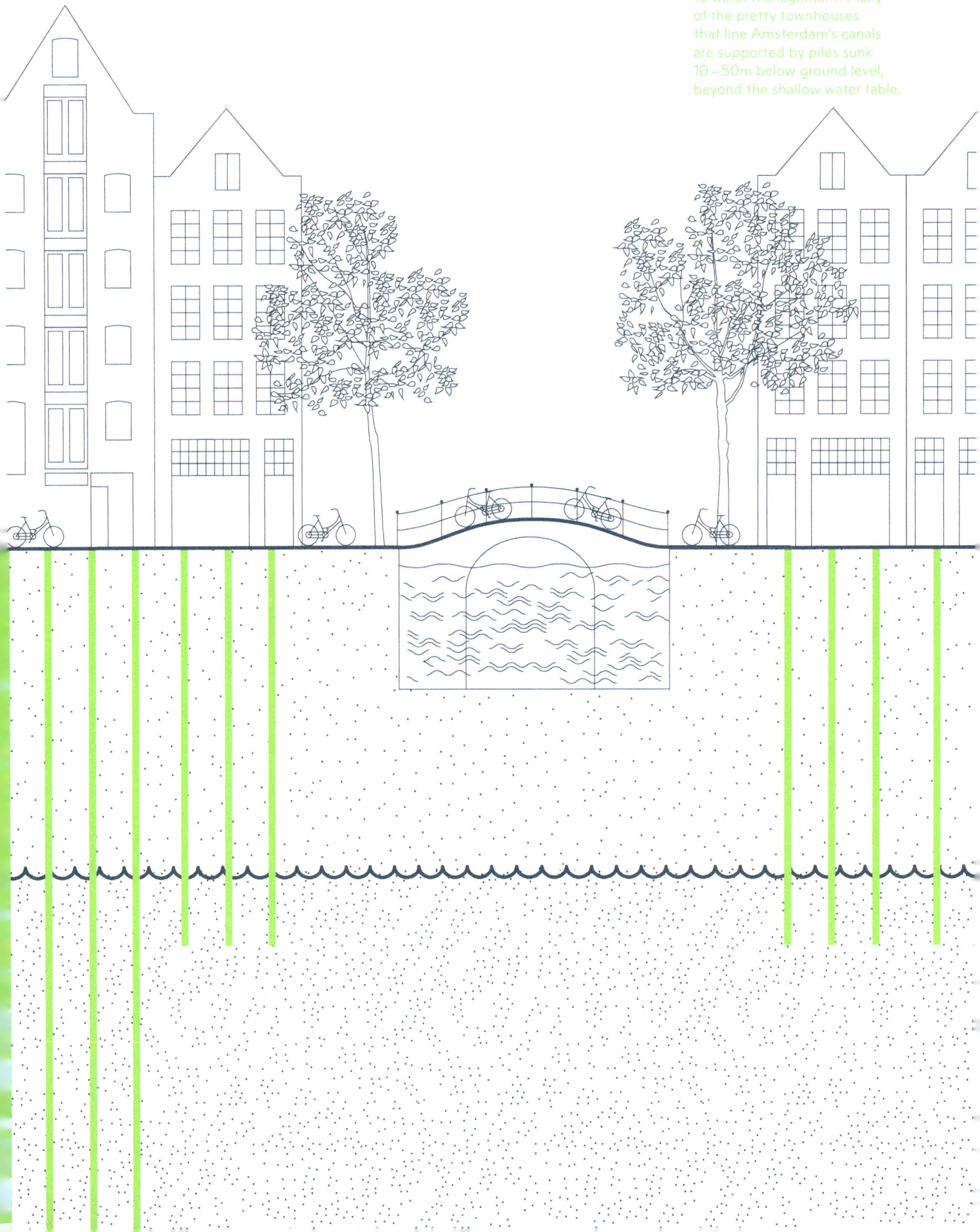

Fig. 3.2
Similar to Venice, construction in Amsterdam relates largely to water management. Many of the pretty townhouses that line Amsterdam's canals are supported by piles sunk 10 – 50m below ground level, beyond the shallow water table.

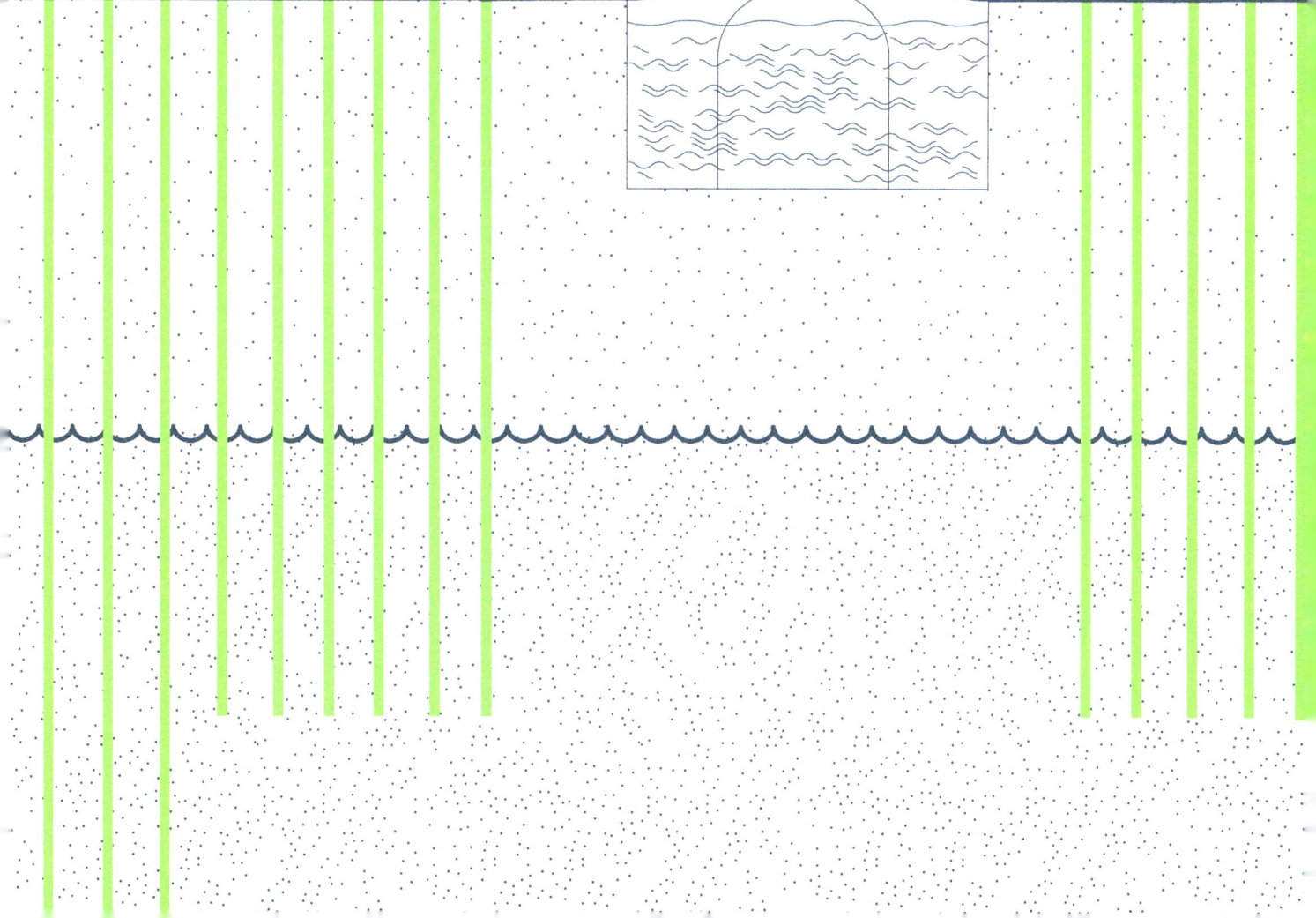

Beijing

Beijing is home to an immense 22 million residents, living in 16 districts across an area of 16,411sqkm. In addition to the formal residents, there are also a large number of people living and working in the city informally. Migrants from poorer rural areas often travel from cities in pursuit of work, although the Chinese Hukou system of household registration can stigmatise and exclude rural migrants who are not permitted to access local services. Like other megalopolises, Beijing faces challenges with traffic congestion, air and water pollution, a lack of open space, community integration, and waste treatment. Similar to Mexico City and Bangkok, Beijing is also sinking. Groundwater extraction is a key factor in the subsidence to parts of Beijing by up to 11 centimetres per annum (Leavenworth, 2016). As part of a central government drive to cure the "ills" associated with city life, Chinese cities including Beijing are the focus of efforts to create smarter, greener and better-quality places to live and work. On 30th March 2017, the Beijing Municipal Commission of Urban Planning (BMCUP) released the draft Beijing Urban Master Plan (2016 – 2030) for public consultation. The plan includes a 1,000km metro system by 2020, a target of 80 per cent green travel by 2030 (with at least 12.6% of bicycles), air pollution controls in line with national standards, targets for urban greening, and access to public parks. The primary planning document in China is the Five-Year Plan (FYP). The current, Thirteenth Five Year Plan (2016 – 2020) was released by the Communist Party of China (CPC) in 2015, on the basis of an earlier document, the 13th Five Year Plan for National Economic and Social Development of the People's Republic of China Outline (2013). The Outline contained seven development priorities including finding new models of coordinated regional development; advancing green development and putting ecology first; and building a more inclusive society with an improved quality of life. In a report on business opportunities associated with the plan, professional services firm KPMG state that 'pursuing new urbanisation is one of the key strategic areas in the 13th FYP'. According to the Outline, China will nurture the development of a number of emerging small and medium sized cities that are self-contained and each have their own distinctive features; develop small towns in desirable geographic locations with convenient transportation, unique natural resources and rich cultural heritage; improve municipal infrastructure and public service facilities; and strive to build cities that are harmonious, liveable, vibrant and distinct. During the 13th FYP period, opportunities for both Chinese and foreign businesses to invest in these new forms of urbanisation lie predominantly in the areas of new 'distinctive cities' and the construction of underground utility pipeline corridors (KPMG, 2016, p 42).

Underground development is a theme that also runs from national to city level planning. Within the Outline for the 13th Five Year Plan, the creation of underground pipeline corridors and networks is highlighted as an infrastructure priority. By 2020 the General Office of the State Council responsible for promoting Urban Underground Utility Tunnel construction aims to complete a 'significant number of world class underground integrated pipeline corridors', make clear progress in eliminating the practice of digging up roads and streets to repair utilities, improve the resilience of existing infrastructure to natural disasters, remove overhead cabling along main roads, and improve the appearance of the urban environment (KPMG, 2016). At an estimated cost of RMB 40mn per km, and an estimated total five-year investment of RMB 5tn, it is a daunting undertaking, but one seen as necessary to supporting the creation of smarter, greener, more functional and attractive cities. Private capital (both foreign and local) is estimated to contribute 55% of the investment for construction of the underground corridors, pipes and cables, with some of those costs returned through charges for access to the corridors and supply of the associated utilities. In an article titled Diagnosing Beijing 2020: Mapping the Ungovernable City, Professor Robin Visser describes Beijing as having 'One of the most aggressive underground space plans in the world, it maximises development use rights in the urban core by allotting 430 million square metres in the shallow layer (up to 10 metres underground) and 630 million square meters in the middle layer (10 – 30 metres underground), largely clustered around traffic hubs and subway transfer stations. In a classic case of interests driving planning, these use rights are primarily granted to the private developers underwriting Beijing's massive public transportation system to serve the new towns' (Visser, 2008 pp 24–25). Understandably, Visser questions the need for extensive subsurface development to achieve a compact urban form, when elsewhere in Beijing (and across China), low-rise gated residential communities are being created on greenfield land.

As explained in Chapter 1, Beijing has an extensive network of underground bunkers, and notwithstanding the poor condition and inaccessibility of some, they represent a considerable resource for the city. If a comprehensive planning and regeneration strategy were to be devised for the estimated 85sqkm of bunkers that are situated 8 – 18m below street level, they could be a great asset to Beijing.

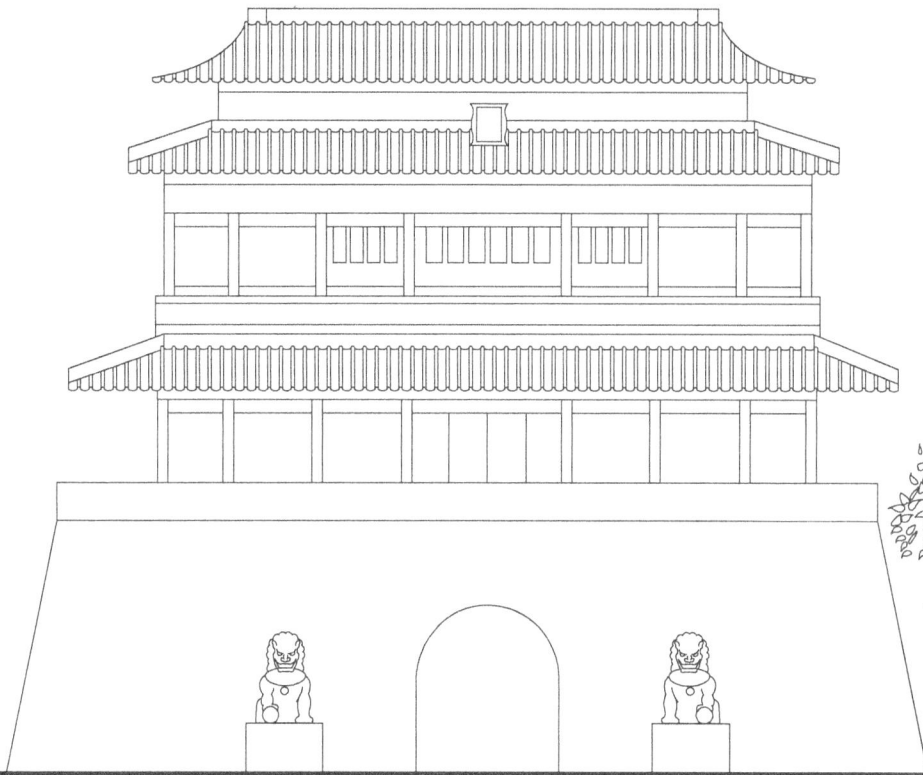

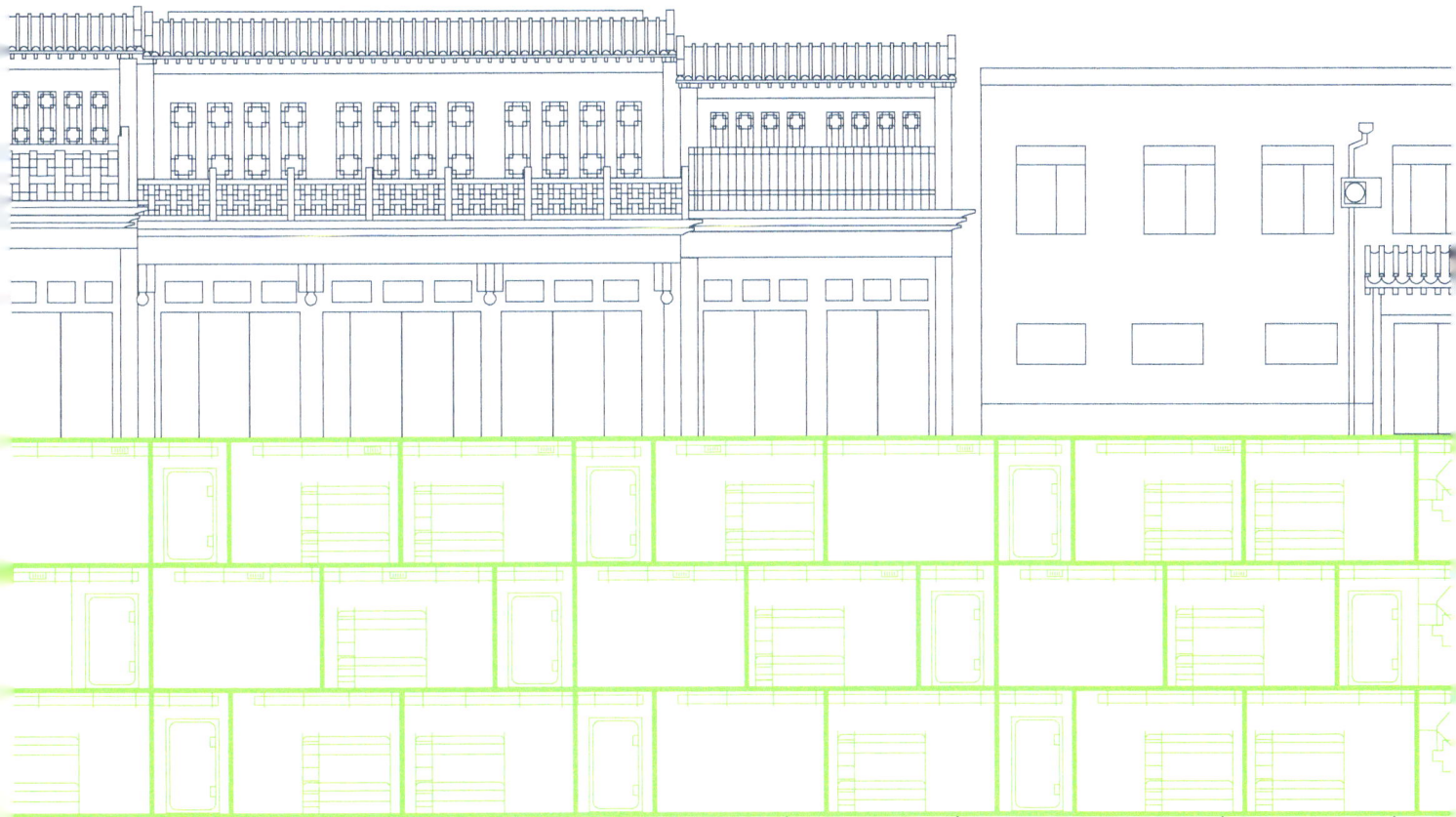

Fig. 3.3
Small doorways, shopfronts and ramps lead from Beijing's busy streets to an 85sqkm network of bunkers, many of which are adapted for residential accommodation or commercial purposes. Some are accessed from Qianmen Street, near the Archery Tower and "front gate" of an historic city wall.

Helsinki

The historic centre of Helsinki is located on the southern tip of a peninsula facing the Gulf of Finland. The City of Helsinki has a population of approximately 630,000 people, within a broader metropolitan area of 1.4 million people. In 2015 the City population grew by 7,493 people, and it is estimated that the population will grow by a further 250,000 people by 2050. There are constraints to accommodating this growing population, and therefore the city proactively seeks to optimise the resources beneath it. Buildings in this older part of the city are relatively modest in scale, with new buildings over 16 storeys classified as high-rise. Although the limited number of tall buildings has helped the city to retain its historic character, it also places pressure on the centre of the city to densify, or risk sprawling further to the north and west (with associated increases in journey to work times and traffic congestion). To disperse demand on the city centre, a number of neighbourhoods are targeted to provide improved places to live and work, including Jätkäsaari, located on the site of a former cargo port. The existing Metro system (that is supplemented by commuter and long-distance trains) was built in the 1980s and is also currently being expanded by 21km to create 13 new stations. At a wider scale, an 80km subsea tunnel is also proposed beneath the Helsinki Gulf, to connect Helsinki with Tallinn in Estonia, thereby supporting economic growth of the wider region. Surveys have been undertaken to understand the geological structure of the sea bed, and the technical challenges involved in delivering the ambitious project. If successful, the project would reduce the current Tallinn / Helsinki journey from a 1.5 – 2.5-hour ferry ride, or 500-mile drive via Russia, to just a 30-minute train journey.

In Finland, the Land Use and Building Act (2000) is the primary piece of legislation with which the built environment is managed. The Act is supported by three types of development plan: the regional plan (maakuntakaava), the masterplan (yleiskaava) at the citywide or district level, and the detailed plan (asemakaava) for sites. In the Capital City of Helsinki, a local plan (osayleiskaava) may also be prepared to mediate between the masterplan and detailed plans. Beneath the detailed plans, in some cases there are also Design Guidelines. In 2013 the City of Helsinki 2020 Master Plan was released, covering the entire city. The Plan designated land into five broad categories (mixed metropolitan uses, housing, public utilities and technical services, commercial and recreation and parks). This plan is now superseded by the Helsinki City Plan: Vision 2050, adopted in October 2016. The Vision 2050 plan took four years to draft and involved the community in activities such as a map based survey where local residents mapped some 33,000 suggestions for locations where urban conditions needed improving, or protection from future development — in total some 33,000 suggestions were mapped.

In parallel to and informing the city-wide masterplans, the City of Helsinki also prepared an underground masterplan. The objective of the Helsinki Underground Master Plan (2011) was to identify and safeguard locations for public and private sector developments including waste water treatment plants, utility and transport corridors, recreational facilities, and civil defence. The master plan included two maps that identified the location of existing and proposed subsurface developments, and a written report explaining the rationale behind the selection and categorisation of the various underground resources. The 2011 Underground Master Plan continues to have legal effect, but is now being revised to ensure consistency with the long term strategic objectives contained within the Helsinki 2050 Plan. The design principles informing the plan were approved in 2017 and it is anticipated a revised draft of the Helsinki Underground Master Plan will be adopted in 2019. The design principles being used to prepare the revised Underground masterplan include:

- Promoting a diversified use of underground facilities
- Safeguarding only the most significant underground space reservations
- Ensuring the safety of underground facilities
- Cooperation between owners of safeguarded land and the government
- Upgrading the future underground space needs of the infrastructure
- Prepare for underground space requirements for different modes of transport
- Assessing the feasibility of geothermal heat plants
- Updating the safeguarding of planned underground parking facilities
- The transport needs of emerging urban nodes

The City of Helsinki Underground Master Plan coordinates, connects, safeguards, and provides a framework for the use of over 600 underground spaces. Land uses ranging from public swimming pools to data centres can be found in some of the 400 existing underground spaces within the city (many of which are naturally occurring bedrock caverns). The actively used spaces such as running tracks, churches, and aquatic centres provide shelter from the cold winter climate and the potential to be used as civil defence shelters in case of emergency. Helsinki's underground spaces are not only prolific, but often also interconnected. An extensive network of tunnels stretching over 300km in length accommodates the majority of energy, water, telecommunications and waste infrastructure for the city. In Viikinmäki, the placement of a waste water treatment plant below ground level meant that a residential development for 3,500 people is being created above. Other underground developments planned for Helsinki include the New Amos Anderson Art Museum designed by Finnish Architects JKMM, who will create a 2,000 sqm exhibition space beneath Lasipalatsi Square, with organically shaped skylights protruding like portholes into the square above, allowing people in each of the spaces to share contrasting viewpoints. Although the natural geology and climate of Helsinki act as strong drivers for the exploitation of underground space, its success is also the result of several other factors. Approximately 62% of the area covered by the Underground Master Plan of Helsinki is within government ownership. Vertically, although not defined in law, where land is privately owned, rights are generally considered to extend to a depth of 6m below ground level, beyond which land is able to be used by the government without the payment of compensation. For those private companies who wish to lease underground space from the government they have an incentive, paying only half the corresponding ground rent.

> Helsinki's role as a world leader in the integration of surface and underground masterplanning is the result of excellent cooperation between technical government departments and private businesses. This has enabled previously disused underground spaces to be converted into functional places that are accepted by the public as important parts of their city. As Helsinki continues to plan for its future, lessons are sure to be learned from its approach to the urban underground.

Underground Urbanism

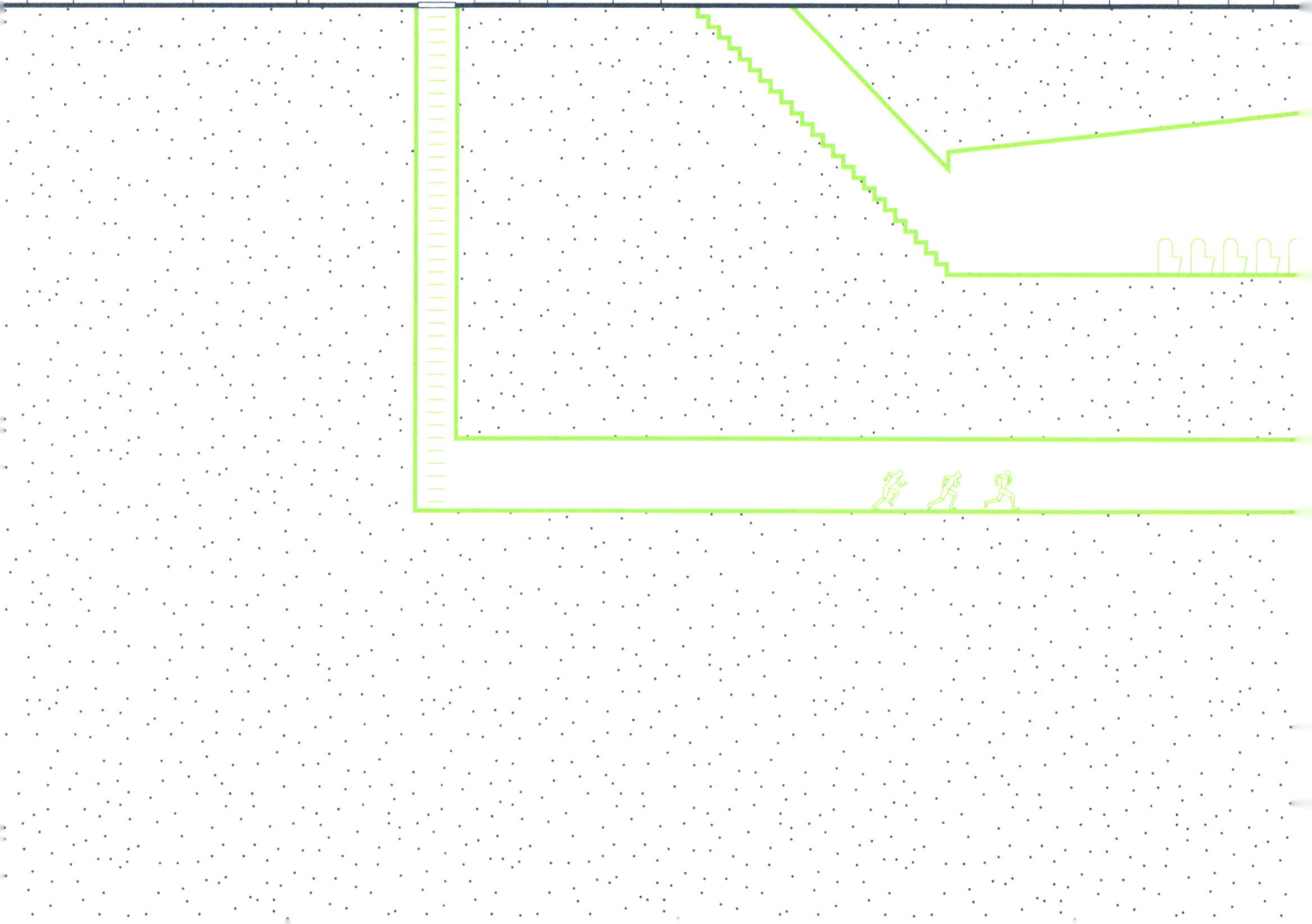

Fig. 3.4
Helsinki has a historic city centre
facing a harbour to the gulf of
Finland. The city shows an
innovative approach to use of its
subsurface, with utility corridors,
running tracks, churches and
swimming pools carved from
the bedrock.

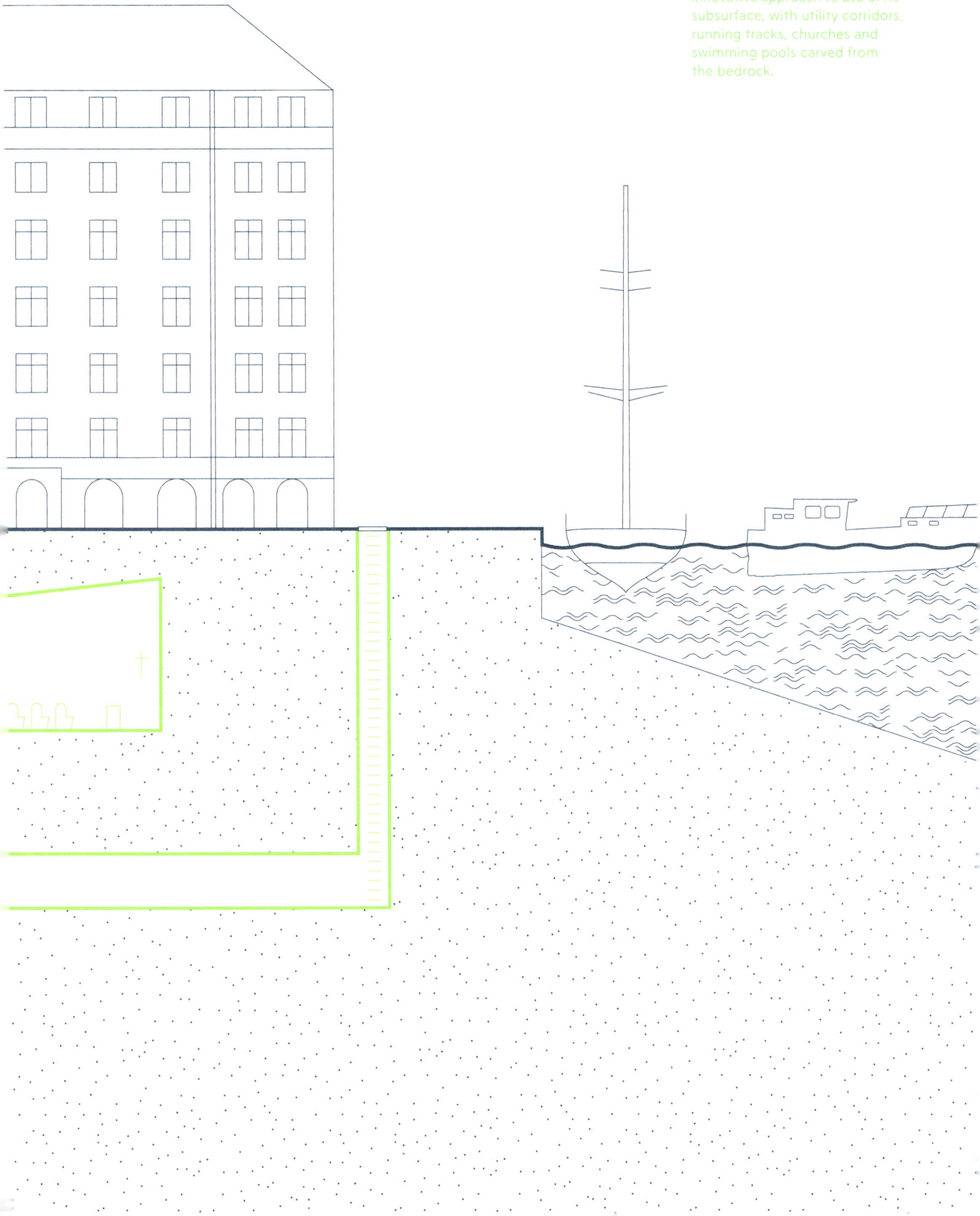

Hong Kong

Hong Kong's dramatic skyline clings to the edge of Kowloon Bay, a ribbon of towers between the mountains and the waterfront, connected by ferries and fast rail links to New Towns. The city's population of 7,320,000 is densely packed at an average of 27,330 people per sqm, with 26% of built up areas constructed on reclaimed land (Planning Department Hong Kong, 2017). Yet this is only part of the picture, with Hong Kong, Macau, and nine cities within the Pearl River Delta being linked to form a mega city region of 80 million people by 2030. This region is in turn part of even bigger plans known as the Belt and Road project to create a new international silk trading route stretching from Europe to the top of Australia.

The system for managing urban growth in Hong Kong is different to other Chinese cities as it is designated as a Special Administrative Region, recognised through a national policy of "one country, two systems". Hong Kong is uniquely managed by a Chief Executive and Council, ministries and secretaries. The planning system is committed to being based on a British model until 2047 (50 years after reunification). The current (draft) strategic plan is Hong Kong 2030+: Towards a Planning Vision and Strategy Transcending 2030, which replaces the previous territorial development strategy written in 2007. Key themes for the strategy are smart, green and resilient and these are based on three building blocks:

- Planning for a Liveable High-density City
- Creating Capacity for Sustainable Growth
- Embracing New Economic Challenges and Opportunities

Hong Kong is well regarded in its ability to deliver technically complex major infrastructure projects. Experience gained in projects such as Chek Lap Kok Airport, the West Island Line railway, and various land reclamation projects, has benefitted the development of various underground facilities such as pedestrian walkways, waste water treatment plants, ammunitions storage, and flood water storage facilities (some of which are located within naturally formed rock caverns). The Happy Valley Underground Stormwater Storage Scheme opened in 2017 and is the largest of its kind in Hong Kong, providing 220,000cbm of non-potable water annually. The water is sourced from the capture of stormwater runoff during heavy storms when the 60,000cbm tank is used to prevent flooding of the surrounding area. The $1.07bn facility has a BREEAM platinum rating and is situated beneath sports fields and a running track (DSDHK, 2017). Detailed feasibility studies are underway for other infrastructure projects including the relocation of the Sea Tin Sewage Treatment Works to rock caverns, thereby reducing odour impacts on surrounding communities and allowing the site to be redeveloped for housing or other uses (DSDHK, 2017). Rock caverns were the subject of a 2011 study by the Geotechnical Engineering Office of Hong Kong that 'identified 400 potential government facilities for future relocation underground. Five areas with over 20Ha of underground space have been identified for further exploration' (Wang, 2015). A topic paper contributing to the evidence base for the Hong Kong 2030+ Plan describes why underground development could be an appropriate form of "land production", namely: 'to help improve the urban environment, especially in densely-populated and congested areas while creating usable space for commercial and community uses, relocating incompatible facilities and thereby freeing up surface land for other beneficial uses, and enhancing urban connectivity and/or unlocking development potential through the provision of pedestrian-cum-retail links and connections with existing developments, subways, transport facilities, etc. (Hong Kong Special Administrative Region Government Planning Department, 2016).

In order to consider the feasibility of retrofitting parts of the city with various types of underground development, a Pilot Study on Underground Space Development in Selected Strategic Urban Areas was undertaken in 2015 for Tsim Sha Tsui West, Causeway Bay, Happy Valley and Admiralty / Wan Chai (CEDDHKSARG, 2017). Underground masterplans are now being prepared for each of these areas, with the overarching vision being 'To Create Coherent, Connected, High Quality and Vibrant Network of Underground Space'. In looking at the opportunities and challenges associated with each of the Strategic Urban Areas, the study considers:
- 'Geotechnical, Structural and Infrastructural Constraints;
- Interface with Existing Underground Uses including Basements, MTR Stations and Tunnels;
- Fire Safety;
- Financial Viability: Construction, Operation and Maintenance Costs and Recovery Period;
- Land Ownership and Town Planning Issues;
- Implementation Agreement;
- Impact to Above-ground Facilities / Activities; and Traffic and Social Impacts during Construction Stage'.

In the case of the Causeway Bay study, concerns have been raised regarding construction, environmental and visual impacts. Oren Tatcher of the Hong Kong Institute of Urban Design questioned one proposal to introduce a large car park beneath Victoria Park, as it would require the removal of tree lined paths, and introduce equipment to the park landscape such as ventilation shafts and emergency exit stairs. Rather than automatically accepting the proposals within the pilot study,

Tatcher said 'Underground development should be considered, and planned carefully, as part of a holistic approach to improving walkability and public space in Hong Kong' (Tatcher, 2017). The need for integrated, high quality urban design is also mentioned briefly within the Hong Kong 2030+ topic paper Planning and Urban Design for a Liveable High-Density City, that says 'With underground space developments becoming more prevalent in the future, the holistic planning of underground pedestrian networks would also need to be carefully considered' (HKSARGPD, 2016). For the Hong Kong 2030+ plan to effectively meet its Key Strategic Direction of 'Fostering efficient use of urban spaces', and the associated action to 'unlock development potential through innovative use of land, especially underground spaces', holistic urban design will indeed be important.

Ultimately, Hong Kong's future relies on the vertical and lateral integration of space to ensure that land use is optimised. This will need to carefully balance competing demands, limit construction impacts, be cost efficient, and create quality urban environments — a big task even for Hong Kong's world class built environment professionals.

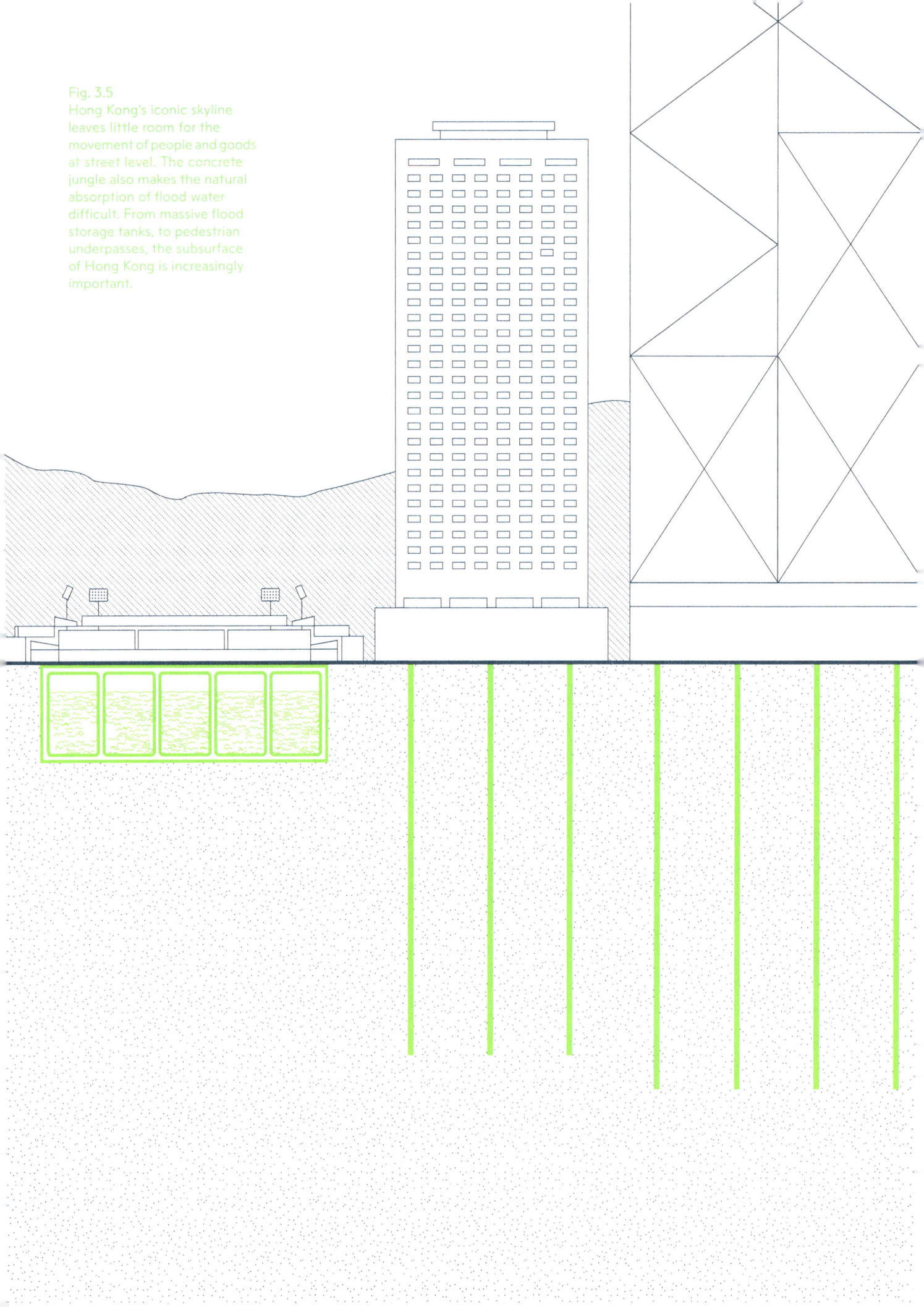

Fig. 3.5
Hong Kong's iconic skyline
leaves little room for the
movement of people and goods
at street level. The concrete
jungle also makes the natural
absorption of flood water
difficult. From massive flood
storage tanks, to pedestrian
underpasses, the subsurface
of Hong Kong is increasingly
important.

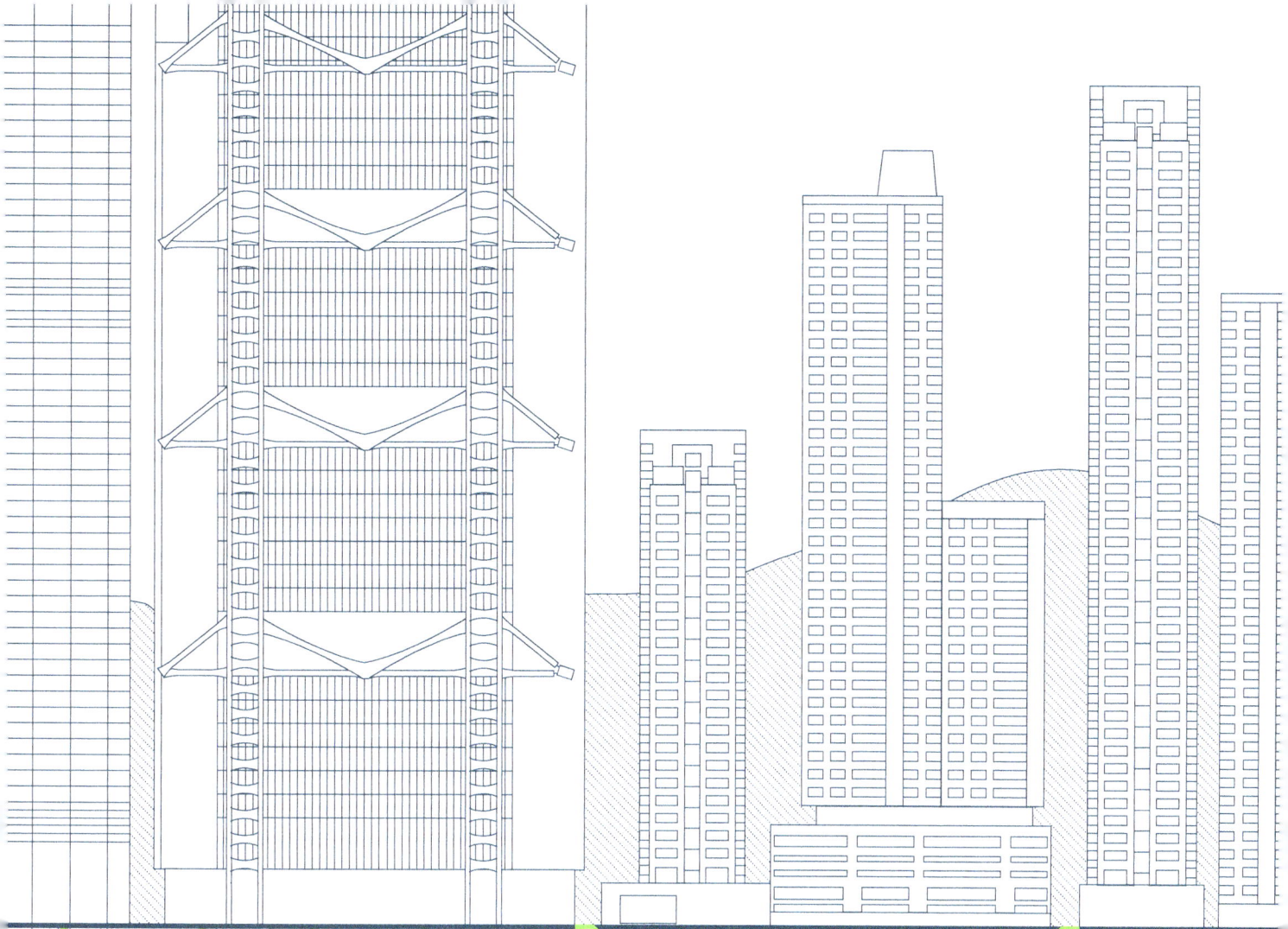

London

London is to an extent defined by its relationship with the underground, yet this isn't reflected in planning policy. Before explaining the current urban planning and development context, it is worth explaining the origins of land use planning policy and how it has evolved. In 1875 the Public Health Act was introduced to the United Kingdom. It required urban authorities to make bylaws for new streets; to ensure the structural stability of houses; prevent fires; provide for the drainage of buildings; and air space around them. However, when the London County Council was created in 1889, it wanted to tailor legislation, and so sponsored the London Building Act of 1894. Following the Second World War, the Town and Country Planning Act 1949 established the framework for modern planning policy by replacing historical building controls such as the London Building Act (1894) with a plan-led policy approach. The system has evolved multiple times in the years since, but many of the central tenets have endured. In March 2012, the National Planning Policy Framework (NPPF), the latest of these evolutions, was introduced. The NPPF is the highest tier in a plan-led system that informs the production of local policies by City and borough level organisations, with community groups also able to prepare Neighbourhood Plans. The NPPF contains 12 planning principles that should inform plan-making and decision-making, one of which is that 'planning should always seek to secure high quality design and a good standard of amenity for all existing and future occupants of land and buildings'. Importantly, the NPPF also contains a presumption in favour of sustainable development, meaning that applications for development consent should be approved unless they are contrary to sustainable development criteria set at a national and local level. The NPPF also states that Local Plans should 'reflect and where appropriate promote relevant European Union (EU) obligations and statutory requirements', these include EU Directives on Strategic Environmental Assessment. It is not yet clear how the EU requirements will feature in British law and policy after the United Kingdom leaves the European Union.

As the top-tier planning body for London, the Greater London Authority (GLA) produced and continues to revise a Spatial Development Strategy (SDS) known as the London Plan (consolidated with alterations since 2011). Under the terms of the Greater London Authority Act (1999), the London Plan can only provide direction on things of strategic importance to Greater London, within the themes of:

- Planning for a Liveable High-density City
- Creating Capacity for Sustainable Growth
- Embracing New Economic Challenges and Opportunities

The London Plan is also informed by other legislation and policies including the European Spatial Development Perspective (European Commission 1999). The Plan currently provides a strategy for growth of the city through until 2036, and is structured around six over-arching objectives, including 'to be a city that becomes a world leader in improving the environment'. Policies within the Plan are grouped around the themes of places; people; economy; climate change; transport; living spaces and places; and implementation. The policies do not include any instruction for the planning or management of the subsurface per se. Whilst the GLA has strategic planning oversight, and can decide on applications for major developments, the majority of planning is undertaken by the constituent Boroughs (32 plus the Corporation of the City of London), each of whom produce their own Local Plans (which must accord with the directions contained within the NPPF and London Plan). Whilst a growing number of London's 32 boroughs consider residential basements within their Local Plans or Supplementary Planning Documents (SPD), the focus is primarily on the environmental and structural impacts potentially associated with construction. In the Royal Borough of Kensington and Chelsea (RBKC), the Basements SPD (RBKC, 2016) provides guidance on the design of basements, how to manage construction impacts (such as noise vibration and dust), trees, flooding and drainage. The SPD is a material consideration in applications for planning permission to construct basements, it does not provide a view as to which parts of the borough are more or less appropriate for subsurface development, and is unable to control cumulative environmental impacts associated with applications from multiple property addresses.

With a population of 8,663 million and having grown at 7% over the past 5 years (GLA, 2017), London faces considerable pressure on its natural resources and aging infrastructure. To support the needs of a growing population, a number of underground infrastructure projects are planned or under construction. These major projects include Crossrail which is described as 'essential to delivery of the strategic objectives of the London Plan'. Europe's largest infrastructure project, Crossrail has built over 100km of track including 21km of new twin-bore rail tunnels and nine new stations. The new railway will increase London's rail-based transport network capacity by 10 per cent, reduce journey times, ease congestion and improve connections for approximately 200 million passenger journeys annually. Crossrail was granted government planning consent using a special hybrid bill of parliament in 2005. Bills are policy proposals that with approval from the House of Lords, the House of Commons, and formal approval by the monarch (known as 'Royal Assent'), then become law as an Act of Parliament. Hybrid bills are those that affect individuals directly as well as the broader public through their nationally significant status. Individuals and organisations can oppose a bill or seek its amendment before a Select Committee, in either, or both the House of Commons and House of Lords.

One of the most significant costs associated with the delivery of major infrastructure projects, is the compulsory purchase of land. Although a flat rate of £50 has traditionally been accepted as the nominal value paid when acquiring subsoil property rights, increasing property prices in London are changing the perceived financial value of the subsurface. The (planned) High Speed 2 project faced challenges from 204 parties who claimed that £50 was an insufficient payment for their subsoil. A number of respondents also sought confirmation as to whether their future ability to develop their property at basement level would be restricted. There is therefore a concern that the physical cost of acquiring or insuring against damage to private subsurface developments could add unnecessary cost to future urban infrastructure projects. In some situations, even where subsurface land rights have been acquired, the ability to develop is still not guaranteed. The Marylebone Cricket Club are entangled in a long running battle to expand their facilities at Lord's cricket club, yet have been scuppered by their failure in 1999 to acquire three former rail tunnels beneath their property (Engel, 2014). A property developer, the Rifkind Levy Partnership, saw value in the cavernous 38m tunnels that were formerly a part of the Great Central Railway, and acquired them on a 999 lease (for a sum that today would scarcely buy a one-bedroom apartment in the area). However, the leaseholder of the tunnels, is also constrained, as access to the tunnels is currently only provided via the basement of an adjacent private hospital, who in turn have their own long-term development plans. The three organisations were unable to align their development interests, or agree an appropriate financial compensation, and therefore the tunnels remain disused, despite their prime location.

> In 2017 the MCC put two alternative masterplans to their committee. The first incorporated the railway tunnels (above which housing would be constructed); and the second, funded entirely by the MCC using their land. The decision made on 27th September 2017 effectively ruled out the MCC acquiring the leasehold of the rail tunnels (and associated land / air above). The decision was reached after extensive technical analysis and consultation with members, many of whom objected to the introduction of two, ten storey apartment blocks above the rail sidings beneath the nursery. Whilst

the members' decision is understandable, the club remains effectively held to ransom, and the Rifkin Partnership constrained in their development potential — not an ideal outcome for either party. A joined-up approach to subsurface property rights could potentially have avoided this protracted situation.

London is fortunate enough to have geological conditions that are conducive to excavation and tunnelling; however, there is a risk London could run out of "good" geology, and areas of the subsurface that are unencumbered by obstructions such as building foundations. If tunnels can no longer be constructed, then future transport and utilities infrastructure might have to be installed at street level, in turn leading to significant changes in the character of London's streetscape. Although the London Plan has no clear strategy for the future of its subsurface, there a few policies that could be revised or supplemented to address this concern. Policy 7.20 states that development proposals should 'wherever possible, make a positive contribution to the protection and enhancement of geodiversity', it is primarily concerned with the protection of 14 Regionally Important Geological and geomorphological Sites (RIGS). As detailed in the report London's foundations (GLA, 2009), the sites were selected according to their educational, historical, aesthetic and scientific values. Additional areas of geological importance could be added to Policy 7.20 if their ability to facilitate transport infrastructure or environmental services is at risk (such as clay that is suitable for tunnelling or areas where groundwater is not able to recharge on account of hard surfacing). Policy 5.4 Retrofitting could support the repurposing of abandoned or underutilised spaces below ground. Disused underground train stations, car parks, bomb shelters and document storage facilities could be promoted to the GLA by their owners as potential redevelopment sites, then (where it is safe and practicable to do so) added to Annex A Opportunity and Inten-sification Areas. Policy 6.2 — Providing public transport capacity and safeguarding land for transport, seeks to protect the alignment of planned infrastructure projects such as Crossrail 2, however, these routes are already informed by constraints such as the building foundations described in Chapter 2. Taking a strategic spatial approach, it could be possible to speculate where subsurface infra-structure is most likely to be needed next. As explained in Chapter 2, the central area of established cities like London are often very congested beneath the surface, however as London's town centres strengthen and the city becomes more polycentric, it might be that transport infrastructure and surface level pressures are experienced more in towns and metropolitan centres such as Stratford, where the density of new residential development is also high. Policy 5.12 Flood Risk Management requests that in preparing Local Development

Frameworks (LDF), local authorities 'utilise Strategic Flood Risk Assessments to identify areas where particular flood risk issues exist and develop actions and policy approaches aimed at reducing these risks, particularly through redevelopment of sites at risk of flooding and identifying specific opportunities for flood risk management measures'. Underground flood storage facilities could be created beneath sports fields, or integrated with other types of development including road tunnels (similar to the SMART project in Kuala Lumpur). Lastly, in Policy 5.4A Electricity and Gas Supply, local boroughs are directed to work with energy companies to establish the future gas and electricity infrastructure needs arising from the development of their area and address them in their local plans. It might be that this Policy needs to instruct local authorities to take a step further forward by identifying locations for emerging technologies, such as the Bunhill Energy Centre in Islington where waste heat from a London Underground train line is captured and redistributed to local residents (GLA, 2017). The London Plan described above (as consolidated 2016), is being replaced by a New London Plan. Currently in draft format, the New London Plan is due to be adopted in Autumn 2019. Through awareness raising, and active engagement on draft policy making, voluntary professional group Think Deep UK are seeking to ensure that responsible planning of the urban subsurface is acknowledged as a priority within the New London Plan. It is encouraging that the Draft Plan contains a policy on Basement Development (D9). Ultimately however, if London is to make the most of its underground assets, then basements are only the beginning.

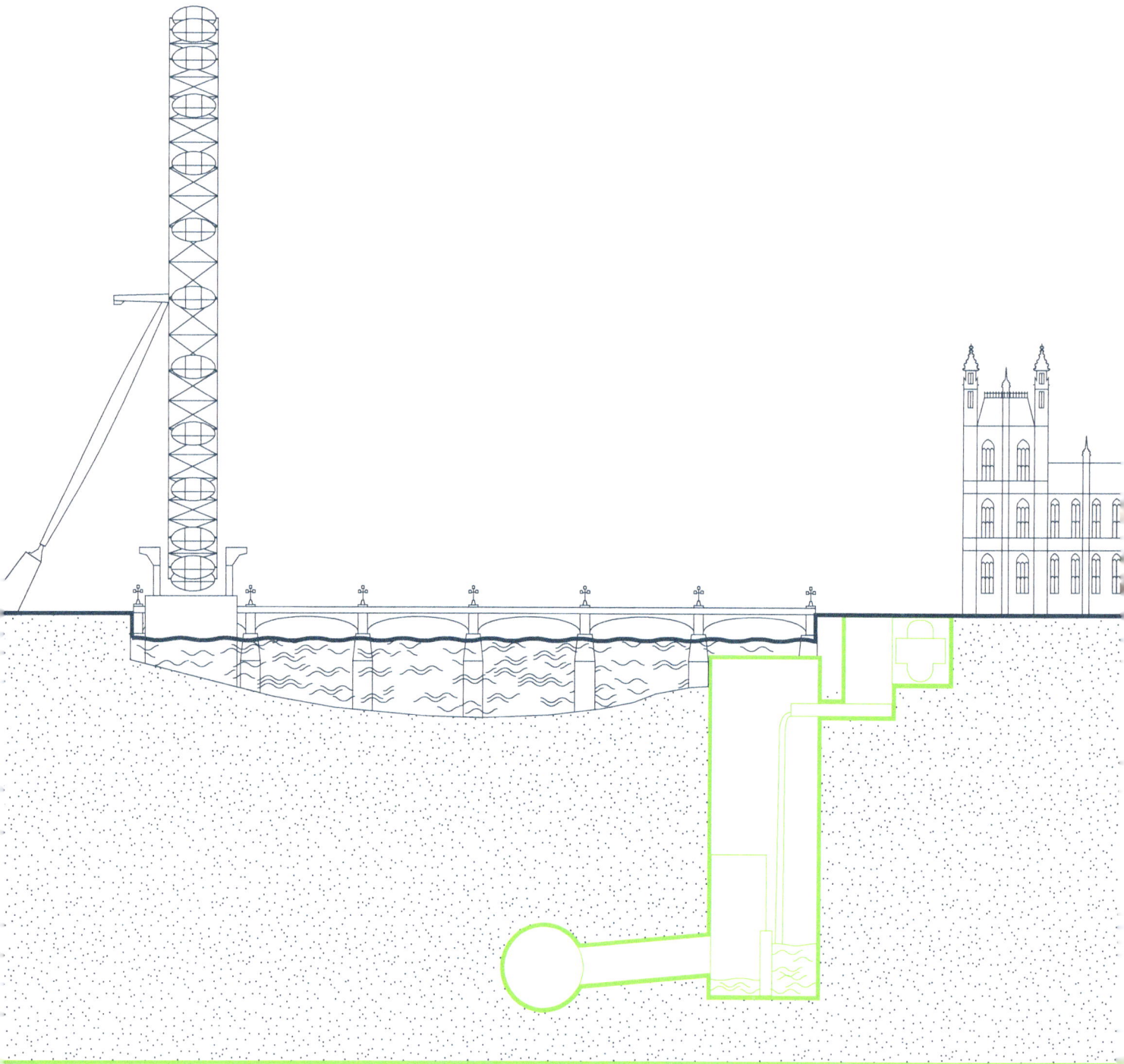

Fig. 3.6
It is possible to traverse much of London without ever seeing daylight, moving rapidly between historic monuments and new corporate edifices on the London Underground (or "the Tube"). But what and where next for this city synonymous with the subsurface?

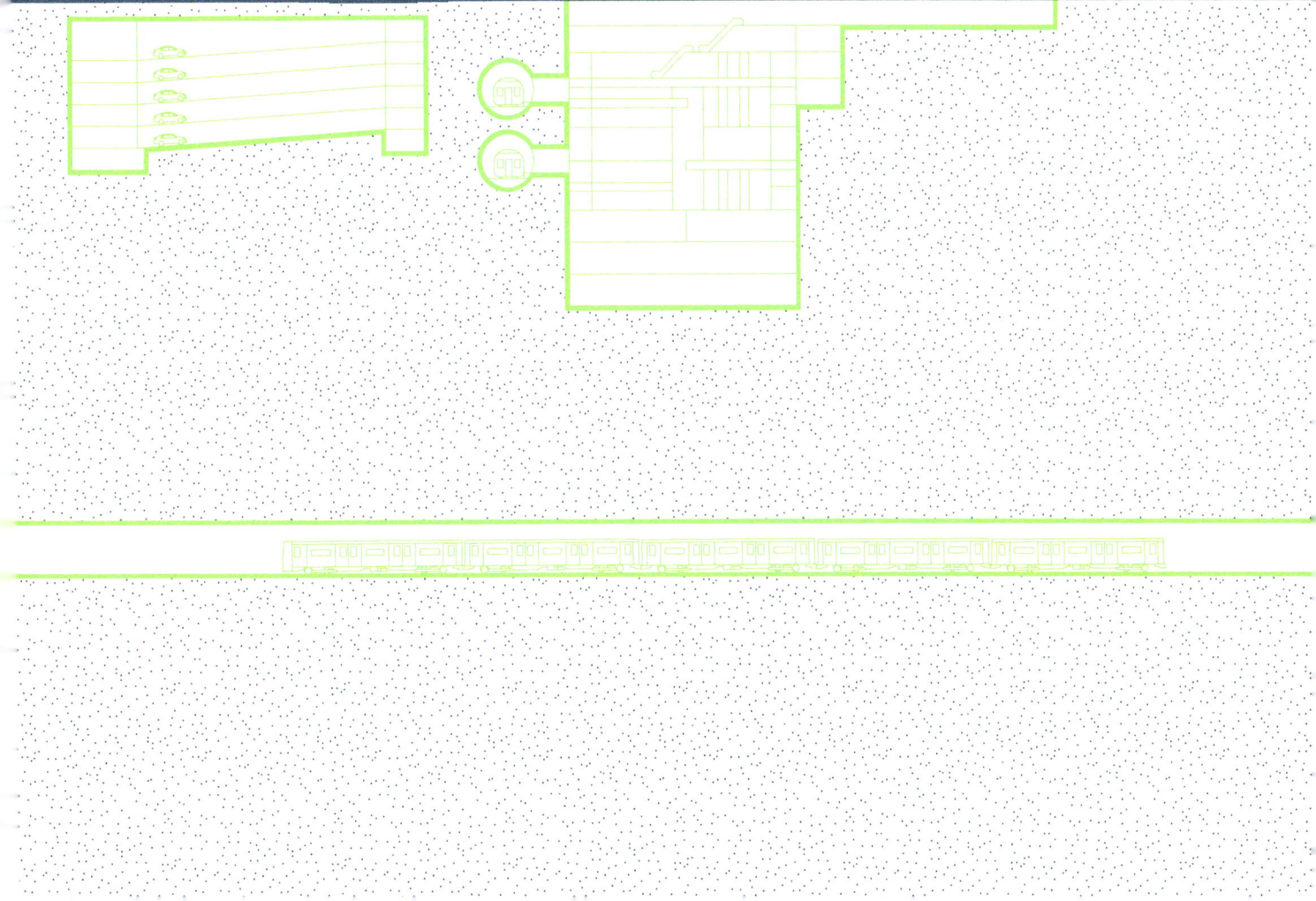

New York

In a city famed for its skyline, how is New York planning for the future of its subsurface? New York's population of 8,537,673 (within the five boroughs of The Bronx; Brooklyn; Queens; Manhattan; and Staten Island), is supplemented by long distance commuters, as well as national and international visitors - a total of 58.5 million visits each year (City of New York, 2016; NYC and Company, 2017). This is a tremendous amount of activity to have concentrated on the island of Manhattan, particularly during peak hours as commuters access the bridges and tunnels that connect the island with the remainder of the city, and elsewhere in New York State. Due to a combination of geology, history, geography, commerce and planning policy, the city has grown dramatically upwards (Reynolds and Reynolds, 2015). Although the New York subway is iconic, the city does not have the same historic legacy of underground construction as Beijing, London or Paris. This is, however, beginning to change, as the city attempts to use land more efficiently, and become more resilient to the effects of climate change. The impacts felt from Hurricane Sandy, and a critical need to upgrade ageing infrastructure, are also encouraging the city to think more about managing the spaces beneath the city's busy streets.

All cities are settled upon layers of made ground and tangled webs of utilities beneath them, but in New York untraced and ageing infrastructure is a particular challenge. In a Vanity Fair article titled 'What Lies Beneath' William Langewiesche described the complications beneath Manhattan as including '(in variable order of ascent) the tunnels and tracks for five independent passenger railroads (Long Island Rail Road, Metro North, New Jersey Transit, the PATH system, and Amtrak); the train stations (current and planned); the subways; the subway stations (current and planned); the under-river tunnels; the foundations of tall buildings; the combined sewer-and-storm-drain lines; the steam tunnels; urban detritus, such as the pneumatic tubes that once carried mail under the city; the water mains; and, generally closest to the surface, the webs of proprietary power and data/cable lines'. Continuing, Langewiesche says 'All this infrastructure was forced underground not through some grand plan that can easily be sorted out but rather through two centuries of competition and compromise as the value of New York's surface space increased and the streets grew more crowded. Taken as a whole, underground New York is an incoherent three-dimensional space that defies simple visualization' (Langewiesche, 2017).

The layers of New York continue to accumulate. Although they sometimes seem to progress at a glacial pace, New York is heavily committed to major infrastructure projects, several of which are currently under construction. The City Water Tunnel Number Three, East Side Access (rail) project from Long Island to Grand Central, phases 2 and 3 of the Second Avenue Subway; and extension of the No. 7 Subway from Times Square to a new terminal on the west side of Manhattan. These major new infrastructure projects are badly needed to supplement ageing infrastructure under pressure from a combination of residents, commuting workers and tourists. Similar to Paris and London, New York also has a number of historic subway stations not currently in use, but with the potential to be reactivated. Perhaps the most iconic station is City Hall, which closed in 1945 but remains in excellent condition. The station features vaulted tile ceilings, with electric chandeliers, and glass skylights. Occasional tours of the station run by the New York Transit Museum for its members are always sold out, giving an indication of people's great affection and curiosity for these abandoned places.

Despite the increasingly chaotic layers of structures and utilities beneath Manhattan, the development of the city has in fact been guided by spatial development plans since 1811, when the grid shaped Commissioners Map and Survey of Manhattan Island was released. The primary mechanism of land use planning in New York is zoning, and the first city was the first in the country to implement a zoning resolution in 1916. All land in New York City falls into one of four zones: residential, commercial, manufacturing, or mixed use; however, a "special district" (of which there are currently 60) can also be declared. The City Planning Commission and the Department of City Planning are now responsible for the orderly growth and development of New York City and operate under rules in Title 62 of the Rules of the City of New York. In 2007, the (then) Mayor of New York Michael Bloomberg released a strategic planning document to overlay the regulatory planning system. PlaNYC was revised in 2011 with the objective of setting a 2030 vision for a 'A Greener, Greater New York'. When Bill de Blasio became Mayor of New York in 2015, PlaNYC was superseded by One New York: The Plan for a Strong and Just City. Also known as OneNYC, the strategic plan for the city continues to build on the themes of sustainability and resiliency contained within PlaNYC, but also focuses on the principles of growth and equity. PlaNYC does not discuss subsurface, basement, geological or hydrological matters, though it does make several references to the underground development including 'Many of the city's gas, steam, sewer, and water lines are not only aging, but are made of materials not in use today, and prone to leaks and breaks. Much of the city's underground infrastructure is not mapped, making it hard to pinpoint issues to make efficient repairs or improvements' (p.32). The need to upgrade New York City's transit system is also acknowledged (p.32), along with the vulnerability of heat and electricity facilities that are often located within floodplains. Private property and lives are also at risk from storm surges, heavy rainfall and high winds. New York City's 1% annual chance floodplain is described as 'vast — 71,500 buildings and 400,000 residents' and it is estimated that by the 2050s 'the number of people living in the 1% annual chance floodplain could more than double to 808,900' (New York City, 2015).

Although the City of New York is constrained by Bedrock Geology, making it difficult to excavate or tunnel (see case studies in Chapters 2 and 4), there is potential for the city to make better use of its under-ground assets. As indicated above, the subway system is in extremely poor condition, and would benefit from concentrated efforts to upgrade stations, rolling stock and railway infrastructure. Perhaps in undertaking these upgrades, opportunities could be identified to improve the comfort and efficiency of the system through initiatives such as capturing waste heat for energy. The potential for disused subway stations to be repurposed could also be examined, as could rationalising utilities into dedicated corridors, or creating under-ground stormwater storage facilities.

The subsurface of New York has the potential to play an important role in improving the resiliency of the city and the efficiency with which land is used in the city. However, to make the most of these opportunities, it is also important that lessons be learnt from projects such as the Second Avenue Subway (or at least its first phase). In summary, without taking a proactive approach to integrating their subsurface assets, New York City will not be able to achieve the goals contained within OneNYC.

Fig. 3.7
The bedrock of New York makes
it difficult to excavate for deep
level tunnels, and although the
rock is able to be blasted away,
most subsurface infrastructure
is shallow and constructed using
a cut and cover technique.
Despite these challenges,
steam rising through grates in
the street, and the ubiquitous
New York subway is a reminder
that the underground is a vital
part of this dynamic city.

Paris

The grand Metropolis of Paris is not only home to some of the world's greatest cultural artefacts and buildings, but also many physical layers of history, rather like the famous French pastry, mille-feuille. From the establishment of Parisii by the Gauls in the third Century BC, to the Napoleonic swagger of the 19th Century, Paris is an ever growing and changing city. Although expansion and evolution are trends consistently experienced by most cities, few seem to have the rhythm of Paris — with long periods of preservation, followed by intermittent shocks of reinvention. The modern city of Paris is vast — with a population of 12mn stretched across a 12,012sqkm area (Paris Region, 2017). Ever popular with tourists, and a major business capital, Paris' three airports handle 95.4mn passengers per annum. It is acknowledged that some communities within this grand metropolis have suffered economic decline, and become ghettos isolated from Paris' better-known and more prestigious neighbour-hoods. However, in recent years there has been a concerted effort to revitalise Paris, and to provide an improved sense of cohesion amongst the city's residents. Both strategic, macro level urban planning, and micro level subsurface design, are helping Paris reinvent itself as a more liveable, sustainable, and economically competitive city.

The physical layers of Paris tell the stories of a lengthy and eventful human settlement. Gypsum, Limestone, Chalk, and Clay are found in the earth beneath Paris (Share, 2014). The resources of the city have been extracted through quarrying materials such as limestone and gypsum (the latter being used to make "Plaster of Paris"). The soft ground conditions have made excavation and tunnelling relatively easy, and combined with centuries of made ground from human settlement, have created a complex web of underground spaces. The city's famous catacombs are thought to hold the remains of 6mn Parisians, and are understandably important to the cultural heritage of the city. The honesty with which death is addressed within the catacombs is also a reminder that as many cities grow, they also face pressure to find sufficient, and appropriate space for human burials — yet another (perfectly natural) demand on the subsurface. Some of the catacombs are open for tours, but the majority of Paris' 280km long network of tunnels, caves and catacombs is closed to public for safety and security reasons, with a dedicated police force fining urban explorers who access the space. Above, and alongside these spaces, are a raft of other interventions in the subsurface, including the usual metro lines, utilities, car parks, building basements, defence bunkers, road tunnels and aquifers (Clement and Thomas, 2001). With all of this activity, what potential is there for the city to optimise a long history of subsurface development?

Like London and other European cities, the planning policies of Paris are influenced broadly by National and European Union policy directives. Paris also a member of the (voluntary) 100 Resilient Cities network, sponsored by the Rockefeller Foundation. Paris' resilience challenges relate to housing shortages, neighbourhood segregation, and heat waves (100 Resilient Cities, 2018). At a National level, there are regulations that determine the types of changes possible for land and buildings. At the opposite end of the scale, local plans ('Plan Local d'urbanisme') also contain guidance on land use zoning controls, and these are legally binding (Maurice, 2013).

The Metropolis of Greater Paris was incorporated in 2016, bringing together 130 separate communes. The objective of this overarching municipal authority is: 'the sustainable development of the region's economy and employment with a view to maintaining and even strengthening, the Greater Paris position among the most attractive global cities' (Metropole du Grand Paris, 2017). The Metropolis of Greater Paris tasked itself with producing three key policy documents: a masterplan; economic development strategy; and a metropolitan climate action plan.

In recent years, the various levels of French government have co-operated to significantly redevelop Paris through two key projects — the Grand Paris Express and Reinvent Paris. The Grand Paris Express is the largest transport project in Europe. The Grand Paris Express will provide four entirely new metro lines, with 200km of new track, and 68 new stations to serve 2 million passengers a day. Significantly, 90% of the new lines will also be built underground (Societé du Grand Paris, 2017). Arranged in a ring formation, the new lines will connect to and extend existing metro lines, connecting also to the city's three airports, major business districts and research hubs. The new system will rapidly reduce the time currently taken for some journeys. Yet, more than simply providing new transport, the project will act as an enabler to improve access to economic opportunities for Paris' poorer communities. Planning transit oriented development nodes around the new stations is also hoped to attract investment for science and research clusters, clean industry, office space, and new homes.

Alongside the Grand Paris Express, the Reinvent Paris call for projects was launched in 2014 and invited the public, designers, and property developers, to consider how 23 different locations across Paris could be used to reinvent the French capital. Due to overwhelming response, a second call for projects was released in 2017, with Reinvent Paris II focused on "The Subterranean Secrets of Paris". In launching Reinvent Paris II, the Mayor of Paris, Anne Hidalgo, said: 'By doing so, we are rejecting a Paris fossilized by nostalgia or, conversely, drowned in a contemporary movement towards standardization. By opening up the scope of possibilities, by articulating urban, ecological and democratic revolutions, we are going to fashion the City of tomorrow: an open, decompartmentalized, vibrant and radiant place' (City of Paris, 2017). The 34 sites selected for Reinvent Paris II include car parks, tunnels, former nightclubs and substations, as well as the space beneath a metro viaduct. Detailed information is provided for each site, including land ownership, utility constraints, and suggestions for possible future uses. The public are able to propose their own suggestions, and comment on shortlisted entries. The winning entries might well progress to development, helping to reinvigorate previously neglected pockets of the city. The Deputy Mayor of Paris, Jean-Louis Missika, (who is responsible for 'town planning, the Greater Paris projects, economic development and attractiveness'), further explains Reinvent Paris II by saying: 'With this new competition, we want to unveil the incredible potential of Paris's underground and invent the Paris of tomorrow'...' The underground is essentially viewed as spaces relegated for municipal services. Necessary for Paris to function, via its transportation, sewage and heating networks, parking lots and cellars, it is often hidden and underutilized'...'By bringing in natural light and creating a new vertical relationship between the subterranean city and the one on the surface, these projects will open up a new dimension in city planning. Tunnels, unused gas stations, parking lots, reservoirs, these are all infrastructures that deserve a second life' (City of Paris, 2017). It is rare for a city to innovate on such a scale, let alone to integrate above and below ground spaces. In doing so, Paris has surely now thrown down the gauntlet to other global cities like New York and London, to also reinvent the forgotten spaces beneath their cities. Cumulatively, these two key urban redevelopment initiatives look certain to ensure that Paris remains one of the world's greatest cities for many years to come, both above and below ground.

Fig. 3.8
The striking pyramid of the
Louvre in Paris contains a
surprise below ground, where
it continues inverted, before
concluding like an exclamation
mark in the light filled atrium
space of a shopping centre,
metro station and museum
entrance below ground. The
physical and historical layers
of Paris are in the process of
being reinvented through a call
by the Mayor for innovative
projects to adapt neglected
underground spaces — an
initiative it is hoped that other
cities will follow.

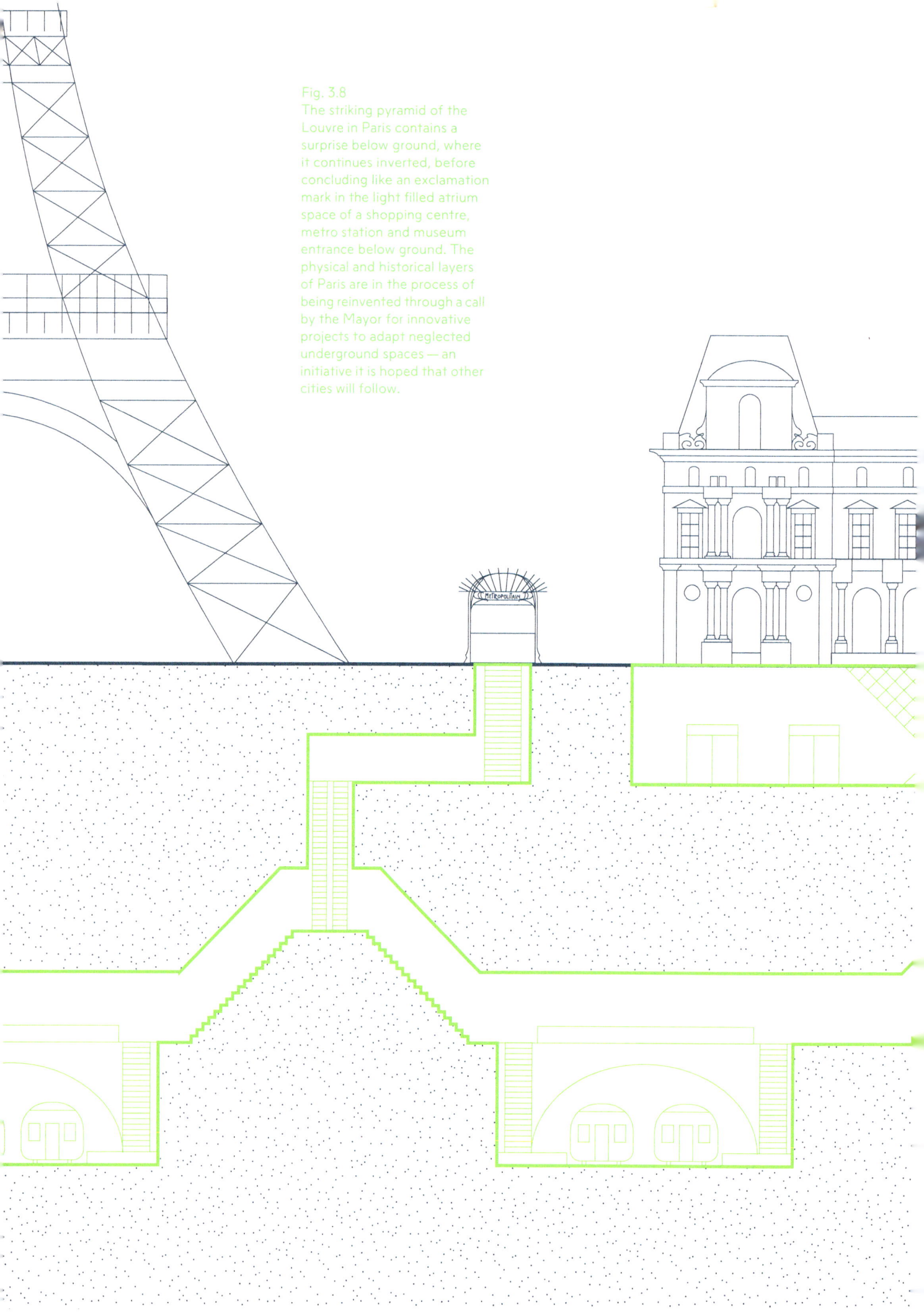

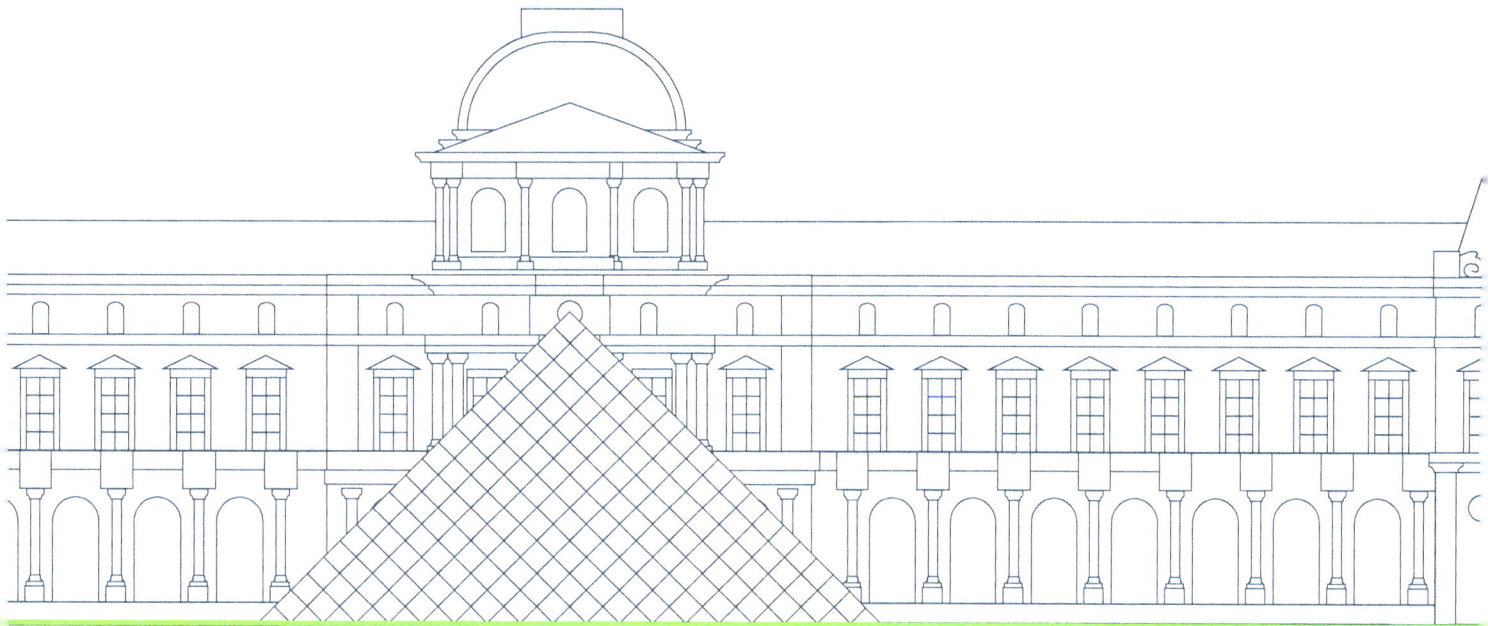

Singapore

Singapore is a city state of modest scale but major ambitions for urban growth, including making the most of its subsurface. Measuring 719.2sqkm with a population of 5.612 million — Singapore is looking, up, out and down to enable its population and economy to continue to grow. Planning for the urban growth of Singapore began in 1822 with the Plan of the Town of Singapore (also known as the Jackson Plan), which adopted a grid formation that divided residents of the colony by ethnicity. Fortunately, ethnic segregation is no longer a part of the plan making process, although some of the districts retain their original names and characteristics. The extent of the 1822 plan area was not adequate to cope with the rapidly growing population and in 1927 the Singapore Improvement Trust was established to upgrade transport and other infrastructure. Following the Japanese occupation from 1941 to 1945, Singapore had a critical housing shortage, leading to establishment of the Housing Development Board in 1960. In 1963 British rule ended and Singapore became part of Malaysia. Two years later in 1965 Singapore left Malaysia to become an independent republic (though it remains a member of the Commonwealth of Nations). In 1964 the HDB had set up an Urban Renewal Unit, which was later restructured and renamed the Urban Renewal Department. These sections within the HDB were tasked with cleaning up overcrowded slums, providing public housing and stimulating economic development, with the scale of this challenge recognised by establishing a dedicated Urban Redevelopment Authority in 1974. In just over 40 years the urban fabric of Singapore has undergone a remarkable transformation, with the country now boasting some of the highest living standards in the world.

The Urban Redevelopment Authority (URA) of Singapore is responsible for spatial land use planning and development control, with the primary both including the production of spatial plans and policies, and assessment of applications for planning consent.

The URA is responsible for the following Acts and their subsidiary legislation: Urban Redevelopment Authority Act; Planning Act; Housing Developers (Control and Licensing) Act and Sale of Commercial Properties Act. Urban Design Guidelines have been produced for nine geographical areas and include a Circular on the 'Central Area Underground Pedestrian Network — Revisions to the Cash Grant Incentive Scheme'.

The Singaporean Government has undertaken several major underground storage and utility projects to create more usable space at ground level. In 1999 the Ministry of Defence began to adapt a former quarry to create a state-of-the-art ammunition storage facility. The new facility required 90% less land than an equivalent above ground facility, and was created for the new Seletar Airport and 120Ha aerospace business park. In 2008 the Public Utilities Board completed Phase 1 of a Deep Tunnel Sewerage System, whereby a 48km tunnel is connected to a plant capable of treating 90,000cbm of waste water per day. In 2014, after an eight-year construction program, the Jurong Rock Caverns were also opened — comprising five rock caverns converted to store liquid hydrocarbons in a facility 150m below ground. The facility frees up approximately 60Ha of much needed land at ground level (Yan Min, 2014). At a smaller scale, cash grants have been offered by the URA to encourage building owners to create underground linkages between existing and proposed buildings, primarily the shopping malls along Orchard Road. The initiative was intended to reduce overcrowding at street level and improve comfort for shoppers (including many international tourists) affected by the hot and humid equatorial climate. Although many building owners decided not to build the underground pedestrian linkages, the locations of the proposed walkways have at least been safe-guarded to enable better pedestrian connectivity in the future. The cost of undertaking boring, drilling, tunnelling or blasting activities can make underground construction costs unfeasibly high. However, where natural rock formations can be exploited and in places where timber and other construction materials are scarce, constructing underground can be a more cost-effective solution. These projects are significant, but by no means the end of underground development in Singapore. Research into the potential of underground development is supported by a $SIN 130mn programme of National Innovation Challenges: Land and Liveability.

The URA's Group Director for Strategic Planning, Richard Hoo says: 'There is potential for a wider use of underground space by tapping on engineering and scientific expertise and to continue to invest in innovations in these and other related fields. We will continue to explore ways to better utilise our underground space and to seek innovative urban solutions that may make underground developments more viable and attractive' (URA, 2012). Singapore is a well-planned and managed city state, with a vision of the future that is not only environmentally sustainable, but also prosperous. The physical scale of the country might be seen as a barrier to achieving these ambitions, but instead, Singapore is using it as an opportunity to innovate and plan strategically for a future both above and below ground.

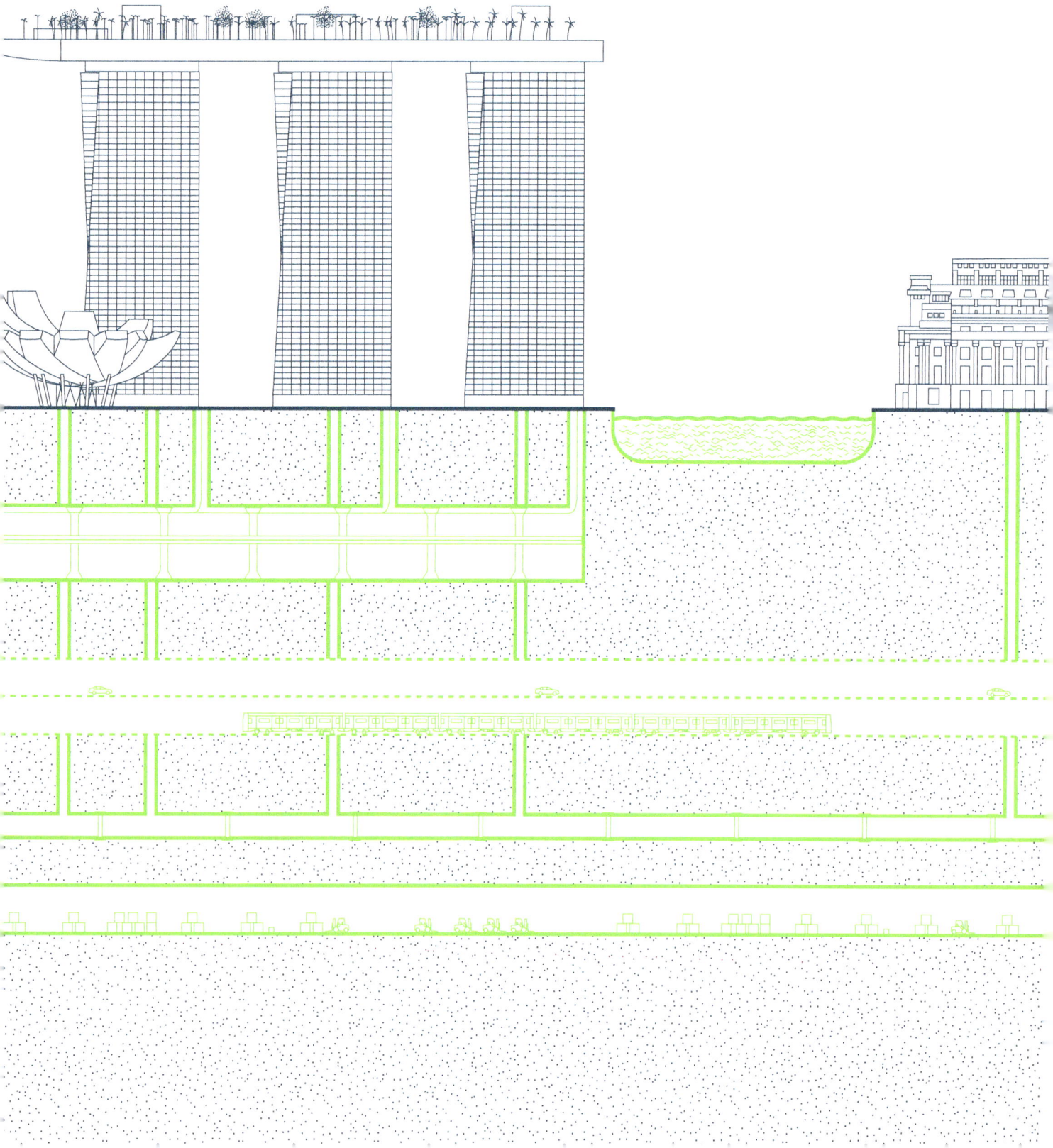

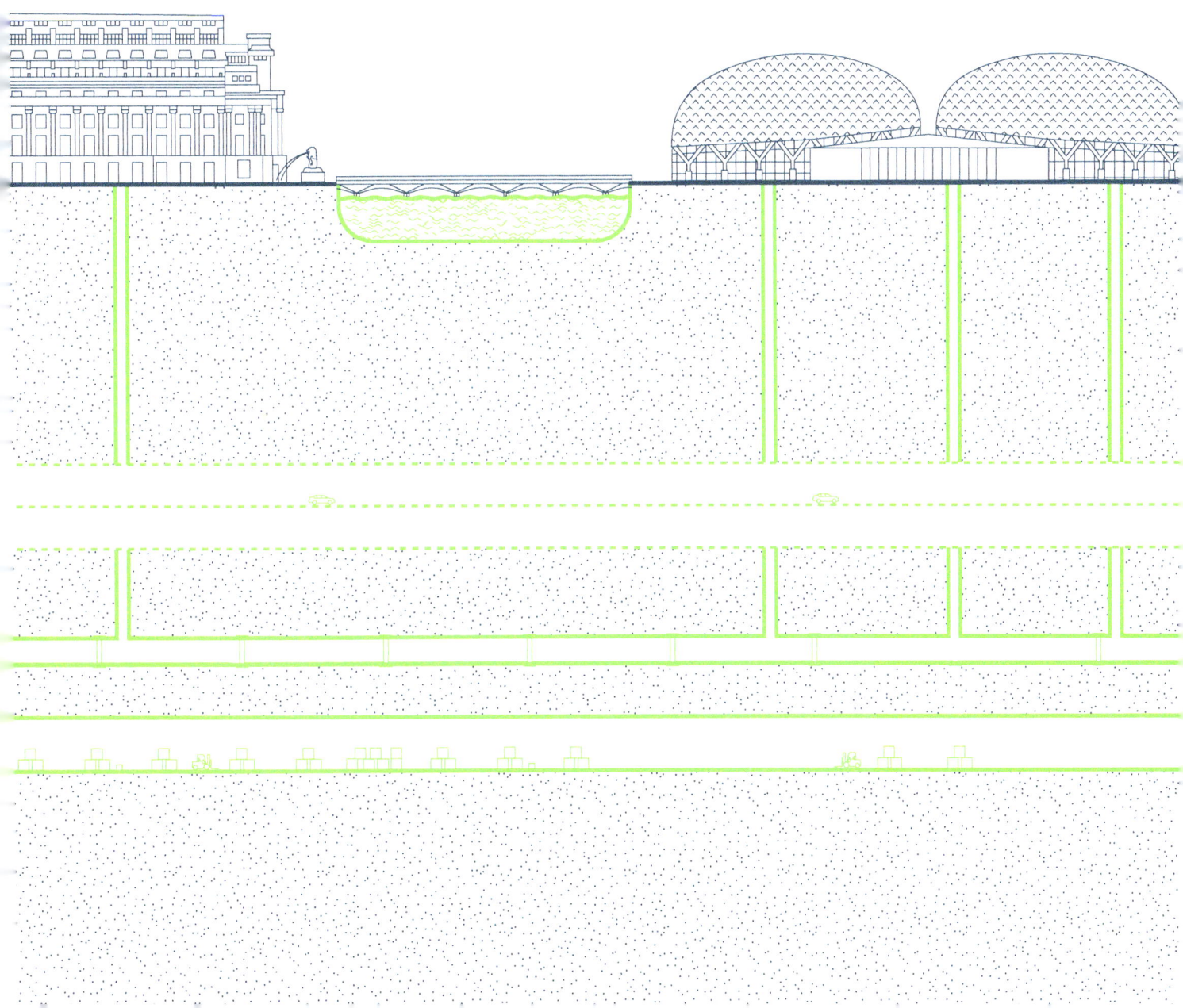

Fig. 3.9
Singapore is a small island state with big plans for its subsurface. The Urban Redevelopment Authority has visualised the subsurface in layered zones of current development and future potential uses – beginning at a shallow level with pedestrian linkages, progressing to utility corridors, transport infrastructure, waste water and deep level storage of hazardous items in rock caverns.

Tokyo

The Greater Tokyo area comprises four prefectures centred around Tokyo Bay, set within a larger National Capital Region. Tokyo Metropolis itself is on the western side of Tokyo Bay and is divided into 23 special wards, plus a western hinterland (the Tama area) which contains 26 cities, 5 towns, 8 villages and two island chains. The official Tokyo population of 13,389,584 people is deceptively low as the broader Tokyo area is the world's largest urban agglomeration, containing over 37.8 million people. Within the Special Ward Area, Tokyo has a population density of 6,032 people per sqkm, with an estimated 1,177 people moving to the city each day. Space is understandably at a premium within Tokyo, but this has led to innovations in technology and design that create a high standard of living, with the city voted as the world's most liveable by Monocle magazine in 2017.

The Japanese land use planning system operates at four levels: National; Regional; Prefectural; and Municipal. The principle legislation for planning and development was the Comprehensive Land Development Act of 1950, but in 2005 the Act (and its associated plan) was significantly revised and renamed the National Spatial Planning Act (2005). The National Spatial Planning Act is accompanied by National Spatial Strategies (revised 2008) which set five strategic goals for the development of the country. The goals are focused on themes including transportation and communication; disaster prevention; and the conservation of natural resources. For Tokyo, the primary spatial development plans are those produced by the Tokyo Metropolitan Government Bureau of Urban Development, namely the City Planning Vision for Tokyo, the Master Plan for City Planning, and the Master Plan for Housing. The Urban Development Vision (2009) contains six goals and seven strategies to support a broader objective to evolve Tokyo into 'an environmentally advanced city with charms and vitality that will serve as a model for the world'. The Master Plan for City Planning (2014) supports the vision by setting out four key policies, which should in turn inform the plans for individual cities. A separate masterplan is also produced for Housing (2012). In 2014 the Tokyo Metropolitan Government released Creating the Future: The Long-Term Vision for Tokyo which contains eight strategies, a successful Tokyo 2020 Games; Evolving Infrastructure; Omotenashi (the Japanese spirit of hospitality); Safe and Secure; Supportive Environment; Leading Global City; Sustainable City; and Tama Area and Islands. An aspiration within the strategy for evolving infrastructure is to create safe and pleasant streets, and to do this it is explained that measures are underway to put more power lines underground and make sidewalks more barrier free.

In 2007 the Law on Special Measures for the Public Use of Deep Underground was introduced to legalise the development of spaces at least 40m below ground level, or 10m greater than the layer on which the deep foundations of a building rest, for public utility infrastructure. The most significant attribute of this law is that when a road, railway or water utility company for example wishes to build a tunnel at deep level, they are not required to receive the consent of parties owning or renting the land above the tunnel, nor are they required to pay them any compensation (Nishioka et al. 2007). Deep level public infrastructure projects are essential to navigate large volumes of people, utilities and waste beneath and around foundations of the very tall buildings above. Masuda et al. (2004) have researched the potential for the Deep Space Utilisation Law to be used to support a deep level combined utility tunnel running across Tokyo Bay from Ariake to Otemachi. The proposed tunnel would be buried deep enough below the bay to withstand damage from earthquakes. If the project proceeds, it will join several other major subsurface infrastructure developments in Tokyo, including the Yamate Tunnel (at 18.2km it is the second longest road tunnel in the world and is constructed 30m below ground), and the Metropolitan Area Outer Underground Discharge Channel which is the world's largest underground flood water diversion facility, capable of pumping 200 tons of water per second.

Not all of Tokyo's underground infrastructure is designed at such a massive scale. On some of the city's critically overcrowded streets and transport interchanges, pedestrian walkways are being constructed beneath ground. The opening, in 2014, of the 900m Tsukiji-Toranomon road tunnel is not a significant achievement at first glance, however, finding the physical space to construct the tunnel (which is only 2m below ground and 30cm from a major utility conduit), was not easy.

> In writing about the complexities of the Tokyo subsurface, Jun Hongo says: 'If you think the urban sprawl of Tokyo looks impressive from above, wait until you factor in the areas below ground'... 'The metropolitan government says Tokyo has approximately 63,000 underground areas, with underground paths, subway systems and shopping complexes comprising 40 percent of the total' (Hongo, 2014). This tension between the physical capacity of both above and below ground spaces, is at least raising awareness of the relationships between the different layers of the city, and how their use needs to be prioritised. What is clear is that as Tokyo invests heavily in urban improvements ahead of the 2020 Olympics, the subsurface is certain to have an important role to play in the future of this dynamic city.

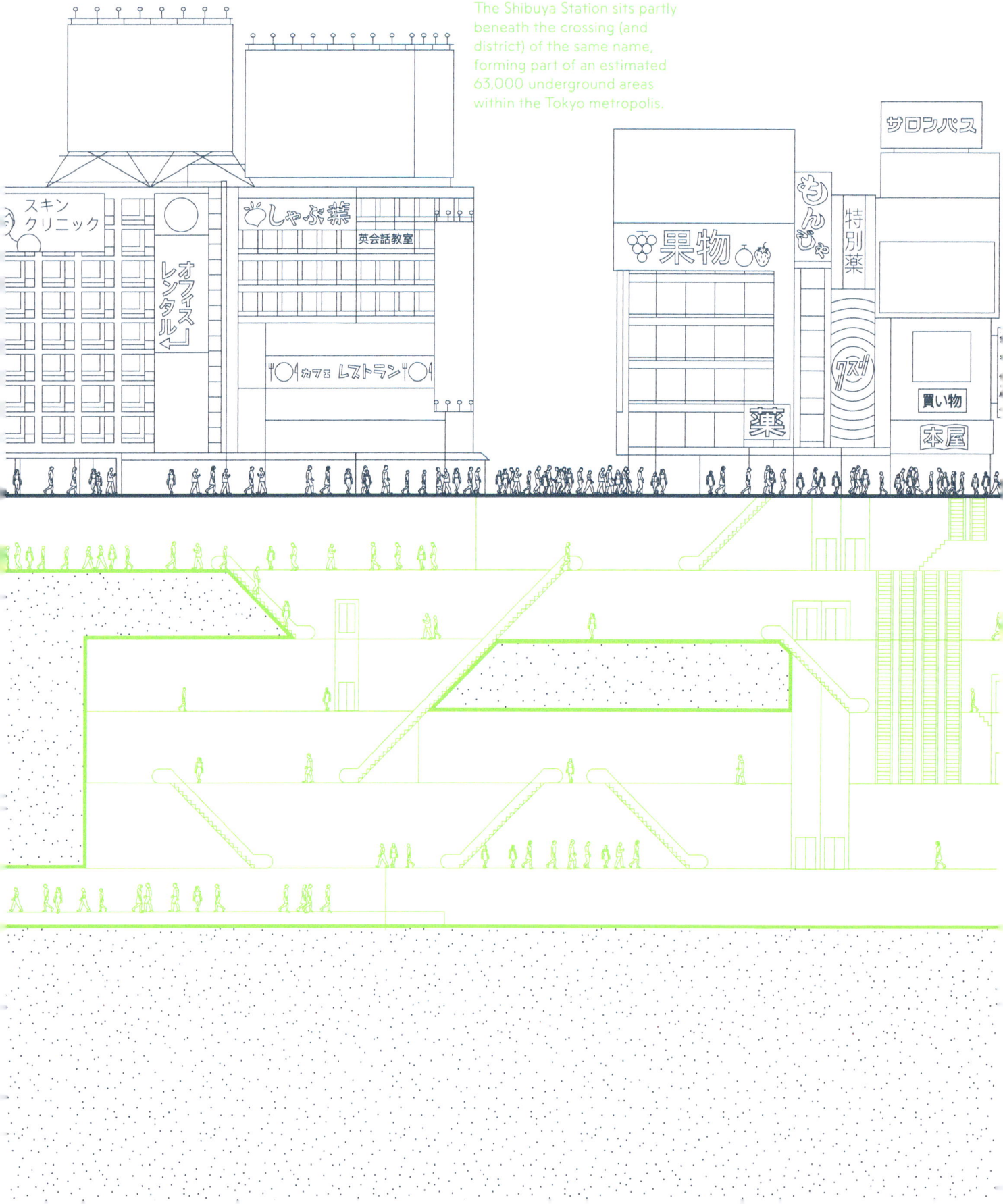

Fig. 3.10
The Shibuya crossing is the world's busiest and when the signal is in their favour, up to 2,500 pedestrians cross the junction as part of their journeys across, above and below Tokyo. The Shibuya Station sits partly beneath the crossing (and district) of the same name, forming part of an estimated 63,000 underground areas within the Tokyo metropolis.

スキン
クリニック

オフィス
レンタル

しゃぶ葉

英会話教室

カフェ レストラン

果物

特別薬

サロンパス

もんじゃ

クスリ

薬

買い物

本屋

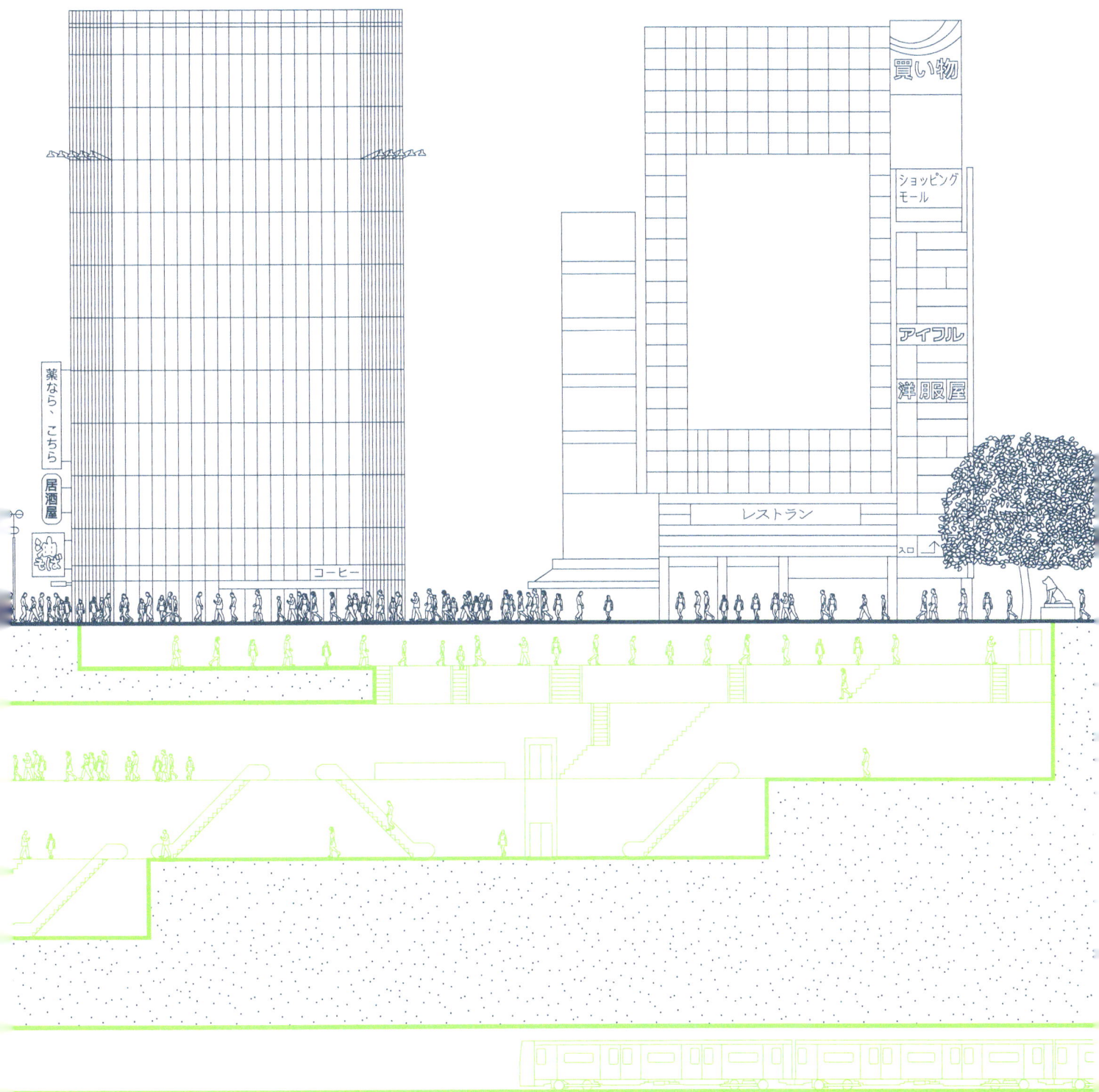

買い物

ショッピング
モール

アイフル

洋服屋

薬なら、こちら

居酒屋

レストラン

入口

コーヒー

Conclusion

So, in conclusion, what lessons can be drawn from these cities? Although not all cities are suited to underground development beyond the typical utilities infrastructure, a strong case exists for planners to better understand and proactively plan for the use of natural resources in their cities. Helsinki is the quiet world leader in addressing this particular built environment challenge, and although similar pragmatic, evidence based work is being undertaken in a commendable fashion by Governments in Singapore and Hong Kong, there remains a great deal more to be done.

> In some cities, it seems that a great (underground) space race is underway, leapfrogging planning policy — the absence of which is also causing other future opportunities to be overlooked or compromised. There is generally an absence of pro-active, spatial planning or design policy for underground spaces. Notwithstanding a subterranean building boom of sorts occurring in London with residential basements and large infrastructure projects (Allen, 2014), there is no strategic spatial plan and very few policies to guide how new or existing underground spaces should be developed in a safe, resourceful manner. Therefore, in addition to geotechnical and structural skills, it is also vital that cities involve urban planners and designers in creating high quality, functional underground spaces.

In considering the case of proposed underground pedestrian walkways in Hong Kong, it is a reminder that there are no easy choices in cities, just different combinations of wicked problems. In ultra-dense cities, parks are vital pressure valves for residents needing space, relative tranquillity and somewhere to connect with nature. However, parks are also places that are relatively unencumbered with existing infrastructure, potentially making them an easy target for other equally necessary urban infrastructure, such as freeways, car parks and pedestrian walkways.

> What is important is that in a variety of ways, cities are beginning to address subsurface development through planning policy, and this is a necessary part of managing their overall long-term growth. Although these nine cities are different in many ways, they share similar objectives, and have a great deal to learn from one another. Perhaps the next step in the long-term planning of these and other cities, is for an international dialogue on how to make sustainable and holistic development of their subsurface a shared development goal.

4.

Adapting

Underground Spaces

Underground Urbanism

For those cities wanting to undertake a three-dimensional approach to spatial planning, the first step is to consider the potential to better use existing underground spaces. By mapping existing underground spaces, a sifting process can begin to identify those with the greatest potential for more intensive, or different uses. Existing underground spaces could include rock caverns, disused metro stations, or underutilised commercial office basements. For cities to make more efficient use of valuable resources such as land, it is necessary to consider how existing underground spaces could be adapted and their use intensified.

When considering the potential to repurpose existing underground structures, the integrity of existing structures can be key. Some, like Joseph Bazelgette's London sewer network, or the grand railway stations of Manhattan and Moscow have an enduring sense of quality. Public infrastructure of the Victorian era was designed to reflect the values and aspirations of a city, somewhat overshadowing the minimum viable infrastructure development often created by contemporary, cash strapped governments.

Rather than waiting for strategic spatial plans to map out public assets, the individuals and business on the following pages have found underground spaces and adapted them for a diverse range of uses. From a public convenience that became a cafè, to vegetables that grow 33m below ground, the following case studies represent pragmatic approaches to making the most of neglected spaces beneath our cities.

Attendant Cafè London, United Kingdom

The Attendant is a petite but ambitious repurposing of a former public convenience in central London. Measuring just 42 sqm the conveniences were built in the late 1800s for use by market stall holders working in the streets above, yet by the 1960s they had fallen into disrepair and were closed by the local council. A private developer purchased the conveniences in the 1980s hoping to turn them into a design studio, yet the conversion was never fully completed. The site remained vacant until 2011 when friends Pete Tomlinson and Ben Russell saw the potential for a cafè serving excellent food and coffee in a unique location.

Convincing people to eat in a former public toilet located underground was a considerable challenge and therefore a passionate attention to detail was key to making the space a success. Beginning by peeling back 11 layers of paint which had accumulated on the wrought iron exterior at street level, the pair gradually transformed what had been a dark and unpleasant environment, into a bright, clean and welcoming place. Original architectural features such as the 1890s porcelain urinals and wall tiles were retained, with new orange tiles used as a detail to respond to the colour of the original attendant's office. To entice customers down the stairs into a venue they couldn't see into from street level, an A-frame sign was placed at the entrance and lighting was used in the stairwell and cafè to reinforce the message that the cafè was a warm, bright place.

In addition to the refurbishment demonstrating authenticity, to entice people to such an unusual space the food and beverages also needed to be exceptional. Tomlinson and Russell brought together coffee from the Caravan Roastery in Kings Cross, milk from Ivy House organic farm in Somerset, coffee cups from NotNeutral in Los Angeles, and a chef from a Michelin-star restaurant. Since opening in 2013 the combination of quality produce and a unique venue has attracted a steady stream of tourists and travel writers curious about the transformation of the place. Interest in the venue has also prompted a trend for the conversion of other underground public conveniences across London such as the cocktail bar Ladies and Gentleman.

4. Adapting Underground Spaces

Digua Shequ Community Beijing, China

Below the streets of Beijing lies a network of bunkers built to protect the city during the Cold War, long disused they have now become home to workers not able to afford accommodation at ground level. The bunkers, along with common basements are estimated to house approximately 1 million people, within a megacity of 21 million people that is continuing to grow. The Digua Shequ (or sweet potato) community group was founded by designer Zhou Zishu and provides an interesting case study on the design interventions that could be used to improve of the quality of life for Beijing's so called "Rat Tribe".

As explained briefly in Chapter one, Beijing is estimated to have over 10,000 concrete bunkers hidden beneath the surface of the city, many of which were constructed for the purposes of protecting residents from a land or air invasion during the Cold War. In addition to the government bunkers, many privately owned buildings also have basements beneath them that also have so called common basements. The average underground apartment measures just less than 10 sqm sometimes shared between several people, the apartments act as bedsits with communal toilet facilities. The apartments are typically located 1–2 storeys below ground level, with some having access to natural light from highlight windows onto the adjacent street, or light-wells built as part of the bunkers. Standards of living in the apartments vary considerably, some of the bunkers have a wide ramp down to a basic reception with a security guard and are also provided with heating, gas, air conditioning, internet, hot running water, and furniture such as a TV, bed and washing machine.

The Digua Community aims to build trust and a sense of community between Beijing residents of all socioeconomic groups, using basement spaces as a focus for their work. Digua Shequ has created a bright and welcoming community centre in a basement in Beijing's Anyuanbeili neighbourhood. The community centre is intended to provide residents living in the bunkers with a third space in which to socialise, learn, and share with their neighbours (Kong, P.Y. et al., 2016). Zishu explains that the principle behind the community centre is one of spatial justice as described by geographers David Harvey and Edward Soja. Drawing on knowledge he developed when studying for his Masters of Creative Practice in Narrative Environment at Central Saint Martins college in London, Zishu applied a clear methodology of research, consultation and practical trials. Ethnographic research is firstly undertaken to ensure that places and experiences are designed in a manner that is relevant to the local community as they are the ultimate custodians of the bunkers, even for a temporary period. Government agencies, entrepreneurs and artists are then brought together to deliver innovative programming of the space. In addition to physical projects, the Facebook page for the Digua Community acts as an online network to connect residents living in other underground spaces and to reach out to their neighbours above ground.

> The Digua Community centre in Anyuanbeili features co-working space, a 3D printing station, movie theatre, gym and cafè in which to socialise with other residents. Site specific design interventions include brightly coloured ventilation ducts created using their 3D printer, and used to improve air quality. A barber's shop created in part of the basement was also included in the Beijing Independent Art Spaces event in 2016, further encouraging interaction between different sectors of Beijing society. Vibrant colours, lighting and materials have been combined to create basement spaces that feel clean and welcoming, rather than neglected. The group have also captured their experiences in the "Digua Wallpaper", published to 'help people living in temporary accommodation to improve their living environment' (Digua Community, 2016).

The Digua Shequa community group have created a great example of subterranean place making, however, it is their efforts to allow underground residents to live with dignity and create links with surface levels neighbours that could yield the greatest long-term benefit. Although the use of Beijing's bunkers should be optimised, it is, however, questionable as to whether they could be adequately improved to provide a permanent housing solution for residents. To integrate the bunkers with Beijing's urban fabric it will be necessary not only to better connect buildings vertically, but to improve necessities such as air quality and emergency access. The Sweet Potato Community have undertaken important steps to opening up dialogue with city officials, and in time it is hoped that Beijing's basements could be integrated into a long term spatial strategy for the city.

> *The phenomena of people seeking affordable accommodation beneath city streets is not new. In his 2000 film Dark Days, the model, musician and producer Marc Singer records his time living with the Freedom Tunnel community in New York's abandoned tunnel systems.*

Fig. 4.3
Digua Shequ
Community

Fig. 4.4
Digua Shequ
Interior

Retrofitting Grout Shafts London, United Kingdom

When new infrastructure is needed deep below cities, there is potential for tunnelling to damage buildings at ground level, compensation grouting is used to mitigate this risk but creates a by-product of grout shafts which increasingly dot city landscapes in a cookie cutter effect, prompting the question — how could we better use these new spaces? In 2014 London based consultants Urben were granted a Design Innovation Award to work with the Royal College of Arts (RCA) to consider how grout shafts left over from construction of the Crossrail project could be repurposed to support urban activities in London. The project was intended not only to enable a creative and commercially viable repurposing of a space that would otherwise be wasted, but also to lead a broader discussion on the need for cities to use their resources far more efficiently.

As the new Crossrail tunnel (also known as the Elizabeth Line) winds its way beneath central and historic parts of London, grout shafts are used to stabilise ground beneath buildings that might otherwise be damaged by subsidence. Crossrail built 13 grout shafts measuring 4.5 m in diameter by 15 m to 20 m in depth. The shafts are open topped, concrete lined spaces in which technicians inject grout into long tubes running deep into the earth (tube a manchettes or TAMs), thereby backfilling any void created by the construction. Prior to Crossrail opening in 2018 the grout shafts will have fulfilled their purpose, at which stage they would usually be backfilled with soil and returned to their original finish at ground level. However, considering the natural and human resources needed to construct the grout shafts, and the new physical spaces created by them, it seemed logical to consider how their life could be extended.

By drawing inspiration from innovative projects such as Growing Underground and the Late Night Chameleon Club fashion store and bar, the project team decided to focus on two grout shafts that could offer the greatest potential to create amazing, inspirational and useful spaces. The first space, on South Molton Lane is located opposite the entrance of the future Crossrail Bond Street Station west ticket hall. The South Molton Lane shaft is also situated within the context of a wide paved area beside a Plane Tree, outside the Grade II listed Greys Antique market. The second grout shaft is located on Davies Mews, at the rear of Greys Antique market. Both of the grout shafts are located close to Oxford Street and its many retail stores, but also within a short walk of world renowned galleries and auction houses in Mayfair. New land is rarely created in such a desirable area, and with record property prices of up to £1,350 sqm, there is an imperative to achieve highest and best·use of land. Furthermore, the grout shafts present an opportunity to provide community services or retail space for organisations that would otherwise not be able to afford space in the area.

South Molton Lane

For the South Molton Lane grout shaft, the intention was to create a functional space that could support the large number of tourists and workers moving through Bond Street station. A welcome hub was therefore proposed to help people safely store their shopping whilst going for dinner or to the theatre; pick up online shopping orders after retail closing hours; meet friends; or get directions from local welcome ambassadors. The interior of the grout shaft would be used as an automatic storage and retrieval system paid for by users on a time charge basis. At ground floor level, the shaft would be integrated with a cafè / local tourist information centre. A first level roof terrace would also assist with wayfinding; activate the streetscape; provide an informal meeting place; and generate revenue. The multi-function space could also be used to hire or store Brompton or other folding bikes; host small performances or act as a community police station after hours.

Davies Mews

Our concept for the Davies Mews grout shaft was provocative and playful. The character of the mews had potential to be further improved, with new cobblestone paving, careful lighting and the installation of a water fountain. Yet the water fountain in Davies Mews was designed not only to improve the public realm, but also to conceal an exciting hidden space. Given the high land values in the area and the established community of art galleries, the team proposed to convert the grout shaft into a small but spectacular art gallery and bar. RCA architect Jordan Jon Hodgson was instrumental in developing the concept of a space which could be closed during the day, laying submerged until the evening, when using hydraulics, a structure could emerge into the streetscape and open up to the public. The notion of topping the gallery with a water fountain began as a joke amongst the team when discussing potential options for dewatering the shaft, but became a legitimate tool for visually integrating the shaft into the surrounding mews. The concept could be seen as an architectural folly, but one with the potential to become a popular space for art exhibitions, product launches and private parties.

One of the greatest challenges to the success of this project was people's ability to visualise something they have not yet experienced. Trying to look at a concrete lined hole in the ground and see an attractive, state of the art gallery lined with LED screens, hidden beneath a water fountain was not an easy task. However, despite the project only being speculative research it received broad support from land owners, local government and Crossrail — and as a result the contractor's methodology changed to infill the shafts with a lean mix concrete that could be extracted at a later date. By recognising that grout shafts could have an afterlife beyond their original purpose, many cities could benefit from these small but potentially important urban spaces.

Initial trials by Crossrail at their Whitechapel grout shaft have found that TAMs are able to be reused for ground source heat collection, potentially enabling them to become part of local heat networks at a later date.

Fig. 4.5
South Molton Lane
Section

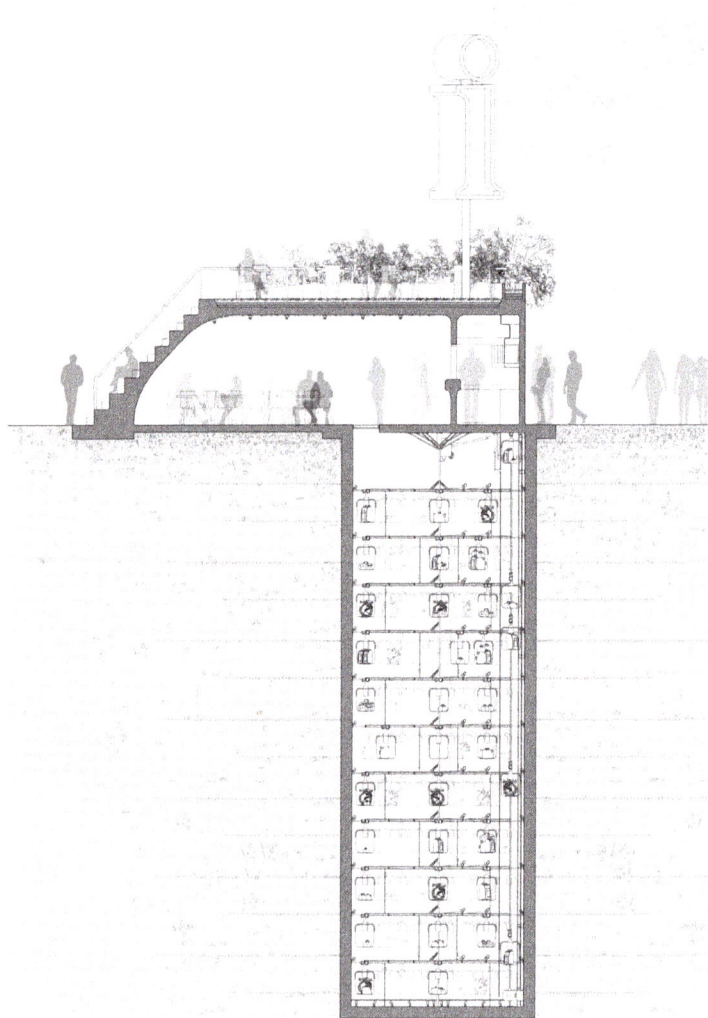

Underground Urbanism

Fig. 4.6
Davies Mews Section

4. Adapting Underground Spaces

Growing Underground London, United Kingdom

Lying 33 metres below a busy London street, a series of World War II air raid shelters have experienced an unlikely transformation — into a farm. Growing Underground was established by the Zero Carbon Food Company who set out to address London's food security challenges and provide fresh produce as close as possible to restaurants and consumers. Although a tunnel deep below ground with no natural light isn't a typical location for a farm, this innovative project has so far proven very successful and is likely to lead to other aspiring urban farmers seeking to replicate the idea in their cities.

In 1940 when London was subjected to increasingly intense bombing by the German air force, a decision was taken to construct air raid shelters beneath train stations that were already being used each night to shelter families from attack. Between 1940 and 1942 a total of eight deep level air raid shelters were constructed, some with the potential to connect with parts of the London Underground train network at a later date. Constructed from concrete rings similar to those used to build the underground rail network, each tunnel measures 16 ft 6 in in diameter and is 1,600 ft long. The tunnels were divided into different sections and lined with bunk beds to accom-modate up to 8,000 local residents whose homes had been, or were at risk of being bombed. The shelters were used in 1944 when newer and more dangerous V-1 and V-2 bombs began to land on London, but by 1945 were no longer required. The shelters were subsequently used as military and civilian hostels, to accommodate migrants arriving from Jamaica on HMT Empire Windrush in 1948, and in 1951 to accommodate school children and tourists visiting London for The Festival of Britain. Aside from the storage of archived docu-ments, the shelters remained unused for almost 60 years until two friends saw an opportunity to use them for their growing business.

Long time friends Richard Ballard and Steven Dring moved from Bristol to London to work in film production and marketing respectively, but met up regularly to talk about the challenges of living in a big city and put the world to rights over a beer. After more than a few pub arguments about oil, energy, food, and the future of London, the pair decided that the only way to feed a growing population was to do it without using any carbon and by having no dependence on fossil fuels. Wanting to reconnect with their West County farming roots and inspired by reading Dickson Depsommier and Jeremy Rifkin, the pair then made the brave decision to establish their own company — Zero Carbon Food. From founding the company it then took a further year of research to understand the amount of food likely to be required by London over the coming years, and to research different urban farming techniques. During their research Ballard and Dring were put in contact with Chris Nelson, a specialist Agricultural Consultant whose experience helped identify how food could be grown in a space with no natural light, buried deep below ground.

Locating an urban farm deep below ground was not always the intention, yet leasing a warehouse at ground level warehouse appeared costly. Given Ballard had an interest in cities and their hidden places, he was aware of the air raid shelters and saw their potential to provide affordable and well insulated space for their urban farm. Despite the idea of using the shelters to grow fresh produce being unconventional, Ballard and Dring were able to convince owners Transport for London (TfL) to provide them an initial research and development testing area of 1,000 sq ft (92 sqm) at a rate of £1.30 per sqm. With a tenancy agreement and planning consent in place, they began trading as Growing Underground and raised funding through CrowdCube to implement their bold ideas.

Billed as the 'world's first subterranean farm' Growing Underground produces 12 varieties of microgreens and herbs, most of which are then sold to restaurants in Central London. Able to offer produce 'from farm to fork in under four hours', their urban location also offers the benefit of significantly reducing food miles and associated CO_2 emissions typical when delivering food from producers to consumers. The produce is grown by planting seeds in a wood fibre pulp for an initial few days before being transferred to shelving units under banks of LED lights. The lights are on for 18 hours a day while strong fans maintain the temperature at between 21C and 23C. The combination of LED light and nutrient rich water from a hydroponic system means that plants can be harvested between six and 28 days after planting, the process then continues in a cycle as underground farms, unlike those above ground, are able to operate throughout the year.

The method of farming used by Growing Underground is environmentally efficient, helped in part by their location below ground. The hydroponic watering system is able to grow crops of green leaf vegetables using 70% less water than traditional open-field farming, and because all the nutrients are kept within a closed-loop system there is no agricultural run-off. With the use of simple netting, and given the depth of the space there are no pests, or need for pesticides. Due to the underground location of the farm, crops are also able to be protected from inclement weather and grown in a consistently warm environment. The concrete air raid shelters benefit from a warm, stable temperature and need less heating or cooling than typical hydroponic farms based in warehouses. The LED lights used to stimulate plant growth were a considerable investment but offer significant energy savings in the long term. In recognising their potential, Ballard says that "LEDs are in their infancy in technology, like the mainframe computer in the 1960s, so these are only going to get more and more efficient."

Fig. 4.7
Growing Underground — Farm

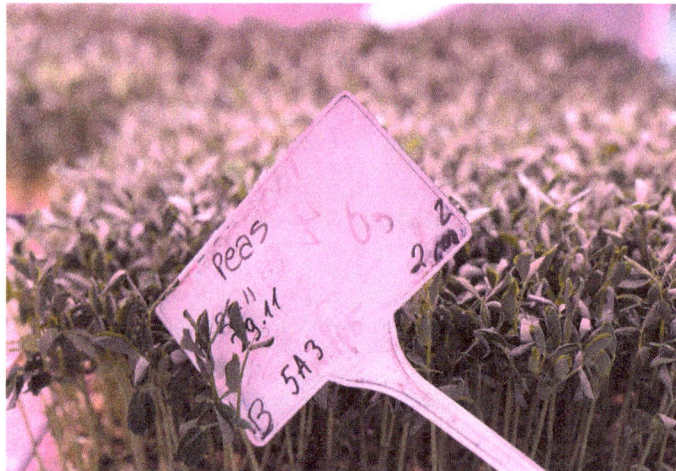

Fig. 4.8
Growing
Underground —
Pea shoots

Following the success of their initial trial, TfL has invested £450,000 in ventilation, electrical repairs and upgrading pedestrian entrances to the shelters. The first section of the shelters to be converted now extends to 6,000 sq ft (550 sqm) of growing area and will be able to produce 700 boxes of goods a day when production has been fully scaled up, with hopes to extend to 23,000 sq ft (2,200 sqm) of growing space within two years. Although the focus is on supplementing rather than replacing exiting farm sources, the approach taken by Growing Underground has great potential to improve food security and bring new life to constrained and currently disused underground spaces. Perhaps just as importantly, the farm demonstrates how advances in LED lighting could fundamentally change the character and function of underground spaces, something with great potential to be applied in cities around the world.

Subsequent to the Growing Underground becoming established, the above ground section of the air raid shelter has also attracted attention, and become the subject of another creative retrofit. The rotunda that sits atop the eastern access shaft to the air raid shelter is to become a café and visitor centre. The café would sit partly above the existing, Grade II listed brick rotunda, and be linked by stairs to a new glass pavilion building at ground level. Both spaces would have views over Clapham Common (park). The aim of the project is to preserve the rotunda, by finding it a suitable contemporary use, as it is currently in poor condition and a target for antisocial behaviour (TfL, 2016). Once complete, the café and exhibition space would support the London Transport Museum to host tours of the sections of the air raid shelter (beyond the area used by Growing Underground), that have been preserved for historic purposes. The 'Hidden London' tours by the London Transport Museum take place in several former underground stations in London, and tickets often sell out shortly after new dates are announced. In the case of the air raid shelter at Clapham South, there is a unique opportunity for visitors to not only explore some of the unique built heritage beneath their city, but also to experience the pleasure of fresh food grown in an extension of the very same space, but used in a radically different way.

Fig. 4.9
"One air raid shelter, many uses"

1940 —	1948 —	1951 —	2015 —	2016 —
WWII	Windrush housing	Festival of Britain	Café	Urban farm
Eight deep level air	accomodating mi-	accomodation	in 2015 permission	Growing underground
raid shelters were	grants arriving from	for school children	was granted to build	microgreens and
constructed.	Jamaica on HMT	and tourists visiting	a café in the rotunda	herbs which are
	Empire Windrush.	London.	over the northern	sold around Central
			ventilation & access	London.
			shaft.	

5. Architectural responses

to the

underground

Underground Urbanism

Successive generations of architects have theorised how underground places could be designed to connect the many layers of our cities. From Eugene Henard's Street of the Future in 1911, there has been an interest vertically separating and stacking land uses within cities. In the 1920s Harvey Wiley Corbett and Hugh Ferriss's Metropolis of Tomorrow was conceived in response to changes in the zoning regulations of New York, and acted as a precursor to the later work of Ville Radieuse by Le Corbusier where (although not underground) pedestrians and vehicles were separated on different levels. In 1969 Oscar Newman responded to Cold War fears by conceptualising an Underground City of some 1.2 miles in diameter buried deep beneath Manhattan, that thankfully no one ever attempted to construct.

Likewise, plans by Paul Rudolph in 1972 to create a Lower Manhattan Expressway thankfully never progressed beyond his designs for a canalised road and rail corridor at the base of an interconnected series of abstract mega-structures for housing. More recently, in 1997 Rem Koolhaas and Bruce Mau illustrated their concepts for The Asian City of Tomorrow in their book Small, medium, large, extra-large. Although contemporary architecture is still interested in layering land uses to increase urban density, the emphasis is now on finding design solutions that improve quality of place.

Underground development in cities is typically associated with large scale infrastructure projects such as rail networks, where the emphasis is on technical excellence in engineering and construction, however, architects also have an important role to play. The role of architecture in underground development must be more than simply putting lipstick on an infrastructure gorilla or interior design in the latter stages of a project. Owing to the complexities of designing underground spaces, skilled architects, specialist lighting designers and artists need to be involved in the early stages of project design and planning.

Within his book 'Below Ground Level' (von Meijenfeldt, 2003) Ernst von Meijenfeldt describes Architect Floris Alkemade of OMA as saying:

'The natural train of thought is that everything above ground is beautiful and good and everything underground is bad, ugly and cheap... you often hear that architecture is only about the recognisable form and the facade, while I believe that it's all about the way in which you organise a building. With underground construction there may be no discussion over the appearance, but I feel this brings far more essential architectural questions to the fore. The discussion therefore gains clarity and is not clouded by inappropriate aesthetic arguments. You design from the inside outwards: how does a room have to function? The outside should therefore be derived from that'.

Evidence of the principles described by Alkemade can be found in the following pages. Although the emphasis here is on completed projects, the case studies begin with a concept by Bunker Arquitectura that challenges notions of where and how we develop in our cities, and is not dissimilar to the radical approaches taken by architects at the turn of the 20th century.

Fig. 5.1
'How You May Live and Travel in the City of 1950', illustration by Harvey Wiley Corbett from the 1925 cover of Popular Science Magazine.

The Earthscraper Mexico City, Mexico

Striking in appearance and revolutionary in design, The Earthscraper concept by Bunker Arquitectura proposes that a new type of iconic building could be constructed in Mexico City without harming the setting of historically significant buildings. The Earthscraper extends 300 metres below ground and takes the shape of a inverted pyramid, with the large lightwell in its centre created through a glass roof to the Plaza de la Constitucion above. The conceptual building design formed an entry to the eVolo skyscraper competition in 2009 and although not constructed, has made an important contribution to the discourse on how cities value and utilise the resources beneath them.

In addition to the geological and hydrogeological context set out in Chapter 1, it is important to understand the cultural heritage that informed the Earthscraper concept. Mexico City is built on many layers of history — from Aztec to Spanish colonial and contemporary architecture, the city has progressively build itself up in layers — from a lake, to pyramids and the colonial city visible now. Mexico City's growing population of over 21 million is continuing to sprawl outwards, yet its historic centre is in need of a physical upgrade. Although it is right for federal and local legislation to prevent the demolition of historic buildings, and also to protect important views through restrictions on building height of up to eight storeys, more intense and well designed buildings are needed to revitalise the city centre. One of the most culturally important places in Mexico City is the Plaza de la Constitucion (Constitution Square, also known as the Zocalo) in front of the Palacio Nacionale, and it is beneath this public square that Bunker Arquitectura have proposed the Earthscraper.

The 775,000 sqm Earthscraper would replace the surface of the Plaza de la Constitution with toughened glass to continue its use for large public events such as concerts and parades, this surface would act as a ceiling for the Earthscraper through which light could filter to the 65 storeys below. The first ten storeys would be a museum displaying Aztec and Mayan artefacts, providing a public interface to the building that would then provide retail shops and housing on levels -11 to -20, the deepest levels accommodating office space, before the tip of the pyramid reaches and capitalises on groundwater to create a source of energy. The CEO of Bunker Arquitectura, Esteban Suarez describes the Earthscraper as an antagonist in a historic landscape where skyscrapers are prohibited and preservation of the built environment is the paramount objective. The Earthscraper is a provocative architectural concept that challenges the priorities of urban governments and our expectations of buildings. Only time will tell if the Earthscraper is realised, but in the interim it provides a helpful example of the potential opportunities laying beneath our cities.

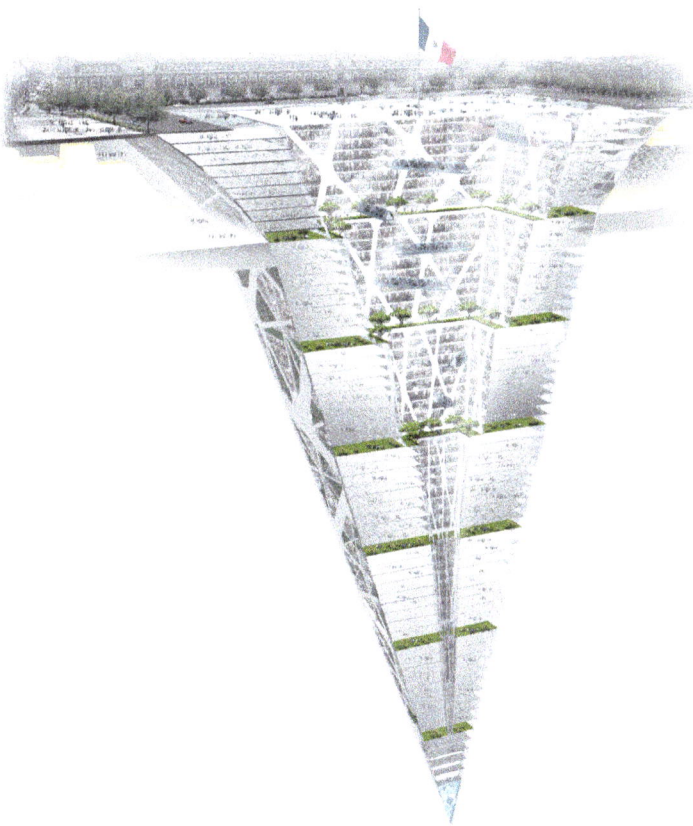

Cuyperpassage Amsterdam, Netherlands

Pedestrian underpasses can be unpopular places, often stigmatised by real or perceived threats of crime, however, the Cuyperpassage beneath Amsterdam station is an entirely different proposition. Designed by Benthem Crouwel Architects in conjunction with the Graphic Designer Irma Boom, the Cuyperpassage is an undercroft space below Amsterdam Central Station created to provide a connection from the centre of the city to the ferry terminal on the IJ-river north of the station.

The 110m long passage is a striking design of two halves, one for pedestrians and the other for faster moving cyclists. The pedestrian side of the passage is finished in 46,000 wall tiles and 33,000 floor tiles, all made by the Dutch Pottery company Royal Tichelaar Makkum in a traditional 13 x 13 cm tile size. Along the three metre high wall on the pedestrian side of the tunnel, tiles form a stunning tableau with a modern interpretation by Boom of a painting by the landscape artist Cornelis Boumeester. Boom's artwork features large and small merchant vessels, herring busses with nets in place, churning waves, and seagulls, but with the crest on the primary vessel depicting Amsterdam's coat of arms. The opposite side of the passage has a more utilitarian design, with two cycle lanes covered in black asphalt and the side wall finished with steel grating. The lanes are set at a slightly lower level to avoid conflicts with slower moving pedestrians. The asphalt surface of the lanes helps absorb noise and provide traction for bike tyres. The wall is finished with steel grates that form an unobtrusive backdrop, that is difficult to graffiti or attach posters to. Described as a 'slow traffic corridor', the passage addresses severance issues caused by the station previously obstructing north/south traffic. By vertically separating the quite different journeys of passengers, cyclists and pedestrians, the multimodal transport hub of Amsterdam station functions efficiently. The passage has proved popular, with approximately 15,000 cyclists using the passage each day.

Fig. 5.4
Cuyperpassage —
entrance

Fig. 5.5
Cuyperpassage — mosaic

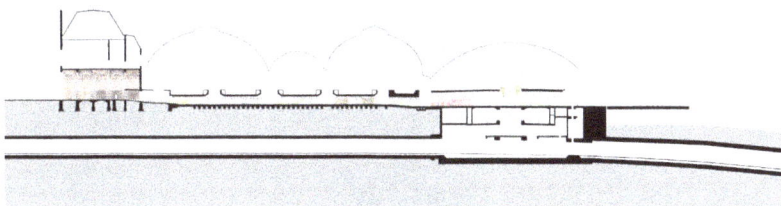

Fig. 5.6
Amsterdam Central
Station — section with
Cuyperpassage on lower
level

Fig. 5.7 (over page)
Cuyperpassage, Amsterdam

5. Architectural Responses to the Underground

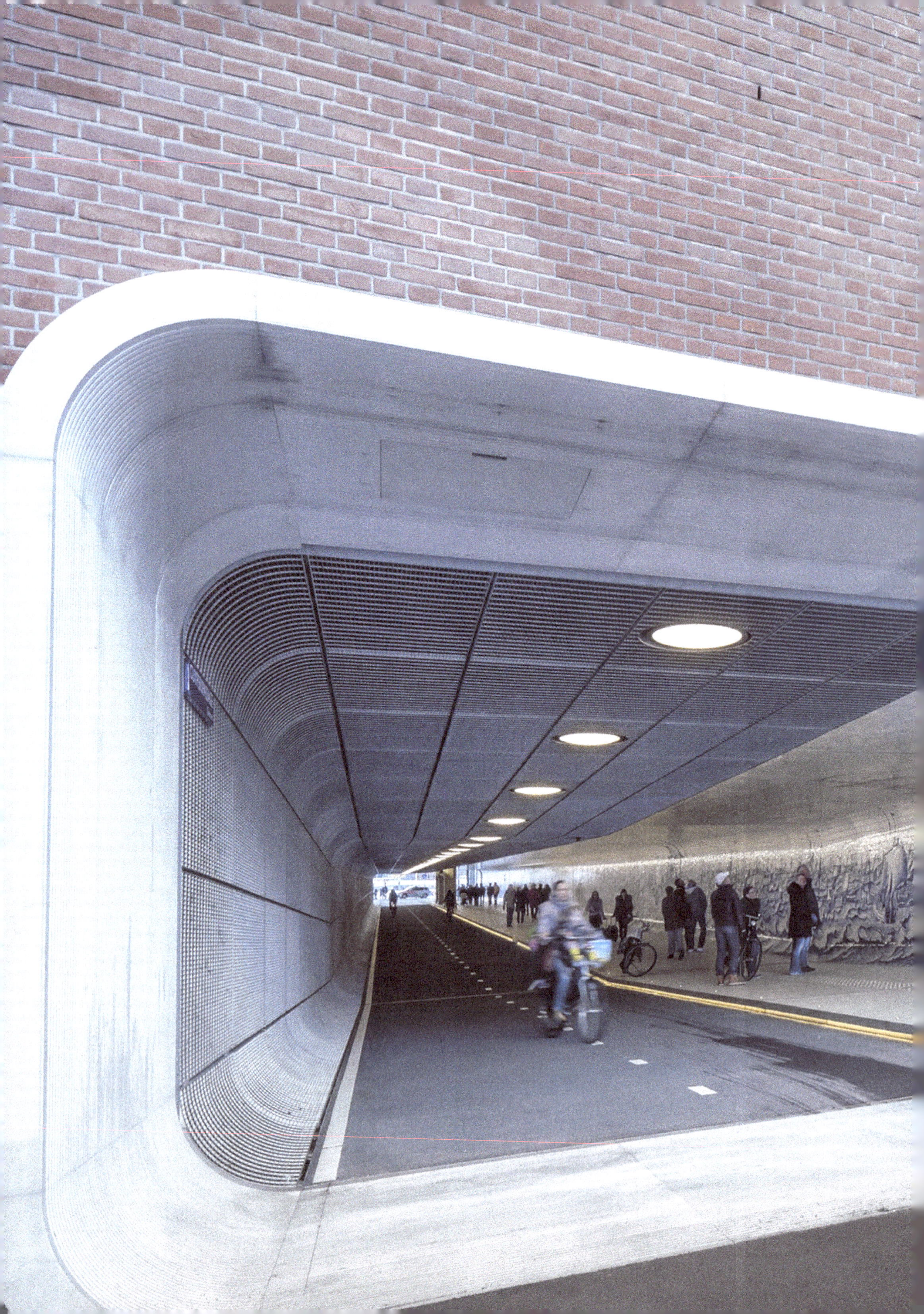

32 Cleveland Street London, United Kingdom

In 2012 Make architects sought to find a new home for their London headquarters, not an easy task given their specific needs, however, by looking underground they were able to see the potential in an unlikely space. Wanting to stay in the Fitzrovia area of London close to good transport; clients; suppliers; other creative industries; and some fine pubs, Make began the search for somewhere to accommodate their growing team. The need to find a large office, all on one level, with street presence, and affordable rent in central London was an ambitious task. During their search, they became aware of a local car park that not only met their size and location requirements, but also offered the potential to showcase their ambition 'to design the best buildings, places and spaces in the world'.

The 1,300 sqm car park is located in Middlesex House, a five-storey art deco building constructed in 1934 which in its early years accommodated factory space on the upper storeys and a car showroom in the basement. More recently the upper floors have been used as office space including by owners Derwent London, with the basement let to National Car Parks. Private vehicle use in central London has fallen in recent years and as a result, the car park was underutilised and attracting a lower property value per square foot than alternative spaces. When Derwent suggested the car park to Make they saw an opportunity to design their own unique studio, in a desirable area, with affordable rent and the security of long-term tenancy. In considering how to adapt the car park for use as an office, Make aimed to maintain the utilitarian, industrial look and feel of the space — with exposed services and pipework and retained original features such as the painted parking columns — yet also create a functional, high-spec studio space which could cater for approximately 160 employees. The office also had to adopt an open-plan layout, in line with Make's non-hierarchical company structure.

Beginning at street level, the first challenge was how to accommodate the original car park ramp which contained a United Kingdom Power Network line, meaning the ramp could not be removed nor tampered with. After much deliberation, the design team decided to retain the ramp feature as part of the overall design in order for Make to maintain a street presence for the sake of their employees, clients, consultants, and visitors to the studio. A new frontage now welcomes guests to the studio, with an animated window display, featuring two of Make's 3D printers, to keep employees, visitors and passers-by entertained. Upon arrival, guests are met by a member of the Front of House team and escorted down the ramp to the main reception area. A series of stepped platforms added to the ramp allows the area to be used as external office and break-out space; forming a natural auditorium, where the covered ramp can also be used for large meetings and presentations. As the vehicle ramp is north-facing it does not receive much direct sunlight, so to shelter and optimise use of this space, a lightweight, translucent ETFE canopy spans the ramp from top to bottom.

> The second challenge in retrofitting the space was to ensure an abundance of natural light. Luckily although located at basement level, the former car park ramp enabled generous floor to ceiling heights of 3.7m to be fitted with full length east facing windows. An existing glass lean-to over the rear light well was removed to make way for a southern facing courtyard garden, accessed by glass doors. A glass block roof light was also installed in the ground floor level courtyard above the centre of the studio, to introduce more light to the basement level.

The third challenge was to provide a flexible but appropriately programmed work space to meet the needs of the business. The studio's underfloor heating and cooling system is zoned to allow for alternative layouts of the space, with ceiling trays transporting power and data throughout the studio to allow data 'drops' to be added at any point. The main open plan work space includes three standing benches to encourage informal, break-out meetings and provide space for sketching. Bespoke, circular desks are "clamped" to the existing concrete pillars, to showcase a unique design feature, provide additional desk area and a more collaborative working environment. In addition to the main studio, a presentation space, model shop, two kitchens with coffee bars, meeting rooms, cycle storage, shower and toilet facilities have also been accommodated.

> Finally, with an aspiration to achieve a BREEAM Very Good rating, the design team carried out a range of measures including the installation of an underfloor heating and cooling system to regulate temperature in the main studio; undertook CO_2 and water consumption monitoring; designed and implemented an environmental management plan; improved the building fabric to reduce CO_2 emissions; installed 100% LED lights with a digital control; and provided recycling bins.

Make have demonstrated resourcefulness and innovation in finding an unlikely home for their architectural practice, and one that despite being below ground level, is a welcoming and professional space.

Fig. 5.8
Make office location, London

Huntley Street

Tottenham Court Road

Googde Street

Rathbone Street

Whitfield Street

Tottenham Street

Charlotte Street

Howland Street

Fitzroy Street

Cleveland Street

Maple Street

Foley Street

Riding House Street

New Cavendish Street

Great Titchfield Street

Clipstone Street

Great Portland Street

Underground Urbanism

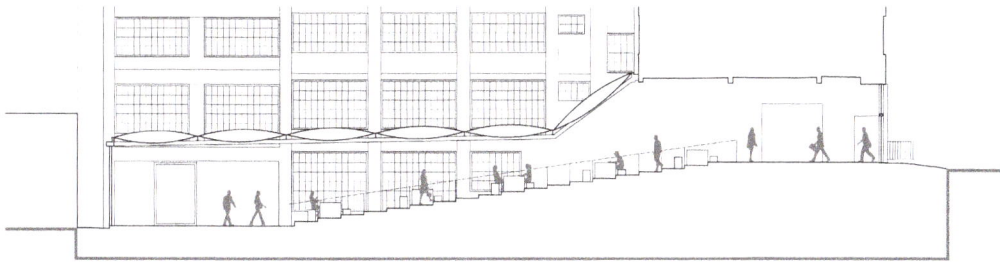

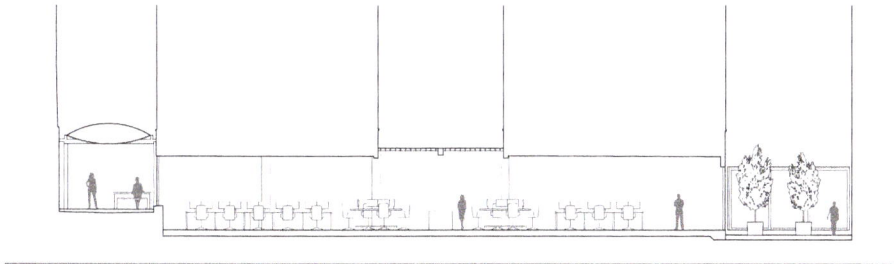

Large, underutilised car parks within central London and other cities have potential to be used differently. Dutch company Q-Park works with artists to host exhibitions and events, suggesting that alternative scenarios for these spaces could exist depending on the time of day or year.

Fig. 5.11
Make office entrance, seating
and display space above former
car park access ramp

Fig. 5.12
Exterior

Fig. 5.13
Interior with roof lights
to courtyard above

Fig. 5.14
interior with former car park
structural columns left in situ

Fig. 5.15
interior showing gen-
erous ceiling heights in
the former basement car
park

The Beach Dubai, United Arab Emirates

In a move that completely transformed the face of Dubai's The Walk at Jumeirah Beach Residences (JBR), one of the area's most popular walkways, The Beach was designed to provide a low-rise leisure and retail quarter. Although created by relocating 600 car parking spaces to a new facility below street level, The Beach is not an underground development per se. Similar to the Rose Fitzgerald Kennedy Greenway in Boston, it provides a good example of how land uses can be separated vertically to optimise the public realm. The project has now transformed an expansive and unsightly surface car park to a well-loved community space.

> The project began from a single sketch when developer Meraas looked at pushing the existing surface car park below ground to create a more active public space along the beach. The existing surface level car park had acted as a barrier to pedestrians moving east to west, and visually dominated the landscape. At night, noise from the car park and groups gathering to race their cars could often be heard echoing between the adjoining residential towers. Furthermore, the long, narrow arrangement of the 600 space car park created tailbacks of congestion to the surrounding road network, further compounding pedestrian/ vehicle conflicts. In order to finance and maintain redevelopment of the car park, the future facility would need to be commercially viable; its upkeep is supplemented by the additional revenue generated from paid parking. To minimise disruption to its surrounding residents and businesses, the project would also need to be fully designed, constructed and ready to operate within 18 months.

The initial sketch for Meraas by masterplanners and architects Benoy set out to rationalise the 600m long beachfront space, and better reintegrate it with the surrounding neighbourhood. The sketch plan showed the 31,400m^2 site broken into four key plazas, with a jogging track and tree lined pedestrian footpaths improving east — west and north — south connections. The arrangement of the pedestrian network enabled views of the waterfront to be enhanced and connectivity with the surrounding JBR precinct to be strengthened. There are now four vehicle and ten pedestrian entrances to The Beach, along with access to the Dubai Tram network.

> A new 1,200 space car park is now discretely hidden below ground, but well connected to street level. By rationalising space, the car park capacity has doubled and improved comfort for drivers who no longer need to park their cars in the intense daylight sun. Pedestrian entrances to the car park are focused around "air gardens" that act as light wells and visually connect the street and basement levels. Both at basement and street levels, bright colours and lighting are

used as part of a clear wayfinding strategy. Technical challenges associated with constructing the car park included dewatering the new basement level structure. However, Paul Priest, Director of Benoy's MENA studios says that these challenges were made worthwhile by the freedom of pedestrian movement the project has now created at surface level. The design has also introduced new routes to the beach for residents of the adjoining apartment blocks. It also provides a unique selling proposition for retailers in a competitive trading environment. Retail units of up to 14m in height are dotted throughout The Beach, interspersed between the walkways and courtyard spaces. The units are important, as along with the increased car park capacity, the provision of 24,000m^2 of new lettable floor area has enabled the project to be a commercial success.

Described as "where urban meets the sea", The Beach has 70 restaurants and shops along with a cinema, beachside kiosks, water park and outdoor gym. A number of shallow water features were included within the courtyards and when combined with the sea breeze, carry cool air to the surrounding spaces. Dynamic media façades have been utilised to activate the space at night and provide flexibility for different seasonal events. A combination of durable, tactile materials have been used, resulting in a style of architecture that is both contemporary and locally relevant.

The Beach has created a new and different typology of space in the Gulf, where retail and leisure uses are set outside, rather than within an air-conditioned mall. Owing to the outdoor, public nature of the space, the demographic of visitors is also more varied than a traditional mall, as tourists, Emirati nationals and expatriate residents come together to stroll along the waterfront in the evening. Perceptions about the comfort of outdoor spaces in summer were quickly changed as responses were overwhelmingly positive and the project has been deemed both a commercial and social success. The Beach now functions as a community space for nearby residents and the wider public, providing a much needed third space in which Dubai's various social groups can interact.

Originally the site of an expansive surface level car park, The Beach has become a key leisure destination for the Middle East. It has imagined a new type of retail and leisure space and proven that outdoor environments can be successful in the Middle East throughout the year.

Fig. 5.16
The Beach — waterfront retail
unit created in place of former
surface level car park

Underground Urbanism

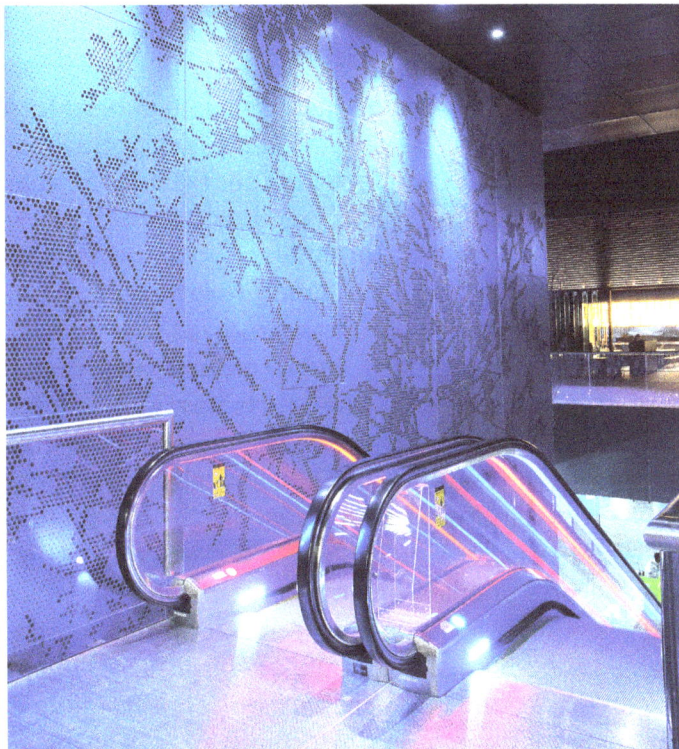

The Dubai Metro is expanding to include a further 15km long section of the Red Line to be known as Route 2020. The route will connect Al Maktoum International Airport and the 2020 World Expo site with seven stations, two of which will be underground.

Gammel Hellerup Gymnasium Hellerup, Denmark

The Gammel Hellerup High School north of Copenhagen was built in the 1950s and gradually expanded, but two projects by Bjarke Ingels Group (BIG) have been critical in shaping its identity and future. Ingels, founder of BIG and himself a former student at Gammel Hellerup explained how the project has transformed the school: 'my high-school, formerly introverted and dispersed, has become open and integrated through two focused interventions. Even though each phase is autonomous and complete — their introduction in to the mix has completely reconfigured the sum of the parts. Like a catalyst or an enzyme — once inserted — all the surrounding substance transforms into something completely new' (Stevens, 2015).

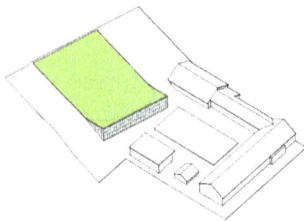

Fig. 5.19
Gammel Hellerup — the sports field curls up to reveal the basement level sports hall

For the first intervention, BIG were commissioned to build a multi-purpose hall in a courtyard surrounded by a perimeter of existing, low rise school buildings. To retain light and views to existing class-rooms, BIG opted to position the hall 5 metres below ground level. To create a light and spacious hall below ground, the 1,100m² space is finished with a vaulted ceiling curved to reflect the trajectory of a ball being thrown. The curved form of the roof reveals itself in the courtyard as a mound, incorporated into a landscaped recreation space. For the roof of the hall to have a curved form and be strong enough to bear the load of children playing above, project engineers Sweco used glued laminated timber ribbing combined with rigid support joints across the 22 metre span of the hall roof.

As the hall was being constructed, the school commissioned BIG for a second project to design a building for the arts. Intended to provide a link between the new hall and sports field to the west, this building was also positioned partly below ground level. The 1,400m² building appears to emerge from the sports field and accommodates classrooms for art, music and drama as well as a student counselling facility. East facing full height windows allow abundant natural light into the classrooms and provide a visual link to the main school buildings and courtyard.

The hall, arts building and existing school buildings are all linked at lower ground level and a new public entrance on the east of the site enables zoning of school facilities for different events and functions. The lower ground level enables students to move easily between classes with improved comfort in winter months. A simple and robust palette of materials link the new sections of the school, with concrete and timber primarily used throughout the interiors. In the gymnasium the floor and ceiling are wooden, and concrete is used for the side walls. Classrooms alternate the same combination of materials, but with an inverse arrangement of timber on the walls and concrete on floors and ceilings. Steel is used for hand railings; window and door frames are light grey; and the gym changing rooms are finished with white mosaic tiles extending across the floor, seating and walls.

Environmental efficiency was important to each of the projects, with the Danish Government Energy Strategy 2050 aiming to cut use of fossil fuels by 33% in 2020, and ultimately achieve independence from coal, oil and gas by 2050. Locating buildings below ground made a significant contribution to reducing energy demands associated with heating and cooling the new buildings, as the surrounding earth provides insulation to regulate temperature. Lighting in the multipurpose hall is partly provided by skylights, with 80% of the energy needed for artificial lighting coming from solar panels on the roof of the existing school buildings. Solar panels on the school roof also provides 30% of the energy needed for hot water, and a subsoil cooling system stores excess heat production.

Each of the projects appear playful, but also represent seriously efficient use of land and natural resources. Finally, although BIG's architectural interventions have won numerous awards including the 2014 Den Nordiske Lyspris (Nordic Lighting Award), the greatest achievement of the projects at Gammel Hellerup is their ability to inspire and educate students on the power of great design.

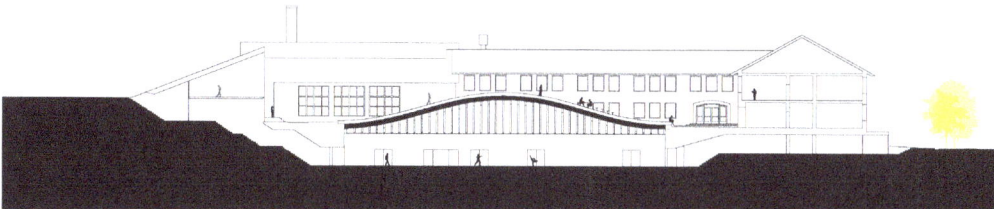

Fig. 5.20
Gammel Hellerup —
section

Fig. 5.21
Gammel Hellerup —
a simple palette of
robust materials feels
light and warm, even
when partly below
ground

Fig. 5.22
Gammel Hellerup —
the roof of the sports
hall is also a fun place
to play

Fig. 5.23
Gammel Hellerup —
interior view of sports
hall with curved cross
laminate timber roof

Fig. 5.24
Gammel Hellerup —
portal from the top of
the sports field into the
arts centre, bathrooms
and sports hall

Lowline New York, USA

In a disused trolley terminal under the busy streets of Manhattan's Lower East Side, testing is underway for the world's first underground park. *'New York is a dense layer cake of history that we don't often celebrate, and there's so much of the city that we don't notice or that remains unseen. So in another respect, the Lowline peels back layers of the city's stratified history to look at and appreciate something which is over 100 years old that is basically hiding in plain sight. The unique nature of the park and the process of walking from the street down into it should should inspire curiosity and feel interesting. It's not just a park that has been dropped 20 feet below the ground, but an altogether new experience.'* James Ramsey, Founder of the Lowline and RAAD design studio.' (Lowline, 2018)

At the turn of the twentieth century, electrified passenger trolleys criss-crossed all five boroughs of New York City, however with the advent of fuel powered transport and regular conflicts between the trolleys and other road users, they were gradually removed from service. The Williamsburg trolley terminal is a remnant of this time, located below Delancey Street on the Lower East Side of Manhattan, the 1 acre site was a large interchange hub for passengers but has been disused since 1948 when the trolley network was discontinued. James Ramsey first became aware of the trolley terminal in 2009 and became convinced that with the right technology, it had potential to become a fantastic urban park. In discussing the project with his friend Dan Barasch (who was separately exploring a project to install underground art in the subway system), the two decided to begin studying if their innovative idea could be viable. In 2011 the pair announced their idea to New Yorkers and after receiving an over-whelmingly positive response, in 2012 they launched a successful crowd funding campaign on Kickstarter to invest in further feasibility studies. The studies undertaken by HR&A Advisors and Arup, provided compelling evidence that an underground park could be possible.

On September 2012 the project (now known as the Lowline) began practical tests of the design concept and invited the surrounding community to participate. An initial two-week exhibition of a full scale model of the planned solar technology and landscaping was attended by over 11,000 people, demonstrating the strong public interest in the project. Almost two years of research, design and community outreach followed the initial exhibition and in October 2015, the Lowline Lab was opened to the public. The Lowline Lab is an interactive laboratory for lighting and horticultural experiments as well as a space in which the local community can gather. Intended as a six-month trial, the Lab had over 45,000 visitors and on the basis of its success, was granted a year long extension by the City.

The Lowline Lab is located a short walk from the trolley terminal and comprises a 464 sqm installation of the plants and lighting that could feature in the Lowline park. Some 3,000 plants including mosses, herbs, vegetables and tropical fruits are growing beneath lighting prototypes that were designed and installed by Ramsey and a Korean technology company Sunportal. The landscape is designed by Signe Nielsen of Mathews Nielsen and built by John Mini Distinctive Landscapes, and it includes over 50 varieties of plants. Helping the plants to grow are optical lighting devices that track the sun throughout the sky every minute of every day, optimising the amount of natural sunlight able to be captured. The sunlight is then distributed into the Lab via a series of protective tubes, directing full spectrum light into a central distribution point. A solar canopy, designed and constructed by engineer Ed Jacobs from anodised aluminium, then spreads out the sunlight across the space, modulating and tempering the sunlight, providing light critical to growing the plants below. The science and technology being used in the Lowline Lab, has become an important part of engaging and educating the community, including through a Young Designers Program that helps children learn about science, technology, engineering, arts, and mathematics (STEAM).

> The Lab is one of many steps in a plan to open the Lowline park in 2020, and if successful it could act as a game changer in the perception of underground spaces. Visitors will enter a glass and concrete lobby which appears to peel back the surface of Delancy Street to reveal a hidden world below. Open all year round, the park will maintain a more stable temperature than at street level and provide a much needed community asset, with space for a range of activities including events, education, passive and active recreation. Given the success of New York's Highline, the Lowline park is also likely to become a popular tourist attraction, providing economic opportunities and the chance to promote the rich cultural heritage of the neighbourhood. If the Lowline succeeds in becoming the world's first underground park it will surely not be the last, with its unique mix of technology and design offering cities the potential to reclaim forgotten underground spaces and turn them into amazing urban places.

Fig. 5.25 The Lowline —
artist's impression of the
pavement curling up to
reveal the park below

Fig. 5.26 The Lowline —
testing prototype
lighting and plants

Fig.5.27
The Lowline —
community engagement
and education

Underground Urbanism

Städel Museum Frankfurt, Germany

Frankfurt's Städel Museum was built in 1878 and despite the gradual addition of gallery space, there was insufficient room to display the museum's growing 20th Century art collection. In 2007 the museum invited eight architecture firms to participate in a design competition to undertake extensive work on the museum. In 2008 local Frankfurt practice Schneider+Schumacher were declared as winners of the competition, with their entry described by the jury as 'A shining jewel at daytime, a carpet of light at night – with this design the architects have achieved something extraordinary'. The undeniably beautiful and unique concept was based on a desire to create a light, contemporary feeling space that did not detract from the setting of existing buildings, or lead to loss of the museum garden, and for this it was necessary to look below ground.

After two years of design and negotiation with the city government, construction commenced on the museum extension, increasing its already significant scale by a further 4,151 sqm. The extension is located below a courtyard garden at the rear of the original museum building. The existing central foyer was rearranged to position the extension on the central axis of the original museum building, thereby clearly linking it to the street entrance, and special exhibition galleries on the ground floor. The new exhibition hall within the extension is vast — 55m long and 47.6m wide, with ceilings between 6 – 8.2m in height. To draw in light, the curved roof of the extension is dotted with 195 circular skylights of between 1.5 and 2.5m in circumference. The skylights enable the gallery to feel bright and spacious, though thanks to inbuilt shading, blackout and ambient light functions, can be adjusted to change the level and type of light in the gallery. From the courtyard above, the centre of the garden now appears to be pulled up by an invisible string, with the other-worldly landscape of glowing dots hinting at the presence of the gallery below.

To balance the multiple constraints of the site with the aspirations of the museum, Schneider+Schumacher adopted a cross discipline approach, with staff from their Architecture; Design; Parametrics; Building and Project Management teams all contributing, along with geologists and engineers. Fixing the extension into the ground without damaging surrounding buildings was the first challenge, followed by the diversion of groundwater and the lack of a dedicated site access for construction. The extension needed to feel light and airy, yet be constructed solidly. The ceiling is 1.5m thick in order to support the weight of the grassed courtyard above, a space which is fully accessible to museum visitors. The circular skylights also needed to be carefully considered, with features such as a transparent layer of dispersed light used to provide privacy for users of the courtyard above. The arrangement of the skylights was influenced by the arrangement of the rooms beneath, but also needed to appear as an easy to read pattern within the courtyard. To balance the project budget the total number of skylights was reduced from 250 to 195, but they still have a striking visual effect when set within the grassed courtyard.

>The success of the Städel Museum extension has been recognised not only by the museum and its visitors, but also through 11 industry awards including the gold German Design Award 2013, and Best Architect Award 2013. Schneider+Schumacher's architectural response is innovative and artistic, providing much needed exhibition space, whilst also retaining the museum's garden but upgrading it to appear as a permanent, sculptural installation within the grounds.

Schneider+Schumacher have recently completed a subsurface extension to another building of cultural and heritage significance. The Mannheim Business School is housed within an expansive, baroque palace and therefore a sympathetic architectural response was needed in order to accommodate new lecture theatres. By converting a former boiler room and coal store, a light filled lecture space has been created at lower ground level, opening into a land-scaped courtyard garden.

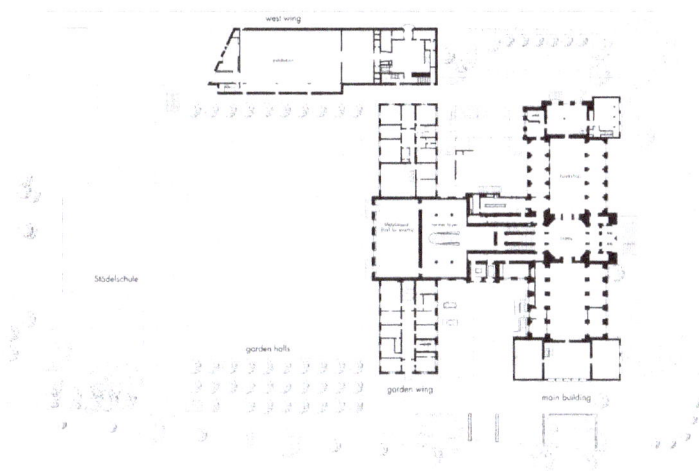

Fig. 5.28
Städel Museum —
site layout

Fig. 5.29
Städel Museum —
the contemporary and playful
courtyard hints at the new
exhibition space below

Fig. 5.30
Städel Museum — gallery
beneath the courtyard garden

Museum of Old and New Art Hobart, Australia

'Everyone, it seems loves MONA's architecture, but they weren't supposed to. They weren't supposed to notice it: it was meant to be neutral, buried, made of such functional industrial materials that it was merely a container, allowing the artworks to be the heroes' (Franklin, 2014).

Buried deep into the earth beneath a winery at a latitude of 42 degrees south, is a 9,500 sqm museum offering an entirely new way to engage with art and antiquities. Located 15km north of Hobart in Australia, the Museum of Old and New Art (MONA) evolved through six years of collaboration between architecture firm Fender Katsalidis and client David Walsh. Despite considerable cost and complexity, the ambitious project has proven successful, with visitors from around the world travelling to experience a subterranean cave of wonders.

Museums of a similar scale to MONA such as the Los Angeles Contemporary Art Museum are typically found in cities, but nothing about MONA is typical. MONA is located within the grounds of Moorilla Estate, a vineyard and winery on a small peninsula in the Derwent River in Tasmania. The Mouheneener Clan of indigenous Australians are the traditional owners of the land and named it Moorilla meaning 'rock by the sea'. In 1947 the Italian textile merchant Claudio Alcorso founded Moorilla Estate and along with his family gradually established a vineyard for Riesling grapes. Alcorso also commissioned the prominent architect Sir Roy Grounds to design two residences for the estate, the Round House (1957) and the Courtyard House (1958) both of which are now protected as buildings of architectural significance and included in the Register of the National Estate. In 1995 Moorilla was purchased by current owner David Walsh, who began to integrate his antiquities collection with the architecture of the estate, opening the Moorilla Museum of Antiquities (MMOA) in the renovated Round House in 1999. As Walsh's art and antiquities collection grew so did the estate, with chalets for accommodation opening in 2000, a microbrewery in 2004, and a larger events and exhibition space known as the Esther building in 2005. As the Moorilla Estate began to establish itself as a credible destination for the arts, construction began on an altogether bigger beast—the Museum of Old and New Art (MONA).

MONA was designed as an antithesis to traditional museums whose grand exteriors can intimidate and exclude, so the subsurface location of the museum is key to the visitor experience. MONA is described as part of an ongoing experiment by its owner to better understand what makes humans tick, and is therefore intended to create a stage for experimentation that is accessible to a wide audience, not just a cultural elite. From its architecture to curation and branding, the MONA brief was for an anti-museum where art could be discovered rather than shown off, hopefully creating a connection built from personal experience rather than being something imposed on visitors. The building was expected to be secondary to the art, but also a surprise discovery after a lengthy journey by river or road. Along with aspirations for how the museum should be experienced, there were other factors to consider in the design brief. The museum needed to be of a scale large enough to house a significant and growing collection of art and antiquities, yet not so large it would prove prohibitively expensive to construct. The museum should also retain and not harm the setting of the listed buildings designed by Roy Grounds.

Fig. 5.31
MONA — basement entrance
bar with rock wall

After $100 million and six years of conversation, design and experimentation, in 2011 MONA opened its (well hidden) doors. The museum comprises 6,000 square metres of gallery space for exhibitions; a 501 square metre gallery designed to accommodate large scale installations (primarily 'Snake' by the artist Sidney Nolan); a 65 seat theatre; and a ground level pavilion dedicated to the 'Sternenfall/ Shevirath ha Kelim' sculpture by Anselm Kiefer. The Courtyard House has been converted into the museum entrance with a gift shop and cafè, and the Round House is now used as a library. Despite the significant scale of the museum, it is conspicuously absent from view unless arriving by river. From the water the southern elevation of the museum looms large, with concrete and corten steel buttress walls appearing like a fortress without windows to indicate what could be hidden inside. After docking at the jetty, visitors climb 99 concrete stairs carved into the Sandstone (an interpretation of the steps to the temple on the island of Naxos in Greece). Only once at a ground level plaza and after walking across a tennis court, is the museum entrance revealed — itself an art installation (Distorted Mirror Entrance by Matt Harding, 2010), through which visitors then begin a deep, dark descent.

Neither approaching by land nor river can prepare visitors for the experience of descending 17 metres below ground into a dark cavern with only the art, a rock wall and stair rail illuminated. Once guests have found their way down into the gallery they are able to reward themselves with a drink at the Void bar, looking back up to the underbelly of the Courtyard House above. The bar is set against the immense Sandstone wall that runs as a feature throughout all of the gallery and circulation spaces within the museum — softly lit but with a rough texture. The rock wall is imperfect but beautiful, with its blemishes of cracks, bandsaw marks and reinforcing steel pins clearly visible to museum visitors who can also touch the small leaks of groundwater that occasionally emerge. Once refreshed, visitors are able to undertake a self guided exploration of the museum using a device called The O — an iPod touch that shows visitors their location within the museum, provides a background to the art on display, and receives feedback. The O is partly needed because there is limited lighting, directional signage and no preferred order in which to explore the museum. The sense of being underground is theatrical and helps visitors feel less self conscious than they might do in a sparse, brightly lit room.

The process of realising David Walsh's vision for MONA not only required thoughtful and creative architects, but also highly skilled construction managers, geotechnical and structural engineers. Principal Architect Nonda Katsalidis worked in close collaboration with owner David Walsh. James Pearce, Director of Architecture at Fender Katsalidis was Project Architect . The Site Project Manager Steve Devereaux and Civil Engineer Peter Felicetti designed the structure of the museum, beginning with reinforcing then underpinning the Courtyard House, so it appears to float above the museum, with its footings visible from the bar below. For this first site enabling phase, more than 35,000 cubic metres of material was excavated then removed from the site. Once exposed, the Sandstone rock wall was softer than expected, and 3m long bolts with grout were used as pins to reinforce the exposed surface. The floor of the gallery is arranged on a 2.5m grid of columns and beams onto which a slab of 2,100 concrete waffle slabs were laid to create the courtyard roof structure. The same waffle slabs were also then used on the exterior, proving visual articulation to the southern facade, but making the scale and function of the building difficult to decipher on approach from the water. The Corten stairway running down through the centre of the museum comprises 13 prefabricated flights of stairs, each of which weighs approximately five tonnes. To minimise the visual impact of mechanical and electrical equipment without internal walls, bespoke solutions were found such as hiding cabling inside concrete beams and columns, and placing the air delivery system and return plenums within walls. A different type of design challenge was also resolved (mid way through construction) when a tunnel was added to connect the lowest level of the main museum building to the Anselm Kiefer pavilion, with the architectural response suitably inspired by the caves and tunnels featured in some of the artist's work. From unlikely beginnings, MONA has grown to become Australia's largest private museum and a popular tourist attraction. Although the museum demonstrates Australian irreverence and humour, the curated works have attracted international acclaim. One of the museum's most popular pieces 'bit. fall' (2006 – 2007) is by artist Julius Popp and uses droplets of water and light to project the most used search terms from google onto the exposed rock face. Over the past year 335,127 people have visited MONA, 16% of which were from overseas (Tourism Tasmania, 2016). The unique atmosphere of MONA has succeeded not only in attracting visitors, but in enticing them to stay longer than many of the world's galleries. In The Making of MONA (2014), Franklin describes research into the tendency of people to spend very little time looking at some of the world's most famous artworks including the Mona Lisa (15 seconds average viewing time) or American museum exhibitions (average tours of only 20 minutes), by contrast tours of MONA can take upwards of five hours, with many visitors returning the following day. The unexpected and inspiring architecture of the museum has also received numerous awards including Australia's top architectural prize, the Sir Zelman Cowen Award.

Fig. 5.32
MoNA—approach from
the River Derwent

Fig. 5.33
MoNA—Distorted
Mirror Entrance by Matt
Harding (2010)

Fig. 5.34
MoNA—a dark and
atmospheric staircase
leads visitors down into
the museum

Fig. 5.35
MoNA—bar with
exposed sandstone rock
wall at basement level

Fig. 5.36
MoNA—exhibition
space with Sydney
Nolan's Snake

Northern Tunnel Stockholm, Sweden

As cities grow, road tunnels are often developed in response to congestion at street level, yet rarely is the result as stylish as the Norra länken in Stockholm. Drivers are able to view five artworks as they travel through 5km of road tunnels between the districts of Karlberg and Värtan. The road tunnels form a section of the partially completed ring road linking Stockholm's islands. Although the ring road has long been contentious, the Norra länken was deemed a necessary alternative to the heavy traffic continuing to use inner city streets. Freight traffic from the port of Värtahamnen was routed through dense parts of the city and the Nationalstadsparken (National Park), contributing to noise and air pollution, and creating potentially dangerous conflicts with pedestrians and wildlife. Although the Norra länken project was primarily a response to surface level challenges, it has created new opportunities for Stockholm to improve on its already high standards of living. By diverting roads below the Nationalstadsparken dedicated access is now provided for pedestrians, cyclists and public transport. Construction of the Norra länken has also enabled the development of two new city districts, with Norra Djurgårdsstaden and Hagastaden providing a total of 15,000 new apartments and 66,000 workplaces.

One of northern Europe's largest road tunnel projects, the Norra länken was commissioned and managed by Trafikverket (the Swedish Transport Administration) who provided finance in conjunction with the City of Stockholm and European Union. Art was an important consideration from the outset of the project, partly as the Swedish Government commits to spending 1% of the budget for each infrastructure project on artistic initiatives. The Swedish Transport Administration could also see the benefit of providing visual stimulation to drivers trying to fight fatigue and the monotony of motorway driving. From the outset, a multidisciplinary team worked to achieve a solution for the interior of the tunnel that would provide for the safe and efficient movement of vehicles, as well as the enjoyment of drivers.

The concept for the artwork within the Norra länken was devised by Architect PeGe Hillinge from Swedish consultants Sweco and sculptor Pål Svensson, who used the park above the tunnel as inspiration for their work. Formerly the King of Sweden's hunting ground, the National City Park (also known as Haga Park), is eight times larger than Central Park in New York and provides a variety of landscapes. Taking inspiration from the artworks integrated into Stockholm's famous Metro, Hillinge and Svensson sought to bring the park down into the tunnels and create an installation in sequences like a film, with drivers having only 7 seconds to view each of the five artworks. The five artworks are located in "rooms" created from the spaces between forks in the road tunnel. The spaces appear like natural caves and each has a separate artwork, focused on the seasons, with water as continuum. Each of the artworks shares three similar attributes — an artwork located at a junction between road tunnels, the use of coloured lights and photography.

Spring
With green colours similar to a meadow in spring, this installation features large butterflies, fluttering beneath the tunnel ceiling. The butterflies are made from stainless steel coloured with the illumination from multiple coloured lights.

Summer
The vivid greens of summer become interspersed with yellow to represent marshlands and reeds. Photographs, light and PVC reeds with translucent tips shimmer and move.

Autumn
Red, yellow and orange colours represent the park in autumn, with photographs and lighting used on the walls and ceilings. In the room created between a fork in the road is a large oak tree made from corten steel, its branches reaching up to the tunnel ceiling and spanning out above the lanes.

Winter
In winter the sky is dark, so too the tunnel ceiling, with small sparkling lights shining like snowflakes. The space between the junctions contains a sculpture in the shape of a snow globe, within this a freezer extracts heat from water seepage and forms a layer of frost that sparkles in the floodlights. The frost gradually forms a chalk white surface in an unexpected environment.

Water
Stockholm is known as the Venice of the north and water is a constant throughout the city's spaces and seasons. Stockholm's many waterways are represented with photographs, an LED screen and blue-white illumination of the ceiling.

In designing the installation safety was a primary consideration, but lighting; legibility; and maintenance were also important factors. Each artwork includes a prelude created by photographs being printed onto metal road signs using reflective paint and placed either side of the tunnels in the 10m before each junction. The materials are robust and easily cleaned like typical road signs, but appear as an integral part of each artwork. Although the tunnels are dark, certain signage needs to be visible to drivers, and the constantly changing levels of light created by vehicle headlights also needed to be factored into the design. The use of coloured LED lights means that dirt from vehicle exhausts isn't easily seen and bulbs can be easily replaced. The introduction of visually distinctive artworks at key junctions has also improved wayfinding for drivers, with the colour and pattern of the autumn forest providing a more memorable prompt to change lanes at high speed, than relying only on road signs.

Expanding road capacity in cities is not always the right decision, but the Norra länken tunnel has improved the quality of life in Stockholm, and shown that heavy infrastructure projects can benefit from the meaningful involvement of architects and artists to improve user experience. Ultimately, this is a project less about traffic, and more about how cities value the land and people within them.

Fig. 5.37
Northern Tunnel —
Spring art installation

Fig. 5.38
Northern Tunnel —
Autumn art installation

Fig. 5.39
Northern Tunnel —
Winter art installation

Fig. 5.40
Northern Tunnel —
Spring art installation

Underground Urbanism

Wehrhahn Line Düsseldorf, Germany

In 2016 the German city of Düsseldorf proudly unveiled its new metro line with the motto of "More Mobility — More Urban Quality", the story of how quality was embedded into the project stretches back over 15 years, and contains important lessons for cross-discipline working. The Wehrhahn Line is a relatively short and shallow underground railway line of 3.4km and six stations, but not only does it make a positive contribution to the lives of Dusseldorf's residents, it also promotes the skill and ambition of the city's professionals. What makes this project unique is the way in which art and architecture have been embedded from the outset, rather than added near completion. The Guardian newspaper was one of many publications who praised not just the final stations, but also the approach taken to their design and delivery.

> *'The new metro represents a rare moment when people who never usually interact — city bureaucrats, engineers, architects and artists — create something bigger than themselves'*

The project began in 2001 with a European wide competition won by netzwerkarchitekten and the artist Heike Klussmann. The design concept proposed a 'continuum' of a singular construction technique and identity for the tunnel, contrasted by 'interstices' of unique stations, each weaving a link between an underground world and the urban fabric of the city above. Key design principles included spaciousness, clarity, and maximising natural light. The continuum has manifested itself as a clear visual concept linking each of the stations along the line. Constructed using precast concrete panels of varying size and shape, the walls and ceilings of the railway tunnel and platforms appear light and dynamic. The detailed design and arrangement of the geometric panels provides a rhythm to pedestrian movement through the stations, and assists with wayfinding. Where the continuum is broken by a station, it is clear where you have arrived, with each station entirely unique in appearance, from platform to street level. Each station appears unique because each was designed by a different artist, working collaboratively with urban planners, engineers, architects and representatives of the city government. The bespoke art installations at each of the stations inform and flow through the design of the space, expanding until entire stations become individual pieces of contemporary art.

Kirchplatz, Enne Haehnle — Track X

Beginning at the three street level entrances, bright orange steel cables unfurl along the white ceiling and walls. From certain perspectives, the cables reveal themselves to be lines of poetic text, able to be read as passengers follow their lead down to platform level. In a light well extending from street down to ground level, the text based sculpture trails up the walls. Through successive visits to the station, passengers can reinterpret the narrative written around them.

Graf-Adolf-Platz, Manuel Franke — Agate

Referencing the quartz agate found in some rock caves, the artist Manuel Franke has painted hundreds of glass panels to create a vivid and immersive landscape. The glass panels that lead down the stairs to the station appear over the arch of the tunnel and are each unique, but layered and arranged to create a singular artwork of intense greens, and dark greys. To create an organic yet surreal visual effect, green paint was applied to the back of glass panels using silk screening, then partially removed with a knife before fixing the initial pattern with hot air. Once on site, dark grey / violet coloured panels were hung on the walls first, with the second layer of painted green panels overlaid to add contrast and give the appearance of visual depth.

Benrather Strasse, Thomas Stricker — Heaven Above, Heaven Below

A conceptual interpretation of the space surrounding architecture is given a literal translation at Benrather Strasse station, where passengers feel as though they are inside a spaceship, looking out to the stars and planets beyond. Heaven Above, Heaven Below uses stainless steel panels embossed like braille, interspersed with monitors that act as large windows through which animated scenes of planets can be seen. The animated scenes are a sophisticated composition realised through working with computer media specialists and images from space agencies, then rendered with a six headed camera to enable visual trajectories in scale with the station. The result is quite spectacular and makes a journey to work feel more like an epic adventure through space.

Heinrich Heine Allee, Ralf Brög — Three Model Rooms

Heinrich Heine Allee Station acts as an interchange with Düsseldorf's original subway; the city's most exclusive shopping street; and basement level shops of the Breuninger mall within the former Kaufhof department store. It is this intersection of places and people which Brög used as the inspiration for an integrated series of artworks comprising sculpture, musical composition and visual media. The three entrances to the station were imagined to be venues — an Auditorium; Theatre; and Laboratory. Working with other artists; a software designer; playwright, director; and musicians; Brög led the creation of unique visual and acoustic installations for each venue. The Auditorium greets visitors to the luxury shopping street Königsallee, with 48 speakers embedded into a white, multi-faceted tile facade. The sound installation Like Birds on a Wire brings together records from over 100 varieties of birds and is layered with music inspired by birdsong then programmed to play in infinite compositions, distributed variably across the speakers.

The Theatre appears as textural and vivid red curtains on digitally printed ceramic tiles beside the escalators to the department store above. The dramatic red colour of the Wehrhahn Theatre by artist Kevin Rittberger draws inspiration from the ancient Greek myth of Orpheus and his descent into the underworld. The accompanying sound installation Orpheo — The Earth is Violently Beautiful plays from three vertical speakers, discretely embedded in the folds of the "curtain".

Finally, the Laboratory extends up a ramp from the western end of the platform, connecting to the original subway line. Here the wall is also lined with digitally printed ceramic tiles, but with a considerably different appearance to those in the Theatre. Interference places copper coloured patterns at the centre of square white tiles, although there is uniformity in their placement, optical illusions are created by each of the unique patterns. Extending from the ramp are two stairwells linking the new and old metro systems, and here the laboratory expands to include hanging metallic sculptures that conceal speakers playing the digital composition Stairs.

Shadow Strasse, Ursula Damm — Turnstile

At Station Shadow Strasse, Ursula Damm has created a complex installation that visually interprets how the station and its passengers connect with the rest of Düsseldorf. A large LED screen placed over the tunnel entrance overlays patterns and images of virtual and real life forms generated from live movements of pedestrians at surface level. The ever changing imagery is also featured on LED screens arranged vertically between the striking blue glass of the station walls.

Pempelforter Strasse, Heike Klussmann — Surround

The monochrome walls, ceiling and floors of the Pempelforter Strasse station might appear to be made from a random arrangement of fragments, however, they form part of a single sculpture, modelled precisely on the station and its entrances. At each of the five station entrances four white bands begin, then spreading out across the station, ricocheting in fragments from the corners. Klussman used 3D computer modelling to calculate the geometries of the bands from CAD files, creating an artwork that was integral to the architecture and vice versa.

Optimising the integration of art into the stations was just one of the many challenges that the project team needed to resolve. The tunnel for the rail line was excavated primarily using a hydroshield process with a tunnel boring machine, working on a southern section then dismantled and relocated to an eastern section where it was reassembled to complete works. As the tunnel boring machine excavated, it simultaneously constructed the tunnel using 45 cm thick precast concrete lined segments, with eight segments combined to create rings of 1.5m in length, each added one at a time. For the station at Heinrich-Heine-Alee, a different construction technique was needed to avoid damaging the Art Nouveau Kaufhof Building, where a 70m long section of the line was constructed using a mining technique to freeze soil below ground level. As with any underground construction project in a busy urban environment, these works are complex, time consuming and require great skill. The search for materials was also not easy, needing to balance affordability, safety, ease of construction, and a certain materiality that could capture each artist's vision for their station. Durability of materials is of key importance for projects where there is a high intensity of use over an extended period of time. To ensure that the materials the artists and architects were proposing could withstand the wear and tear of long term public use, full scale samples were built in a disused tunnel elsewhere in the city.

In conclusion, it is clear that this project had an unwavering commitment to quality and artistic endeavour. The result is a railway line that could change perceptions of what it means to be underground, providing a totally different sensory experience for travellers.

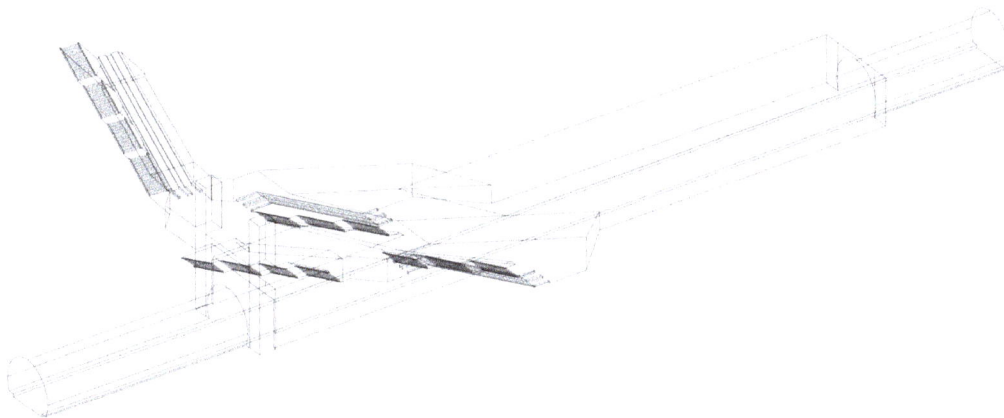

Fig. 5.41
Wehrhahn Line —
axonometric station view

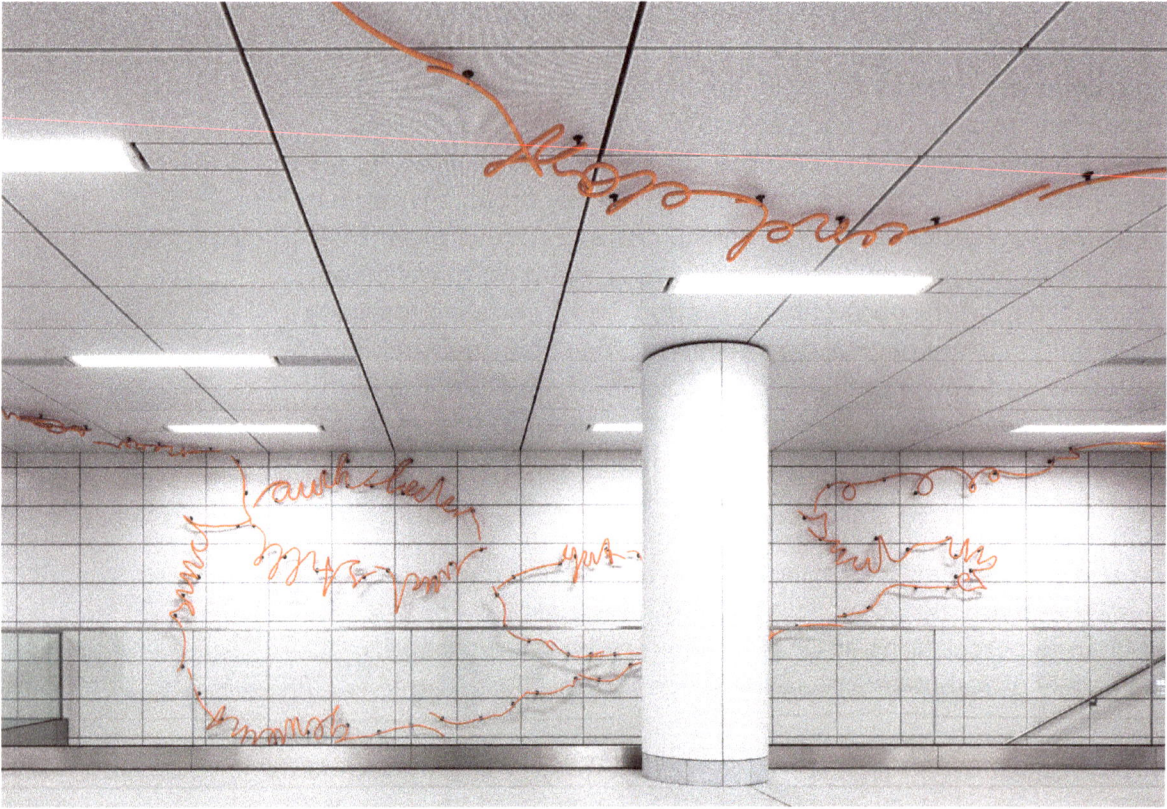

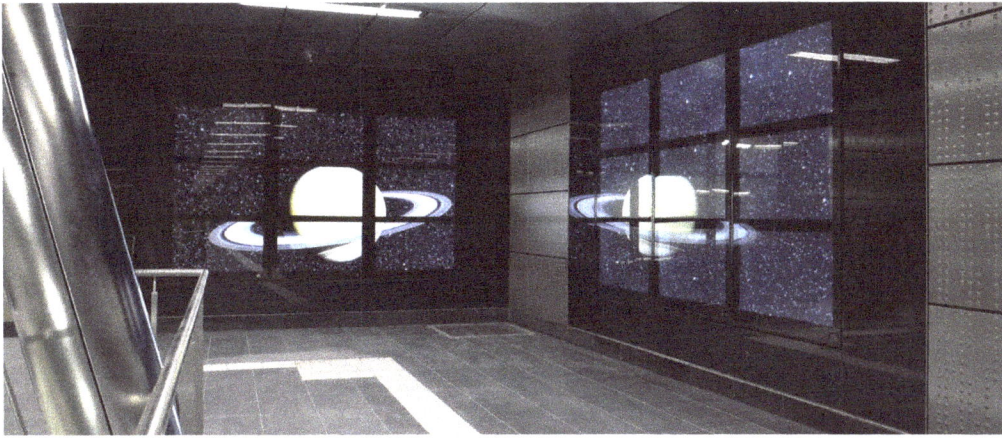

Fig 5.42
Wehrhahn Line —
Track X by Eine Haehnle
at Kirchplatz Station

Fig 5.43
Wehrhahn Line—
Track X by Eine Haehnle
at Kirchplatz Station,
looking down to platform
level

Fig. 5.44
Wehrhahn Line —
Heaven Above, Heaven
Below by Thomas
Stricker at Benrather
Strasse Station

Fig. 5.45
Wehrhahn Line —
detailed view of Heaven
Below by Thomas
Stricker at Benrather
Strasse Station

Fig 5.46
Wehrhahn Line —
Agate by Manuel Franke
at Graf-Adolf-Platz
Station

Fig 5.47 (over page)
Wehrhahn Line —
platform level view of
Agate by Manuel Franke
at Graf-Adolf-Platz
Station

6. Creating quality

underground

places

Although there are a great many underground resources and spaces that are not appropriate for active human use, where people are spending time below ground, it is important that design of those places is of the highest quality. Urban Planners, Engineers, Designers and Architects all have an important role to play in setting standards for the quality of environments that are created through underground development. Rather than considering the design of underground places as primarily structural and interior design exercises, see them as integrated parts of a city whereby a great level of thought and skills is needed to counteract the negative perceptions typically associated with underground spaces. This chapter attempts to define the characteristics of well-designed places and tools for achieving these outcomes.

Well Designed

When considering the wide range of publicly accessible underground spaces in our cities, and also the wide variety of people using them, it is difficult to provide singular design guidance. To address this challenge, this chapter is framed around the principles of user-centric design, and considers the qualities that help people feel better about their interactions with the underground. Although meaningful user-centric design is not possible at the whole city scale, its principals can provide useful direction. Although in a sense, all design should be human centred, there are many examples of public places that are derivatives of other built development, rather than having been designed as a clear response to well understood user needs. Human centred design attempts to inform and guide the process of design, to ensure that places and products go beyond being fit for purpose, and to optimising user experience.

> The City of Gainsville in the United States has an ambition to become 'the most citizen-centered city in the United States'. City Manager Anthony Lyons has said 'think of citizens and users not as customers, but as co-designers of those services, in the end you get a much better experience because it's one based on what they need rather than what the government needs' (Budds, 2016). The city worked with design company IDEO who retrofitted a downtown shop to become a place for ongoing, open ended community engagement. The former retail space had a high footfall and provided a place for residents to drop in, share their thoughts on the city and how it could be improved. Similar to the idea of Urban Rooms or "Place Spaces" recommended by the Farrell Report (DCMS, 2015 p.33), this exercise enabled direct engagement with the community on their terms, rather than through a formally structured consultation exercise. Gainsville's experience was that governance was re-thought from the angle of outcomes rather than compliance. IDEO's extensive work on the subject of human-centred design is captured in their field guide (IDEO, 2015), which encourages organisations to seek inspiration, generate ideas, and then test those ideas through action. The solutions resulting from this design process should ultimately be desirable to the people using them, commercially viable, and technologically feasible.

To design better underground places, it is necessary to understand who will be using them, what their motivations are for engaging with that place, and how their experience can be as positive as possible. Data on user behaviour can be gathered in several different ways. Remote data gathered from mobile phone use, Closed Circuit TV, and open data sources can provide useful information on the volume and direction of travel for pedestrians, drivers and cyclists moving through cities. The London Data Store is an open data platform provided by the Greater London Authority and provides over 700 data sets (GLA, 2017). This information has been an important asset for the development of applications such as Citymapper. Online and manual user surveys are still a useful way of supplementing this baseline data, and obtaining primary qualitative data. By using existing public places as precedents for new development, the behaviour of people using those spaces can be observed. Drawing lessons from the work of William H Whyte in the Street Life Project, and subsequent book The Social Life of Small Urban Spaces (1980), the patient study of people using public spaces can provide an invaluable insight into features that do, or do not work. The New York Project for Public Spaces explain that 'Whyte advocated for a new way of designing public spaces — one that was bottom-up, not top-down. Using his approach, design should start with a thorough understanding of the way people use spaces, and the way they would like to use spaces. Whyte noted that people vote with their feet — they use spaces that are easy to use, that are comfortable. They don't use the spaces that are not' (2010). Finally, where existing users are not available to provide data, characterisation exercises can be a useful way of anticipating potential user needs. By imagining the types of people likely to use a place and their likely experiences, the approach to design is more empathetic, and outcomes more relevant. The research of Samar Hechaime and the London Fusion programme uses storytelling and characterisation to help enhance people's experience of a city (Hechaime, 2014). Similar to IDEO, the Urban Factorisation methodology begins with immersion (in this case through characterisation as an alternative to survey data), this triggers imagination, that in turn leads to implementation. Characterisation describes the process of adopting a fictional persona, in order to experience an urban environment from a different perspective. Seeing a city from the perspective of a child, or someone with limited mobility for example, not only encourages empathy for others, but also helps to brainstorm ideas about how the design of public places could better respond to a wide range of users' needs.

> In 2014 Transport for London (TfL) undertook research into how customer's perceptions of the built environment affect their experience of travelling on the London Underground. The results reference Maslow's hierarchy of needs and range from basic safety, to a sense of order, then comfort, and finally — life enhancing experiences. Using this passenger research as a base, TfL then commissioned Architect's Studio Egret West (SEW) to prepare the London Underground Station Design Idiom. TfL's stated intention was to ensure that future station designs provided customers with welcoming, comfortable and straightforward journeys. The idiom contains nine

design principles to be used as a checklist for good design on projects ranging from small scale repairs to the construction of entirely new stations. Although the Idiom extends into very detailed guidance, the advice also notes that flexibility is needed to ensure that stations can adapt to changes in programmes and emerging technologies. The Idiom correctly identifies that cumulatively, design can create special moments and memorable experiences for passengers, and help to integrate stations with their surrounding neighbourhood.

In describing the drivers behind production of the Idiom, Transport for London have said 'Good design should be the driver of decision-making, should permeate every level of the organisation, and should, ultimately, be celebrated by everyone. The Idiom is more than a set of principles; it is a philosophy, an attitude and a way of thinking. It promotes a joined-up, people-focused and design-minded Underground, the best network in the world' (Garnett, M., 2015).

Building on this methodology of human-centred design, and with an understanding of how to gather the evidence needed to inform good design, the following pages contain research, standards, ideas and examples of how to create great underground places.

Fig. 6.1
London Underground
Design Idiom—platform
level visualisation of a
space designed for
passenger safety,
comfort and clarity

This warehouse looks like the perfect place for a nightclub — no neighbours, the space is affordable. I could create a beer garden with special lighting beneath the underpass next door.

Uurgh... another hot, crowded tube ride, we need more trains — with air conditioning and cooler, more accessible stations.

The lighting in this basement conference room is sooo bright! I know they can't get windows down here, but could they at least try to make it less stark?!

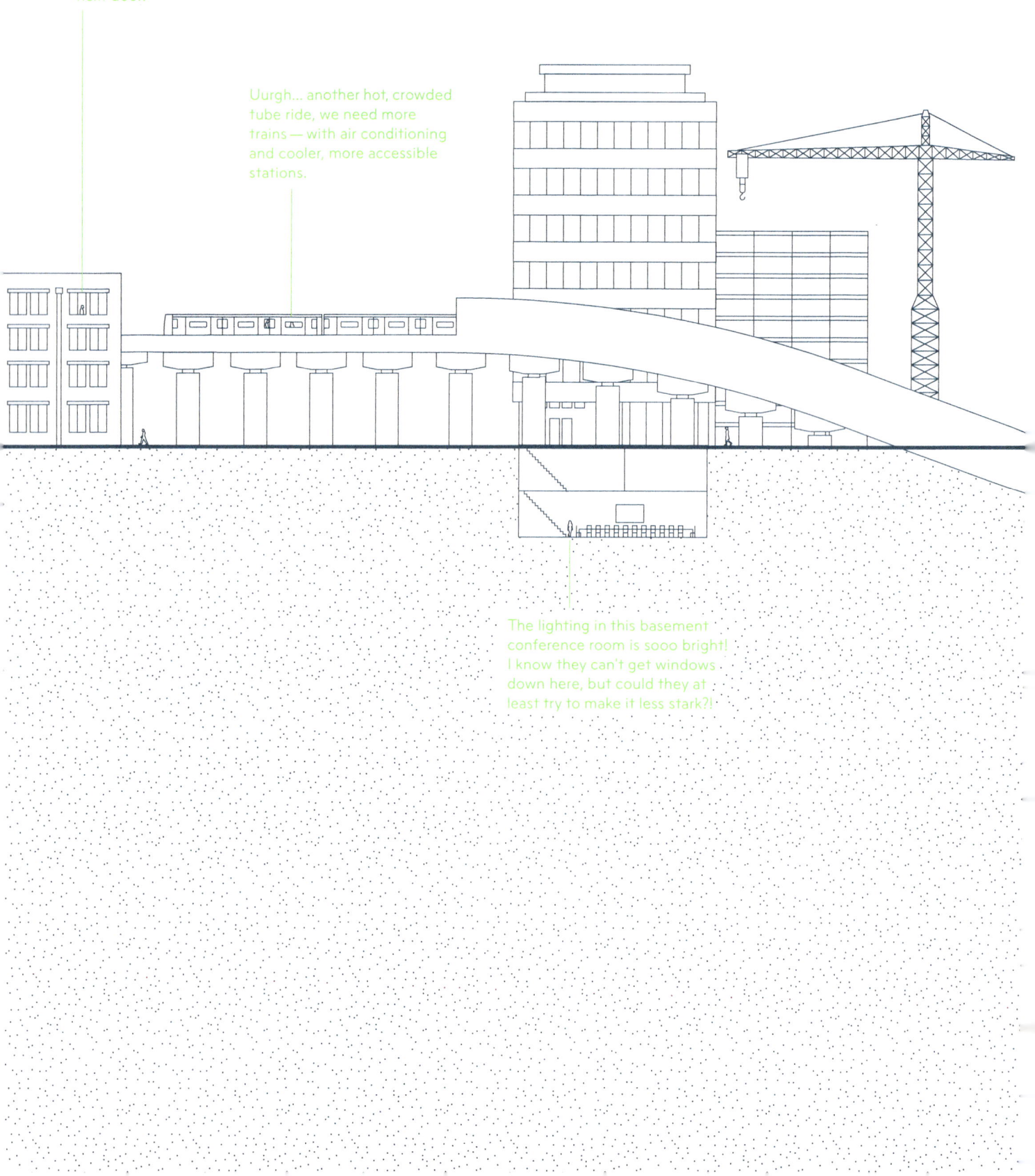

Fig. 6.2
Designing Underground Places
in Cities — User Perspectives

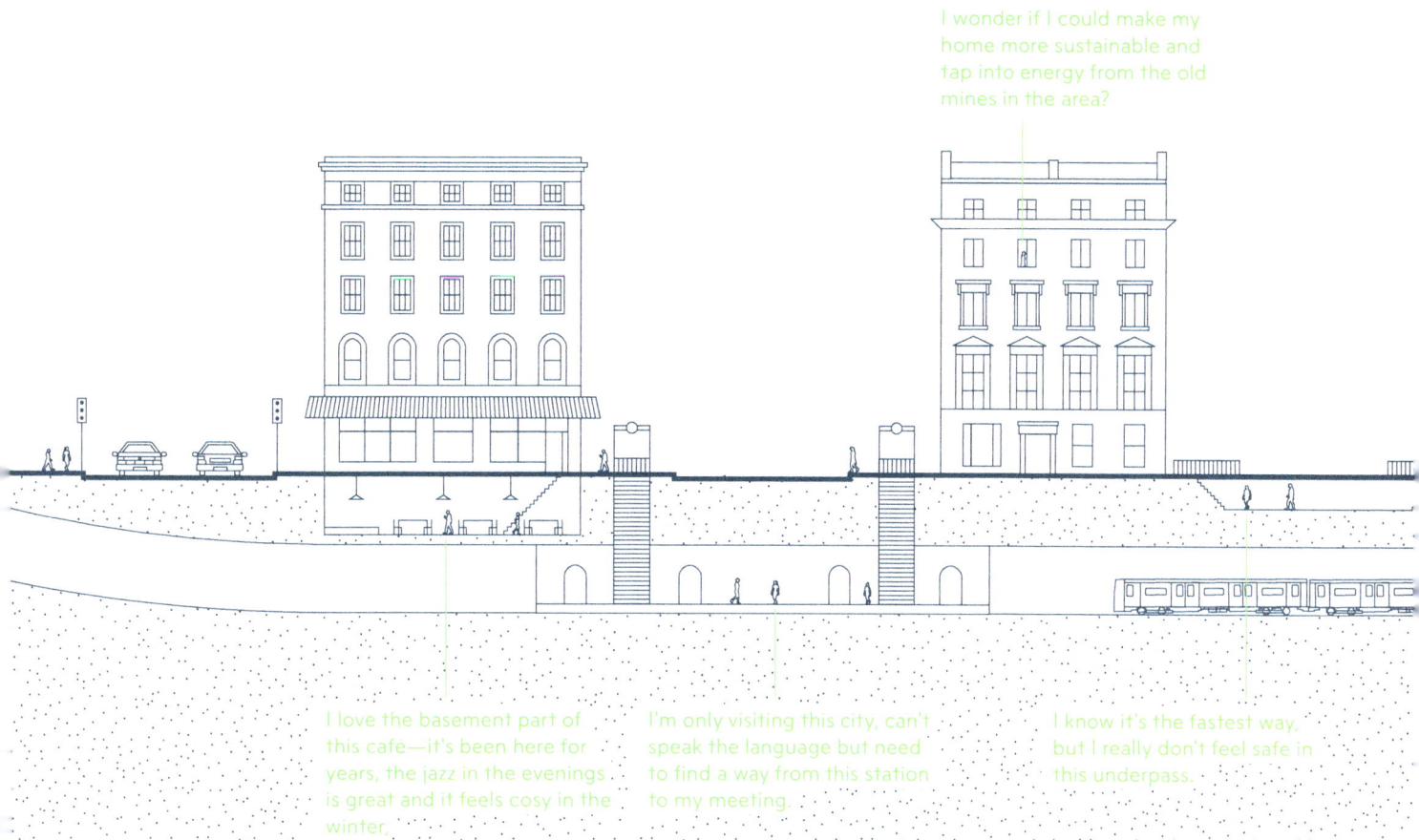

I wonder if I could make my home more sustainable and tap into energy from the old mines in the area?

I love the basement part of this cafe—it's been here for years, the jazz in the evenings is great and it feels cosy in the winter.

I'm only visiting this city, can't speak the language but need to find a way from this station to my meeting.

I know it's the fastest way, but I really don't feel safe in this underpass.

Sustainable

Sustainable development extends beyond strategic land use planning, and into the detailed design, construction and operation of underground places. Whilst there are no universal standards for the sustainable design of underground places, there are opportunities to combine recommendations from a range of professional standards, and lessons learnt on previous projects. Beginning with the high level 2030 Sustainable Development Goals devised by the UN, it is possible to refine down key themes through to green building standards, and design principles. Applying these goals is not just about making them as environmentally sustainable as possible, but also about creating comfortable and attractive places.

Internationally, there are numerous environmental assessment methods including BREEM (UK), Estidama (UAE) and Green Star (Australia), however, the US Green Building Council's programme is the most comprehensive in terms of topic and geography and scope. Leadership in Energy and Environmental Design (LEED) is the certification system of the US Green Building Council, but is recognised by over 20 other countries. LEED Version 4 covers five types of projects, each with mandatory and optional credits to certify projects (with a maximum of 100 credits available). For each type of project the credits are broken into six key areas: Location and Transport; Sustainable Sites; Water Efficiency; Energy and Atmosphere; Materials and Resources; and Indoor Environmental Quality. At an overarching level, there are also LEED System Goals known as Impact Categories. The Impact Categories focus on what LEED projects should accomplish, such as the protection of water resources and enhancement of health and wellbeing. The impact categories provide a weighting to the credits, to provide 'multiple lenses' of sustainability. Whilst none of these categories specifically reference underground development, there are credits that could be interpreted, or adapted as follows:

- Design places in flood hazard areas to ensure resilience in emergency situations, through features such as integral flood barriers, and electrical wiring above flood level.
- Where possible, provide underground places such as shopping malls with direct access to functional entrances from parks / plazas and streets.
- Use underground or multi-storey parking facilities to minimise land consumption and rainwater runoff associated with impermeable surface level car parking.
- Consider lighting levels and thermal comfort ranges when designing energy systems.

- Identify opportunities for waste water reuse from sources such as HVAC equipment condensate, site rainwater and groundwater.
- Work with, and try to accommodate, natural baseline conditions including topography, hydrology, climate, vegetation and geology.
- Concentrate building density below as well as above ground to make land available for outdoor public space.
- Contribute to reduction of the urban heat island effect by extracting and capturing waste heat energy from land surrounding subsurface developments and infrastructure (a significant, unresolved challenge for the London Underground).
- Design in flexibility to enable the joint use of facilities at different times of the day, or throughout the lifecycle of a development e.g. use city car parks for sports when they are less busy on weekends, or use cinemas as lecture theatres during weekdays.
- Reduce water and energy use through materials selection, for example surfaces that refract light could reduce the level of electrical energy needed for illumination.
- Find new uses for construction waste such as compressed earth bricks from tunnel excavation.
- Look for opportunities to integrate surface level landscaping, including through the use of structural columns as tree planters.
- Use renewable materials such a cork on wall linings to improve acoustics and air quality.
- Identify opportunities for renewable sources of energy such as redirected solar power that utilises advanced technology like prototypes on the Lowline, waste energy capture from underground data centres, or ground source heat extraction to charge electric cars in underground car parks.
- Reduce the lifecycle environmental impacts of buildings by reusing or repurposing abandoned or blighted underground spaces.
- Specify building materials that support the physical and mental health of users through acoustic performance, visual and acoustic comfort.
- Although not always possible, attempt to create quality views — potentially through live footage of surrounding spaces at street level (similar to the digital art installation at Pempelforter Strasse station in Dusseldorf), green walls, or site-specific design innovations such as large-scale

periscopes to street level.

- Think differently so that projects can 'achieve exceptional or innovative performance'.
- Identify opportunities for landscaping and local food production (similar to the Growing Underground case study).
- Introduce fun and interactive elements that encourage walking and cycling such as kinetic paving.

The ideas listed above are not intended to provide a comprehensive overview of LEED, but instead use the LEED credits as a starting point to imagine how underground places could be made more sustainable. It is hoped that as subsequent versions of the LEED programme are announced (with V4.1 released in 2018), guidance for sub-surface design is included. In the interim, as with most sustainable design, the ideas listed above are simply good practice, intended to enhance user experience whilst reducing detrimental impacts on our environment.

Fig. 6.3
Piano Stairs, Brussels

Fig. 6.4
Bunhill Energy Centre, London

Fig. 6.5
Groove at Central Mall, Bangkok

Fig. 6.6
SelgasCano Architects' Office, Madrid

6. Creating Quality Underground Places

187

Safe

Managing Risk

When considering the development of new underground spaces or the repurposing of existing ones, it is important that risks be assessed at both a city-wide and sites specific level. In the United States, the Risk Management Process for Federal Facilities: An Interagency Security Committee Standard identifies and attempts to mitigate natural, accidental, terrorist, state sponsored, criminal, and other threats (Renfroe & Smith, 2014). This comprehensive approach to risk assessment can be used as part of scenario planning to identify potential risks to new developments. Essentially the type and probability of a threat (defined / credible / potential / minimal) is balanced against the vulnerability and consequence (devastating / severe / noticeable / minor), giving an estimated risk category of low to very high.

> Transport for London is currently considering the sale of disused underground train stations for conversion into a variety of uses such as nightclubs, restaurants and museums, yet safety and security risks are a key consideration in determining if and how the spaces could be reactivated. The presence of asbestos, a need for safe egress in the event of an emergency, prevention of access to other secure parts of the operational train network and provision of adequate ventilation, are all considerations in determining the feasibility of a project. In New York plans to convert the disused but stunning City Hall Subway station into the New York transit museum were abandoned after the September 11, 2001 terrorist attacks in the city, presumably as a result of the perceived increased risk that such spaces bring (Wert, 2010). Rather than simply preventing access to places like City Hall Subway Station, there is an argument to be made that proactively using and managing these types of places can improve security of the city above.

Fear of the Unknown

Pedestrian underpasses can be intimidating places, sometimes even when they are the most direct route, free of road traffic, and sheltered from the rain, people still go out of their way to avoid using them. Entering a space without being able to see a way out or the next stage of your journey, is counterintuitive to our human nature. Transport for London's Transport Action Plan explains that 'Fear of crime can inhibit walking and cycling along certain routes and to certain locations and is an important factor to consider in promoting active travel. Perceived and actual safety on streets can relate to whether there are other people using the environment, lighting, how well maintained the area is, openness of the space and potential hiding places for assailants' (TfL, 2014 p.53).

In describing an attempt to walk over a railway pedestrian bridge in an area of London known for its drug dealing and crime, the writers of a blog on art archaeology and walking in London, recall a terrifying yet hilarious experience, whereby the fear of who or what they might encounter was overwhelming:

'We were walking one night along Cheshire Street, about to go across the railway footbridge, which cuts through to Pedley Street. It's a very dark and secluded spot. I don't think there's any street lights, maybe there's a little light coming from the windows up above. The railway footbridge cuts through from an alley off Cheshire Street and over the railway. The steps down at the other end of the bridge turn a corner to the left, then turn another corner, leading down into a railway arch. Because of the turn of the stairs you can't see who might be coming around the corner. And as the railway arch is very dark, leading onto a cobbled lane, secluded from any main streets, there's not that many people passing through, sometimes a few during the day' '...So, as we approached the railway footbridge I felt the apprehension of all those things. It was dark. It must have been about eleven o' clock maybe. There was nobody really around. But we wanted to go over to the other side because it was on our route. So we tentatively approached the steps up to the bridge. And, we looked at each other, and we went up a bit further, further up the steps...and one of us thought we saw something at the other side, and one of us gasped. And I don't know who, but somebody shrieked, and we all went running back down again, screaming. And got to the bottom, asking each other 'What happened? What happened?' 'Well, I heard you two getting a bit nervous, and I was getting a bit nervous. Then I screamed. Sort of joking but a bit scared, and kind of trying to make you more scared, but kind of believing it myself... and then we all ran down'... We couldn't believe how scared we'd been. And how stupid it seemed. Because however dangerous it might have seemed to cross the bridge, or whoever might have been lurking, the fear seemed to have nothing really to do with those ordinary fears of being attacked in the street by someone. It had taken on a kind of supernatural quality. Some kind of indefinable fear that was lurking along this bridge' (Burton, Korda & Qualmann, 2010).

Although it is clear that the underpass and footbridge of Pedley Street is part of a cluster of poorly designed spaces that attract anti-social behaviour, what is also striking about this story, is the intense psychological fear that harm was imminent. The alternative route for neighbours living either side of the rail line is four times longer, walking alongside mechanics workshops or warehouses located beneath the railway arches, spaces that are poorly lit and surveilled at night. Whether above ground, at street level, or undercroft, this series of spaces feels unsafe and hostile, particularly at night. Although there are serious functional challenges with the design of the area, there are techniques that can be used to improve this and other spaces to help the people using them feel safer.

- Encourage more people to use underground places, thereby providing activation and a sense of safety in numbers.
- Where possible provide passive as well as remote surveillance.
- Lighting that is well designed and maintained to avoid dark patches of poor visibility.
- Improve detailed design and spatial integration of entrances and exits for underground places, to ensure that these gateway areas are not dark, with recessed areas, or difficult to overlook.

The Art of Distraction

Similar techniques can also be used to improve pedestrian underpasses or walkways linked to busy places such as train stations. The passive surveillance provided by the presence of small retailers such as coffee shops or dry cleaners can provide positive reinforcement in the presence of others. Art installations with cabinets of curiosities, or walls of lights can temporarily distract users from the fact they are below ground, and also make places feel well curated and cared for. However, sometimes these measures aren't enough. Rough sleeping, drug use, littering, criminal damage and generally anti-social behaviour can quickly make places feel unsafe. Policing and proactive management is often needed in these places to maintain their attractiveness and continued patronage. To counteract both the real and perceived fear of crime in public underground spaces, cities might look to examples of the dedicated police force for the Paris catacombs, or the friendly presence of ambassadors for Business Improvement Districts. Once users have full confidence in the level of safety associated with a place, their experience can begin to be optimised.

Underground Urbanism

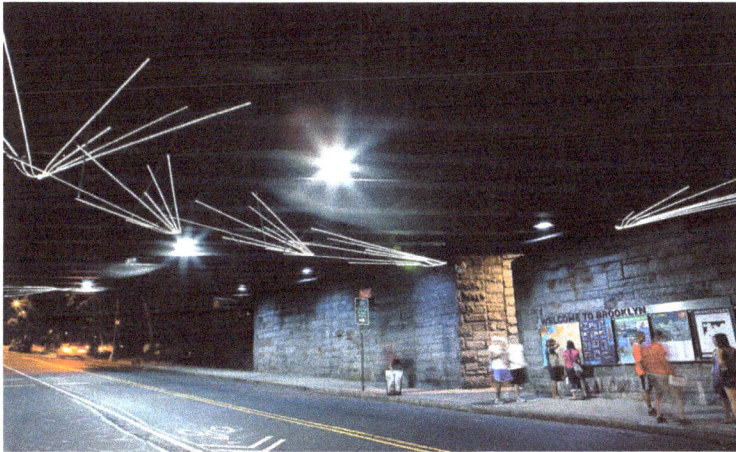

Fig 6.7
Baker Street Wonderpass,
London

Fig. 6.8
Light Installation Brooklyn
Bridge, New York

Fig. 6.9
Campbell Arcade,
Melbourne — entrance

Fig. 6.10
Warwick Junction, Durban —
artwork by Faith47 shown on
scale model of the market at the
Venice Biennale 2016

Fig. 6.11
Warwick Junction, Durban —
artwork by Faith47 at night

Warwick Junction in Durban, South Africa is a hub for the movement of people and the trading of goods. Informally created beneath a highway flyover, for many years the market, bus terminus and taxi station was a busy but dangerous space. One police officer had become so sick of arresting people for repeat offences that he worked with an architecture practice (designworkshop:sa) and NGO (Asiye Etafuleni) to improve the area through better pedestrian linkages, lighting and community capacity building. Perhaps the most striking improvement is the addition of large scale public artworks created by Faith47 to champion the market traders. The improvements have lowered crime and increased confidence in the area, with the project featured at the Venice Biennale 2016.

Welcoming

People are like water, looking to flow as easily as possible through urban spaces to their destination. There is a natural preference to take the most direct route from A to B - whether travelling by car, public transport, bike, or on foot. Following this subconscious desire line, people generally prefer not to change levels, or their direction of travel. Getting circulation and legibility right is vital to the success of under-ground spaces. As per Transport for London's Whole Street approach 'Pedestrians are very sensitive to even very small diversions in their journeys, and weather conditions, noise, aesthetics, perceived safety, wayfinding and many other factors will influence a pedestrian's perception of their access' (TFL, 2014 p54). Transition zones from street level to the subsurface need to be carefully designed. The following principles can help create spaces where people seamlessly move from above to below ground:

- Maximise proportions — avoid entrances and canopies that appear to funnel drivers or pedestrians into immediately smaller spaces. Congestion at road tunnel or underground train station entrances can provoke feelings of anxiety if people anticipate a sense of claustrophobia.
- Maintain levels — maintain ground level as far into the transition space as possible, and then descend on as low a gradient as possible.
- Provide visual clarity — make it clear where people are going and what they might experience next.
- Be consistent — avoid strong contrasts in light levels, physical scale and temperature that can feel disorienting or jarring.
- Keep it positive — lighting, materials and professional management can all make people feel welcome and confident, thereby counteracting some of the negative connotations around underground space.
- Stand out — where an underground space is a standalone destination, landmark entrances help highlight to people places that are worth exploring.
- Make people feel valued — use quality materials, offer a generosity of space where possible with ceiling heights, and create a positive ambience.

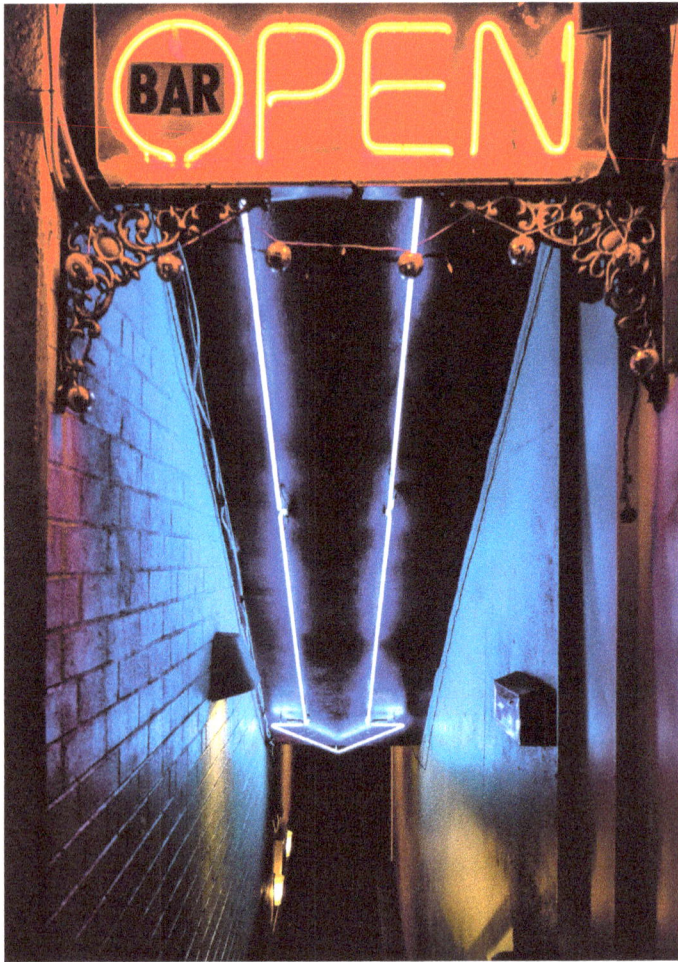

Fig. 6.14
The Tippler Bar, New York

Fig. 6.15
Car Park Entrance, University
of Melbourne

Underground Urbanism

Fig. 6.16
Ion Shopping Mall, Singapore

Fig. 6.17
Apple Store, New York

6. Creating Quality Underground Places   197

Legible

'The directionless infinity of underground space is both attractive and repellent. After all, there is no horizon to get your bearings by, only perspectives depth' (Ernst von Meijenfeldt, 2003).

Beginning at a macro scale, Planners and Designers need to stitch together above and below ground spaces to provide better linkages for movement and to improve user experience. In his book Vertical, Stephen Graham asks difficult questions about the potential consequences for people living in dense, multi layered cities. For example, do citizens have a right to identify and experience "natural ground level"? Is the increased layering / stacking of cities inevitability? Does ground level always need to be signposted as a human navigational tool? What are the moral responsibilities of stacking and layering people and their possessions in cities? People often experience underground spaces as interiors, not as complex assemblies; however, as cities such as Hong Kong and Singapore develop more underground pedestrian walkways, urban designers should proactively design these as coherent sequences within longer journeys.

Providing legible underground places is not just about navigation, but providing users with enjoyment and encouraging confidence in their journey. In his book Townscape (1961), Gordon Cullen explains the principles of Serial Vision, whereby pedestrians travel through existing and emerging views. Describing how turning a corner can reveal a new view, Cullen talks about streets being like the 'unfolding of a mystery, the sense that as you press on, more is revealed. Yet, given the psychological and social reservations expressed about underground spaces, places need to be designed to strike a careful balance between revealing just enough of the emerging view that pedestrians feel safe and interested enough to continue their journey' (Cullen, 1961).

Wayfinding

Wayfinding is the process by which people are able to understand their location relative to a destination, and the route/s able to be taken between those points. Clear wayfinding strategies not only improve user experience, but assist escape in the event of an emergency. Familiar points of reference and clearly identifiable means of escape are particularly important in underground places, that can be confusing due to a lack of typical visual cues such as windows to a street outside. There is a growing amount of research on digital wayfinding applications that use 3D mapping of a building, sensors, and even augmented reality, to help users navigate underground places. These interactive maps build upon products such as Google's Indoor Maps, and enable users not only to identify a route to their destination, but also to understand their own location at any given moment, potentially saving time in the event of an emergency (Yokoi et al., 2015). At New York's Metropolitan Museum of Art, datasets are being used to help visitors navigate their way through 20 different but interconnected buildings using a mobile application (MMA, 2016). These technologies may also benefit visually impaired users, providing them with additional layers of information and audible or sensory (vibrating) responses (Black et al., 2017). One challenge associated with this approach however, is that if the technology (or even just the battery on a phone) fails, then users might not have a manual wayfinding strategy to fall back on.

Graphic Techniques

The use of colour is one of the easiest ways to communicate different wayfinding options. The London Underground map designed by Harry Beck in 1933 is iconic and has been reproduced in various cities around the world. The diagrammatic map shows the relationship between train lines and stations, rather than distance. Each train line is represented by a specific colour, making it accessible to people with limited English language and reading skills. In Toronto, a colour based wayfinding strategy for the PATH network was first proposed in the 1980s. Design firms Gottschalk, Ash International, and Keith Muller Ltd. were commissioned to create a design concept that would enable better wayfinding between the growing network of car parking garages, hotels, department stores, railway and subway stations. Each of the four letters in PATH was represented by a colour that in turn matched an orientation (City of Toronto, 2018). In 2016 the City of Toronto commissioned consultants Steer Davies Gleave to devise a new design concept for the PATH network that has expanded 23 per cent in the past 5 years (Steer Davies Gleave, 2016). Colour is often a key feature of wayfinding systems, but careful consideration needs to be given to what is being communicated, and to whom. Certain colours can be interpreted differently depending on their cultural context, for example the colour red can be associated with danger, good luck, or mourning depending on the beliefs of the viewer. Visual clarity is crucial in wayfinding, particularly for people with deteriorating or poor eyesight (Trust Housing Association, 2011). A limited palette of contrasting colours can therefore assist the widest range of users.

Using colour as the basis for communicating location and direction, different materials and textures can then also be used to emphasise navigational message and respond to specific uses. This might be as simple as coloured electrical tape in a line on the ground, the addition of Braille on signage, or the creation of visual contrast through embossing. Illumination can also be used to enhance colour, and compliment places without natural light. The use of different colours, materials, and lighting to convey information can also be adjusted in scale, with larger markers to improve visibility, and introduce an element of playfulness.

Visual Clutter

As with the public realm at street level, visual and physical clutter is to be avoided to prevent overwhelming and confusing users. Clutter is not only the result of too much signage for directions and information, but also commercial advertising. There is a difficult tension here between places such as pedestrian underpasses needing to be free to use, and yet costing money to construct and maintain. Although these costs can be offset by revenue from commercial advertising, an over-abundance of visual media can be distracting and disorienting. The relentless attention jacking by increasingly interactive forms of advertising can also tire and overwhelm users. A begrudgingly captive audience on the London Underground is surrounded by advertising on almost every surface, as the transport provider seeks additional forms of revenue to fund its core services. This overstimulation can be tiring, and prove challenging for users to get their bearings below ground.

Fig. 6.18
Underhub Language
School, Kiev

Underground Urbanism

Fig. 6.19
Wayfinding at Narita
International Airport
Terminal 3, Tokyo

Fig. 6.20
Wayfinding at Narita
International Airport
Terminal 3, Tokyo

6. Creating Quality Underground Places

Fig. 6.21
MSCP, London

Fig. 6.22
Bangaroo Car Park,
Sydney

Fig. 6.23
Mercedes Benz Museum

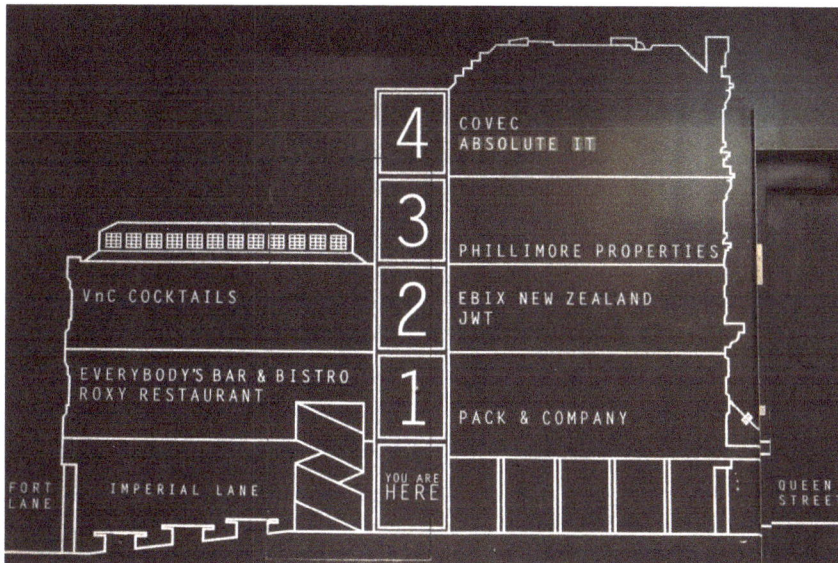

4 COVEC
ABSOLUTE IT

3 PHILLIMORE PROPERTIES

VnC COCKTAILS

2 EBIX NEW ZEALAND
JWT

EVERYBODY'S BAR & BISTRO
ROXY RESTAURANT

1 PACK & COMPANY

FORT
LANE   IMPERIAL LANE

YOU ARE
HERE

QUEEN
STREET

Fig. 6.24
Imperial Lane Cafe,
Aukland

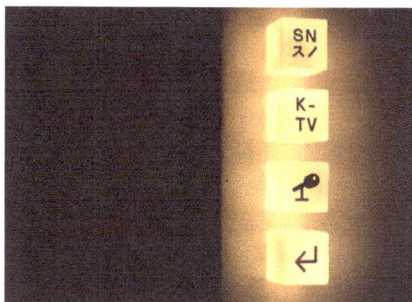

Fig. 6.25 Supernormal
Restaurant & Karaoke,
Melbourne

Comfortable

Temperature

Mechanical heating and cooling requirements are generally less in underground spaces than buildings above ground level, as the embodied energy of the surrounding earth helps maintain an even temperature. Humans are most comfortable in a temperature range of 18–24°C and buildings constructed below ground are generally able to maintain more even, comfortable temperatures. However, where excess heat is being produced, then indoor temperatures can become uncomfortable. In years gone by, the London Underground was promoted as a place to seek refuge from heat in summer, but from an average temperature in 1900 of around 14°C, the earth surrounding some deep level tunnels is now 20–25°C (Elledge, 2017). The increased temperatures make it particularly uncomfortable for passengers in the summer peak hours when train carriages can exceed 30°C in temperature. The reason for the increased temper-ature relates to the heat generated by trains moving and braking in tunnels that are surrounded by clay earth, with the earth gradually accruing the waste heat without any real way of dissipating the heat. Transport for London is investigating different ways of diverting the waste heat produced by trains, however, given the problem has developed gradually over almost 120 years, a quick resolution is unlikely to be found. In other underground places, heat generated by lighting, or electrical equipment also contributes to increasing the ambient temperature and in turn, often requires further mechanical measures to counteract a lack of natural ventilation.

Acoustics

Underground spaces are often well insulated against noise owing to the dense surrounding earth, however, they can face challenges associated with acoustic reverberation, making them uncomfortable for users. High ambient noise levels in cities can have serious mental health impacts (University of West England, 2015). Relatively confined underground public spaces such as the pedestrian walkways that connect shopping malls, airport terminals, and train platforms are often finished with hard materials such as ceramic tiles. Hard surfaces on walls and floors can amplify internal sources of noise, although it is recognised that there is a tension here between specifying materials that are appropriate for high levels of pedestrian traffic (robust and easy to clean), with those that are softer and denser such as fabric panels. The British Standards Institute (BSI) advise that for noise generated inside a building, Designers have options to reduce impacts through noise attenuation, obstruction of the sound path between the source and recipient, or improving the sound insulation of the building envelope (BSI, 2014 p11–12).

Lighting

Given the negative perceptions surrounding underground space, the selection of lighting is one of the most important factors in creating a comfortable underground place. When selecting lighting for underground places, designers should anticipate the response from users — will they feel reassured, calm, or perhaps uncomfortable? Clearly, the ultimate use of the space will determine the best type of lighting to specify, but typical considerations include:

- Source (natural / artificial);
- Shadow and reflection;
- Lux levels;
- Light spill;
- Colour and Tone (warm / cool);
- Energy use and waste heat production;
- Effects;
- Control (manual / programmed / responsive / automated); and
- Type (fluorescent / filament / LED).

Getting a meaningful amount of natural light into underground spaces is challenging. Shallow level spaces can use a combination of roof lights and enlarged glass clad entrances to maximise natural light, and make artificial lighting appear more natural by association. The Jubilee Place shopping centre in London's Canary Wharf has a light, airy feeling through the use of skylights, generous ceiling heights and glazed entrance atriums. At the Potsdamer Platz in Berlin, a combination of glazed paving and light tubes at street level are used to provide light to the shopping centre and railway station at basement level. Built in 2003, the tubes appear at street level like tall, abstract sculptures, which then punctuate the ceiling below. Ranging between 14 and 21m in height, the tubes work by attaching heliostats and light sensors to a steel tube that is wrapped in glass, and within the tube prismed foil refract the available light (a combination of daylight and halogen globes). By magnifying the available sunlight, it is possible to achieve up to a 50,000-lux level below street level (Gasser, 2003). Using similar principles, but new technology, the Sunportal lights being trialled at the Lowline Lab in New York, utilise optical lighting devices to track the sun then distribute it into tubes, before re-dispersing it below ground through solar canopies made from anodised aluminium (Lowline, 2018).

The combination of materials and lighting is also important. The Parc de Celeste is a rare case of shadows consciously being used for (dramatic) visual effect. The shadows unintentionally created from the interaction between lighting and fixtures, can take on a sinister feeling in underground spaces where there is limited natural surveillance (or as Jane Jacobs described, "eyes on the street"). Mirrors and glazed surfaces can help amplify the limited amount of light available in underground spaces, yet bright isn't always better. Excessive illumination and brightness can also make spaces feel sterile and offputting. Therefore, achieving the right amount and quality of light within underground spaces is a fine balance between the needs of the user, as well as financial and technical project constraints. Programmable LED lighting is now revolutionising the way that underground spaces look, feel and perform. Warmer tones of light, and an extensive choice of colours are available with LED lighting, and as indicated in the Growing Underground case study, this can lead to underground spaces being used in unexpected ways.

Air Quality

The advances in light technology improving the appearance of underground spaces also offer the potential to introduce planting to underground spaces. Although green walls can be costly to install and maintain, they have the potential to improve air quality, as well as amenity. In some instances, groundwater and humidity could be recycled to irrigate green walls or other indoor landscaping.

6.26
Sofital The Palm, Dubai —
Green Wall by Patrick Blanc

Underground Urbanism

Fig. 6.27
Carousel Shopping
Centre, Paris — tall
ceilings, a warm palette
of natural materials,
and diffused natural
lighting from an inverted,
pyramid shaped skylight
make this a comfortable
and attractive subsurface
place.

Inspiring

Underground spaces might be misunderstood or even feared, but we can't help but be fascinated by them. Furthermore, the positive impacts of a well-designed public place can't be understated. Let's not take ourselves too seriously — from BIG's smoke ring blowing waste energy plant, to trampolines in Welsh caves, cities shouldn't be afraid to experiment. Underground spaces are quirky, curious, and cool — so embrace the novelty, and have fun designing and using them!

Resourceful

In most cities, land is too valuable to leave the spaces beneath underpasses empty, particularly where they have a knock-on effect of attracting antisocial behaviour, or making neighbourhoods feel unsafe or neglected. Whether it is a microbrewery or a mechanic's workshop, a climbing wall or a community centre, these undercroft spaces offer great potential to reactivate spaces and put eyes back on the street through reintroducing building frontages that were often demolished to create motorways. In London, the design collective Assemble created a temporary performance space beneath a decidedly unglamorous freeway overpass as a side event for the 2012 Olympic Games. The Folly was constructed with help from the local community and played host to 40,000 people over the nine weeks it was in operation. As part of the process to transform a neglected space into a positive place, Assemble prepared a fictional narrative to imagine how such an unusual space could have come to be. The origins Folly are told as the tale of 'a stubborn landlord who refused *to move to make way for the motorway, which was subsequently built around him, leaving him with his pitched roof stuck between the East and Westbound lanes'* (Assemble, 2017).

In Yokohama, Japan the space beneath an elevated railway has also been repurposed for arts and the community, but using a different approach. The Koganecho Studio for artists is located in an area that had been known for prostitution and drug dealing, but working with the local area management and architects, a creative studio with events and retail space has been created. Five architectural practices (Contemporaries, Studio 2A, Workstation, Koizumi Atelier and Nishikura Architectural Design Office) used basic materials of timber, glass, corrugated metal and cement, to transform a 100m stretch of undercroft space beneath the railway overpass (Liotta, 2013). The studios created beneath the underpass now provide a welcoming and practical place for artists to create and exhibit their work.

Hidden

The Ewha Women's University Campus is not immediately obvious when looking across the hills of north west Seoul, as the 70,000 sqm development is sunk into the landscape through acts of deft architectural skill and heavy engineering. Architect Dominique Perrault has created a valley between two halves of a building, covering each with grass to camouflage the building into the surrounding landscape. The two halves of the building each has a full height glass curtain wall, and are separated a sufficient distance apart to allow the space between to act as a sunlit agora. In 2011 the 20,000-capacity campus building was awarded the prestigious Grand Prix de l'AFEX (association des Architects francais a l'Export). The award added to a collection for Perrault, who has long sought to embed his buildings into layers of landscape. Perrault's other notable projects include the National Library in Paris, and the velodrome and Olympic swimming complex in Berlin (De Muynck, 2008).

Adventurous

Sometimes exploring a seemingly hidden or abandoned space appeals to our sense of adventure. Although most people aren't compelled to become urban explorers of the deepest parts of their city, sometimes places that are hidden, or a little rough around the edges yet honest, can hold the most appeal. The Park-Ing pop up store by Japanese DJ and designer Hiroshi Fujiwara was created in the basement car park of a building owned by Sony in Tokyo. The temporary retrofit of the car park was designed by Architect Nobuo Araki and included a grand staircase punched through the concrete layers of the car park, which was otherwise left raw, providing a strong visual contrast to the clothing and art installations on display (Strategy, 2016).

Wondrous

Let's face it, even the most jaded big city commuter can't help but notice and appreciate those little moments of joy and wonder in our everyday places. Unexpected moments of wonder in your everyday travels can improve your mood and maybe even change your direction of travel. Noticing the way sunlight falls beautifully into New York's Grand Central Station like a cathedral, or feeling like an extra from Metropolis when in the cavernous stations of London's Jubilee Line, are experiences that help people pause (even momentarily) for reflection. At Kings Cross in London, Architects Allies and Morrison designed a light wall to line one side of a 90m underground pedestrian walkway linking two train stations with surrounding offices, restaurants and public space. The light wall itself is designed by Spears and Major, and delivered by Light Lab who placed the expanse of LED lights behind a glass wall, creating a canvas onto which light based art installations and animated displays, using a full RGB spectrum and white light spectrum of 3.0 – 6.0K, are reflected off the opposite wall and ceiling to create an immersive and futuristic feel (Light Lab, 2014).

Atmospheric

Beginning with a brief to bring contemporary art into car parks, the atmospheric Parc Des Célestins elevates a typically banal space into an interactive artwork. Voted the world's coolest car park, Parc Des Célestins successfully combines a strong built form, architectural pattern, vertical integration, and the interplay of light and shadows. Designed by Architects Michel Targe and Jean-Michel Wilmotte in conjunction with the artist Daniel Buren, the core of the car park is shaped like a steep, winding cylinder acting as a central light well to cast sculptural shadows on to the walls and floor (Willmott and Associates, 2017). The 435-capacity car park extends 53m in diameter, with parking extending either side of the light well to a depth of 22m below street level (Henley and Barr, 2009). The light well also provides inter-action with a small public square at street level, whereby members of the public can look down a periscope of sorts. A large mirror at the base of the light well rotates to refract light onto different parts of the car park, thereby amplifying the visual impact of the periscope until it becomes a kind of kaleidoscope. The periscope is also an effective and playful way of creating connectivity between the street and subsurface.

Artistic

People want to feel valued, and art has an important role to play alongside architecture. There is a generosity imbued by the presence of public art, particularly when it is a deliberate alternative to the presence of commercial advertising. However, it is not just large scale, integrated artworks such as those found in the Stockholm

Metro that are appreciated, in New York the sculptor Tom Otterness has created a series of petite, but well-loved installations. Life Underground (2001) is part of the Metropolitan Transportation Authority's Arts for Transit program, and comprises a series of bronze sculptures scattered throughout the Subway Station at Eighth Avenue and Fourteenth Street. Often measuring no more than 250mm in height, the sculptures are spread around the ticket halls, stairs and platforms of stations — sometimes slightly hidden and waiting to be discovered. Although the installation provokes commentary on social issues of greed and corruption, their scale; form; and position helps them appeal to all age groups. The New York Times recounts the reaction of a young boy who happened upon the sculpture of an alligator swallowing a man: *"After jumping on the alligator's head and trying to wrestle the little man from his bronze jaws, the observer notes that the boy, "about to give up, he kicked the alligator, his foot connecting solidly with the bronze head. Surprise spread across his face as he ran away, crying, 'Mom, it tried to bite me!' "* (Rogers, 2003). Art creates the opportunity for people to share those small moments of humour and interaction, and in the case of Life Underground, couldn't be a more appropriate way of enriching people's experience of an otherwise transitory, and functional underground space.

Fig. 6.28
The flyover

Fig. 6.29
The folly

6. Creating Quality Underground Places

211

Fig. 6.30
Studios beneath underpass in
Kogane-cho, Yokohama

Fig. 6.31
Kogane Studio for artists in
Yokohama

Fig. 6.32
Ewha University Campus, Seoul

Underground Urbanism

6. Creating Quality Underground Places

Underground Urbanism

Enduring

The cost of constructing underground spaces can be considerable; to ensure they remain useful to cities they should be designed in a manner that is future proof and flexible. Over engineering buildings at an initial construction stage can be costly, but it can also offer long term benefits. Some of the world's greatest cities have a legacy of fine quality public buildings and infrastructure which, thanks to a commitment to quality, are still used and enjoyed today.

Fig. 6.38
Thames Tunnel 1843

Fig. 6.39
Thames
Tunnel 2016

Fig. 6.40
Thames Tunnel Section

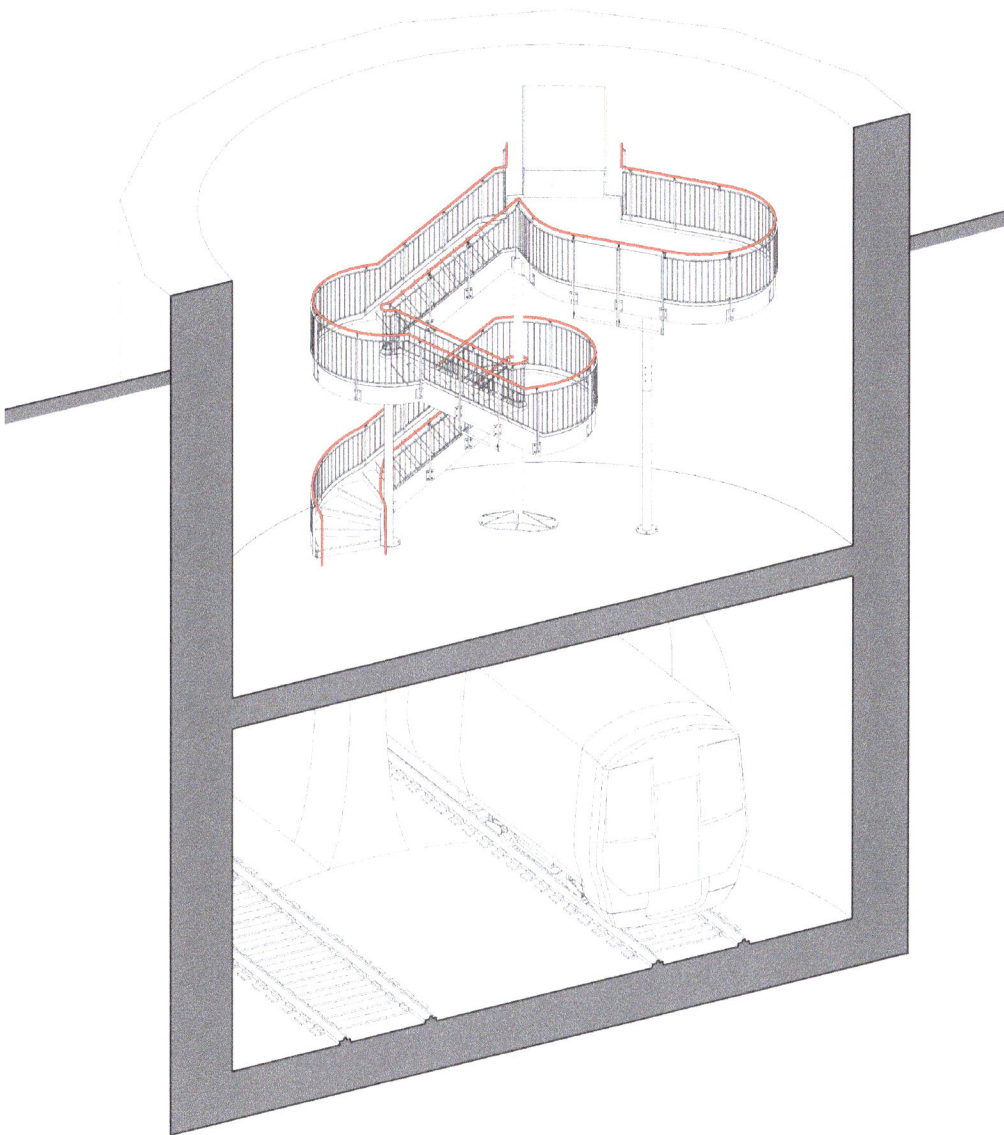

7. As

Above,

So

Below

The Flip Side

Population growth and the subsequent densification of cities is increasing spatial pressure on the urban subsurface. Road and rail tunnels, as well as pedestrian corridors are used to connect cities, yet the spatial requirement for these assets is rarely considered at a whole city scale. These spatial demands are also not balanced with the need to maintain environmental services such as water storage and filtration. In the free market context of most of the world's cities, these dense inner urban areas also attract high land values. These high land values add to the cycle of densification, with higher floor area ratios needed to achieve appropriate returns on land investment. The economic context of cities such as London, Hong Kong and Singapore therefore also makes the construction of major real estate projects viable. Physical soil, or earth, rarely has a meaningful financial value, and yet, once converted into floor area, is very much a valued, and tradeable asset. The creation of enormous basements for private homes in London is driven by these land economics. So too, are the skyscrapers constructed on small, and almost impossibly constrained parcels of land, their basements and foundations stretching deep beneath the surface. The earth extracted for these basements, and the train tunnels needed to connect the buildings, is sent further afield — used to contour golf courses and reclaim land from the sea. The properties of that soil are therefore also lost from the city, and the water previously held within it, either extracted or diverted. Rarely are these dots (or holes) connected. What physical space and natural capital remains beneath our cities, and how we can balance the competing demands and consequences associated with development? It is against this background, that the land beneath our cities needs to be considered. Underground Urbanism hopes to have made a modest contribution to the ways in which we visualise, plan, design, and manage our urban environments — from bottom to top.

Built environment professionals need to be more aware of constraints and opportunities associated with the urban subsurface. Therefore, in considering the long-term sustainable development of our cities, decision makers need to engage with a range of built environment experts, not least Geologists and Hydrogeologists, whose early stage involvement can help mitigate risks such as ground contamination or instability. We also need to acknowledge the perceived, as well as real, concerns linked to underground places, and engage the public so they are better able to appreciate the common resources beneath them. The land beneath our cities is comprised of complex, interrelated layers of natural and man-made objects. Yet despite being vital to our quality of life, these objects are often out of sight, and therefore out of mind. Indeed, it has been said that less is known about the land beneath our cities, than outer space. By painting a novel picture of these layers, it is hoped that readers have a better understanding of what lays beneath their city streets.

So how can we better plan for the responsible development of our valuable urban subsurface? A speculative, first come, first served approach to the urban subsurface can have unintended consequences. The foundations of tall buildings form iceberg like obstructions to the alignment of the rail lines needed to serve them. Although land can be safeguarded for public infrastructure, this is often done on an individual project basis, rather than part of strategic spatial planning. The exception here is Helsinki, and it seems likely that Singapore and Hong Kong will create similar three-dimensional spatial development plans. Overall, unfortunately, there is generally an absence of pro-active spatial planning or design policy for underground spaces. By looking at cities holistically, and fine tuning how different land uses are distributed, cities have the potential to become more efficient and enjoyable places. The public could also have a forum to debate the merits of the various uses competing for subsurface resources. For example, should land uses with a large footprint, but limited need for daylight such as car parks and self-storage facilities be placed below ground, thereby allowing the space above them to be developed for housing? If cities map and then analyse their existing underground spaces, opportunities for future proofing and resilience might reveal themselves. Rather than document storage, could (as with the case of Growing Underground) former air raid shelters be used to grow fresh vegetables and herbs, much closer to market? As existing freeways reach the end of their lifecycle, are there opportunities to place traffic below ground, and create public open space at street level? Without a comprehensive understanding of the subsurface of a city, it is not possible to plan for its responsible use and development.

Taking inspiration from Paris, cities can begin to plan for the land beneath them by cataloguing existing spaces that are surplus to requirements, and inviting proposals for their reinvention. It is hoped that the case studies in chapters four and five of this book give inspiration to others seeking to make the most of forgotten spaces beneath their cities.

Creating successful underground places requires creativity and skill. Contemporary art, quirky design features, and a sense of playfulness are themes in many of the projects highlighted within this book. Focusing on how to experience underground places can guide design. It is important that the journey, for example, of pedestrians through a city, is a coherent and enjoyable one. Instead, too often, it is confusing and disjointed, as a result of individual spaces designed as a functional reaction to transport capacity, with a lipstick of (value engineered) interior "architectural" design then applied. In many ways the spaces that exist underground are most interesting architecturally, there are entrances, but no façades to focus attention on. The exterior of underground buildings is almost irrelevant, as their only interface is with unseen earth. When working with underground buildings, Architects have to challenge themselves to maximise the benefits associated with volume, light, and quality of materials, such that people are able to appreciate the hidden but important places within their cities.

A great deal of time is spent planning land uses and codifying design standards for buildings at surface level, yet the same level of attention is rarely given to the flip side of a city. Until our urban environments are understood as complex spaces made up of interrelated layers, they will fail to meet our collective expectations for sustainability, competitiveness and quality of life. Underground Urbanism has sought to provide a new perspective on our cities, and encourage built environment professionals to collaborate in rethinking them from (below) the ground, up.

Underground Urbanism

Figures

Throughout

Illustrations, plans and sections
Elizabeth Reynolds (www.urbenstudio.com) and BOB Design (www.bobdesign.co.uk): Figures 1.1, 1.2, 1.4, 1.7, 2.01, 2.02, 2.03, 2.04, 2.05, 2.06, 2.07, 2.08, 2.09, 2.10, 2.11, 2.12, 2.13, 2.14, 2.15, 3.1, 3.2, 3.3, 3.4, 3.5, 3.6, 3.7, 3.8, 3.9, 3.10, 4.8, 6.2.

Chapter 1

Cargo Sous Terrain
Cargo Sous Terrain (www.cargosousterrain.ch): Figure 1.3

The Big Dig
The Rose Kennedy Greenway Conservancy (www.rosekennedygreenway.org): Figure 1.5

The Jewel, Singapore
Sam's Studio / Shutterstock: Figure 1.6

Chapter 4

Attendant Café
Conversion and refurbishment by Pete Tomlinson and Ben Russell, photos by Paul Reynolds: Figures 4.1, 4.2

Digua Shequ
Beijing DiGua Technology (www.diguashequ.com), photos by Pop Up City (www.popupcity.net): Figures 4.3, 4.4

Retrofitting Grout Shafts
Jordan Jon Hodgson, Elizabeth Reynolds & Royal College of Art (www.rca.ac.uk): Figures 4.5, 4.6

Growing Underground
Conversion and use by Growing Underground (www.growing-underground.com), photo by Elizabeth Reynolds: Figure 4.7

Chapter 5

How You May Live and Travel in the City of 1950
Harvey Wiley Corbett: Figure 5.1

The Earthscraper
Bunker Arquitectura (www.bunkerarquitectura.com): Figures 5.2, 5.3

The Cuyperpassage
Benthem Crouwel Architects (http://benthemcrouwel.com), photos by Jannes Linders: Figures 5.4, 5.5, 5.6, 5.7

32 Cleveland Street
Make Architects (www.makearchitects.com): Figures 5.8, 5.9, 5.10, 5.11, 5.12, 5.13, 5.14, 5.15

The Beach
Benoy (www.benoy.com): Figures 5.16, 5.17, 5.18

Gammel Hellerup Gymnasium
Bjarke Ingels Group (https://big.dk): Figures 5.19, 5.20, 5.21, 5.22, 5.23, 5.24

Lowline
Raad Studio (https://raadstudio.com): Figures 5.25, 5.26, 5.27

Stadel Museum
Schneider+Schumacher (https://www.schneider-schumacher.com): Figures 5.28, 5.29, 5.30

MONA
David Walsh and Fender Katsalidis (fkaustralia.com): Figures 5.31, 5.32, 5.33, 5.34, 5.35, 5.36

Northern Tunnel
Sweco (https://www.sweco.se) and Artist Pål Svensson: Figures 5.37, 5.38, 5.39, 5.40

Wehrhahn Linie
Netzwerkarchiteckten (https://netzwerkarchitekten.de/en): Figure 5.41
... with Artist Enne Haehnle: Figures 5.42, 5.43
... with Artist Thomas Stricker: Figures 5.44, 5.45
... with Artist Manuel Franke: Figures 5.46, 5.47

Chapter 6

London Underground Design Idiom
Studio Egret West (www.egretwest.com): Figure 6.1

Piano Stairs
The Oval Office Live Communication (www.theovaloffice.be/en): Figure 6.3

Bunhill Energy Centre
Cullinan Studio (http://cullinanstudio.com): Figure 6.4

The Groove at Central Mall
Synthesis Design and Architecture (http://synthesis-dna.com): Figure 6.5

SelgasCano Architects' Office
Selgas Cano (http://www.selgascano.net): Figure 6.6

Baker Street Wonderpass
Bigg Design (https://www.biggdesign.co.uk): Figure 6.7

"This Way" Brooklyn Bridge Light Installation
Linnaea Tillett (www.tillettlighting.com) and Architect Karin Tehved: Figure 6.8

Campbell Arcade
Designer of 1956 arcade unknown: Figure: 6.9

A Study of Warwick Junction at Rush Hour
Artist Faith47 (https://faith47.com), photo Elizabeth Reynolds: Figure 6.10, photo Kierran Allen: Figure 6.11

Canary Wharf Station Jubilee Line Entrance
Foster and Partners (www.fosterandpartners.com): Figure 6.12

Paris Metro Entrance
Hector Guimard: Figure 6.13

Neon Bar Entrance
Designer unknown: Figure 6.14

Car Park Entrance, University of Melbourne
Engineer Jan van der Molen, Landscape Designers Ellis Stones
and Ronald Rayment, with Atlas figures salvaged from Colonial
Bank Building, Elizabeth Street: Figure 6.15

ION Orchard Shopping Centra
Benoy Architects (www.benoy.com): Figure 6.16

Apple Store, Fifth Avenue
Bohlin Cywinski Jackson Architects (www.bcj.com): Figure 6.17

Underhub Language School
Architect Emil Dervish (https://emildervish.com) and
Photographer Aleks Yanchenkov (www.facebook.com/
yanchenkovphotography): Figure 6.18

Narita International Airport Terminal 3
Consultants PARTY (https://prty.jp) and Nikken Sekkei
(www.nikken.co.jp/en): Figures 6.19 and 6.20

MSCP, Queen Elizabeth Park
Haptic Architects (https://hapticarchitects.com) and
BOB Design (www.bobdesign.co.uk): Figure 6.21

Bangaroo Car Park
Wayfinding design by There (https://there.com.au), photo by
Steve Brown: Figure 6.22

Mercedes Benz Museum
UN Studio Architects (https://www.unstudio.com): Figure 6.23

The Imperial Buildings
Fearon Hay Architects (https://www.fearonhay.com):
Figure 6.24

Supernormal Restaurant
Chris Love Design (www.chrislovedesign.com): Figure 6.25

Green Wall at Sofitel, The Palm
Botanist and Inventor Patrick Blanc (https://www.
verticalgardenpatrickblanc.com), photo Elizabeth Reynolds:
Figure 6.26

Carousel du Louvre
Architect I. M. Pei (https://www.pcf-p.com), photo Elizabeth
Reynolds: Figure 6.27

The Flyover / The Folly
Assemble Architects and Designers (https://assemblestudio.
co.uk): Figures 6.28, 6.29

Kogane-Cho Studios
Figures: 6.30 and 6.31

Ewha University Campus:
Architect Dominique Perrault (http://www.perraultarchitecture.
com/en/homepage): Figure 6.32

Life Underground
Sculptor Tom Otterness (http://www.tomostudio.com):
Figure 6.33

Park-Ing Pop Up
DJ and Designer Hiroshi Fujiwara and Architect Nobuo Araki
(http://actp.co.jp): Figures 6.34 and 6.35

Parc des Célestins
Architects Michael Targe and Jean-Michel Wilmotte
(http://www.wilmotte.com/en), Artist Daniel Buren Figures:
6.36 and 6.37

Thames Tunnel (1843)
Isambard Kingdom Brunel: Figure 6.38

Thames Tunnel (2016)
Refurbishment by Tate Harmer Architects (http://tateharmer.
com): Figures 6.39 and 6.40

Text

Urban Growth — Up, Out & Down

Admiraal, H., (2006). 'A Bottom-up Approach to the Planning of Underground Space' *Tunnelling and Underground Space Technology*, Volume 21, Number 3/4, pp464 – 465, 2006. Amsterdam: Elsevier.

Barbara, A., (2017). 'The Challenges of Building Amsterdam's New Metro—the North-South Line' TEDxAmsterdam. [online] Available at: tedx.amsterdam/2015/09/the-challenges-of-building-amsterdams-new-metro-the-north-south-line (Accessed 21 May 2017).

Barles, S. & Guillerme, A., (1995). *L'urbanisme souterrain*. Paris: Presses Universitaires de France.

Bauer, C. & Fletcher, R., (2015). *Under the Elevated*. New York: Design Trust for Public Space.

Belanger, P., (2016). 'Altitudes of Urbanisation'. *Tunnelling and Underground Space Technology.* Volume 55, May 2016. Amsterdam: Elsevier.

Berg, N., (2017). 'Goodbye Highways'. *Landscape Architecture Magazine.* [Online] Available at: landscapearchitecturemagazine.org/2017/02/07/goodbye-highways/ (Accessed 04 June 2017).

Boston Planning and Delivery Agency, (2017). Rose Fitzgerald Kennedy Greenway Planning. [Online] Available at: bostonplans.org/planning/planning-initiatives/rose-fitzgerald-kennedy-greenway-planning (Accessed 04 April 2017).

Broere, W., (2013). 'Urban Problems — Underground Solutions', *Advances in Underground Space Development.* Editors Zhou, Cai & Sterling, for The Society for Rock Mechanics & Engineering Geology. Singapore: Research Publishing.

Cargo Sous Terrain, (2016). Cargo sous terrain: The Goods Transport System of the Future [Online] Available at: cargosousterrain.ch/de (Accessed 15 July 2016).

Cornaro, A., & Admiraal, H., (2012) 'Changing World—Major Challenges: the Need for Underground Space Planning' in Papers of the 48th Annual ISOCARP Conference. Perm, Russia. The Hague: ISOCARP.

Croft, J., (2016). 'London's basement extension boom to be tested in High Court' — Financial Times. [Online] Ft.com. Available at: ft.com/content/9e4b0854-8ca9-11e6-8cb7-e7ada1d123b1 (Accessed 23 May 2017).

Eduardo F. J. De Mulder, C. C. Derk F. Van Ree & Wang, K., (2015). 'Underground Urban Development: An Overview', *Engineering Geology for Society and Territory* — Volume 5 pp25-29. Switzerland: Springer International Publishing.

Erdem, A., (2008). 'Subterranean space use in Cappadocia: the Uchisar example'. *Tunnelling and Underground Space Technology* Volume 23, Issue 5, pp492 – 499 (September 2008). Amsterdam: Elsevier.

Flint, A., (2017). '10 years later, did the Big Dig deliver?', *The Boston Globe* 29 December 2015. [Online] BostonGlobe.com. Available at: bostonglobe.com/magazine/2015/12/29/years-later-did-big-dig-deliver/tSb8PIMS4QJUETsMpA7Spl/story.html (Accessed 23 May 2017).

Graham, S., (2016). Vertical: The City from Satellites to Bunkers. London: Verso.

Harris, A.., (2014) 'Vertical Urbanists — opening up geographies of the three-dimensional city'. Progress in Human Geography, Volume 39, 5, December 2014 pp601 – 620. Thousand Oaks: Sage Publications.

Hong Kong Drainage Services Department, (2014). Tai Hang Tung Storage Scheme (THTSS) [Online] Available at: dsd.gov.hk/EN/HTML/395.html (Accessed 15 July 2016).

Huan-Qing, L., Aurèle, P., Philippe, T., & Xiao-Zhao, L., (2013) 'An Integrated Planning Concept for the Emerging Underground Urbanism: Deep City Method Part 1 Concept, process and application' *Tunnelling and Underground Space Technology*, Volume 38 Pages 559 – 568. Philadelphia: Elsevier.

Kim, A.M., (2016). 'The Extreme Primacy of Location: Beijing's Underground Rental Housing Market', *Cities*, Volume 52, March 2016, pp148–158. [Online] Available at: www.sciencedirect.com/science/article/pii/S0264275115300196 (Accessed 10 July 2016).

Kaur, K., (21 March 2017) 'Changi's Jewel Shaping up well for a sparkling start in 2019', The Straits Times. [Online] Available at: straitstimes.com/singapore/changis-jewel-shaping-up-well-for-sparkling-start-in-2019 (Accessed 22 May 2017).

Parriaux, A., Tacher, L. & Joliquin, P., (2004). 'The hidden side of cities—towards three-dimensional land planning'. *Energy and Buildings* 36(4): pp335-341. Amsterdam: Elsevier.

Rose Fitzgerald Kennedy Greenway Conservancy, (2017). Visiting the Greenway [Online] Available at: rosekennedygreenway.org/visit/visiting/ (Accessed 04 April 2017).

Utudjian, É., (1972). L'urbanisme souterrain, Paris: Presses universitaires de France.

Wainwright, O., (2012). 'Billionaires' basements: the luxury bunkers making holes in London streets'. [Online] *The Guardian*. Available at: theguardian.com/artanddesign/2012/nov/09/billionaires-basements-london-houses-architecture (Accessed 22 May 2017).

Wetherell, (2015). Mayfair Residential Market Update End of Year Report 2015 [Online] Available at: wetherell.co.uk/wp-content/uploads/2015/12/Wetherell-End-of-Year-Report-2015.pdf (Accessed 28 August 2016).

Winston, A., (5 December 2014). Moshe Safdie's huge greenhouse for Singapore's Changi airport gets underway', *Dezeen*. [Online] Available at: dezeen.com/2014/12/05/moshe-safdie-huge-greenhouse-singapore-changi-airport/ (Accessed 22 May 2017).

Zhang, S., (9 July 2016). 'How to Fit the World's Biggest Indoor Waterfall in An Airport'. *Wired*. [Online] Available at: www.wired.com/2016/09/fit-worlds-biggest-indoor-waterfall-airport/ (Accessed 13 May 2017).

Understanding the Underground

Abu Dhabi Urban Planning Council, (2015). Abu Dhabi Urban Street Design Manual [Online] Available at: file:///Users/lizreynolds/Downloads/Urban%20Street%20Design%20Manual%20-%20Overview.pdf (Accessed 19 December 2017).

Abu Dhabi Urban Planning Council, (2016). Utility Corridors Design Manual [Online] Available at: file:///Users/lizreynolds/Downloads/compressed_UCDM_English.pdf (Accesssed 19 December 2017).

Abu Dhabi Urban Planning Council, (2015). Abu Dhabi Urban Street and Utility Design Tool [Online] Available at: usdm.upc.gov.ae/USDM/ (Accesssed 19 December 2017).

Balch, O. (2017). A world without waste: the rise of urban mining. *The Guardian*. [Online] Available at: https://www.theguardian.com/sustainable-business/2016/oct/25/urban-mining-recyling-waste-buildings-offices-cities (Accessed 22 May 2017).

British Geological Survey, (2014). Heat Energy Below Glasgow. [Online] Available at: bgs.ac.uk/research/energy/geothermal/heatEnergyGlasgow.html (Accessed 19 March 2017).

Chaussarda, E., Wdowinskia, S., Cabral-Canob, E., & Amelunga, F., (2014). 'Land subsidence in central Mexico detected by ALOS InSAR time-series'. Remote Sensing of Environment, Volume 140, January 2014, pp94–106. Elsevier: Amsterdam.

Danish Architecture Centre, (2014). 'Reykjavik: The Ground Heats the City'. Sustainable Cities. 21 January 2014 [Online] Available at: dac.dk/en/dac-cities/sustainable-cities/all-cases/energy/reykjavik-the-ground-heats-the-city/ (Accessed 19 March 2017).

Dobraszczyk, P., Galviz, C., & Garrett, B., (2016). Global Undergrounds: Exploring Cities Within. London: Reaktion Publishing.

European Geothermal Energy Council, (2012). Developing Geothermal Heat Pumps in Smart Cities and Communities. [Online] Available at: regeocities.eu/wp-content/uploads/2012/08/ReGeoCities-Final-Report_web.pdf (Accessed 19 March 2017).

Fulcher, B., Menge, S., & Grillo, J., (2013). New York City – Second Avenue Subway: MTA's 72nd Street Station and Tunnels Project Construction of a Large Span Station Cavern, Running Tunnels, Cross-Over and Turn-Out Caverns, Shafts and Entrances. [Online] Available at: me.smenet.org/docs/Publications/ME/Issue/May%201_WebOnly.pdf (Accesssed 19 December 2017).

Goel, R.K., Singh, B., & Zhao, J., (2012) Underground Infrastructures Planning, Design and Construction. London: Butterworth – Heinemann.

Graham, S., (2016). *Vertical: The City from Satellites to Bunkers*. London: Verso.

Kimmelman, M., (2017). 'Mexico City, Parched and Sinking,

Faces a Water Crisis'. *The New York Times* [Online] Available at: nytimes.com/interactive/2017/02/17/world/americas/mexico-city-sinking.html (Accesssed 19 March 2017).

Manaugh, G., (2009). Bldgblog Book: Architectural Conjecture, Urban Speculation, Landscape Futures. San Francisco: Chronicle Books.

Midttømme, K., Banks, D., Kalskin Ramstad, R., Sæther, O.M., & Skarphagen, H., (2008). Ground-Source Heat Pumps and Underground Thermal Energy Storage — Energy for the future. ResearchGate [Online] Available at: researchgate.net/publication/233933871_Ground-source_heat_pumps_and_underground_thermal_energy_storage_-_Energy_for_the_future (Accessed 19 March 2017).

Phien-wej, N., Giao, P.H., & Nutalaya, P., (2006). 'Land subsidence in Bangkok, Thailand'. Engineering Geology. Volume 82, Issue 4, pp187 – 201. Amsterdam: Elsevier.

Revesz, A., Chaer, I., Thompson, J., Mavroulidou, M., Gunn, M., & Maidment, G., (2016). 'Ground source heat pumps and their interactions with underground railway tunnels in an urban environment: A review'. *Applied Thermal Engineering*. Volume 93, 25 January 2016, pp147 – 154. Amsterdam: Elsevier. Sinsakul, S., (2000).

Sinsakul, S., (2000). 'Late Quaternary geology of the Lower Central Plain, Thailand'. *Journal of Asian Earth Sciences*. Volume 18, Issue 4, pp415–426. Amsterdam: Elsevier.

Sneider, J., (2017). 'Stand clear: New York City's Second Avenue Subway is finally here', *Progressive Railroading*. [Online] Available at: progressiverailroading.com/passenger_rail/article/Stand-clear-New-York-Citys-Second-Avenue-Subway-is-finally-here--53202 (Accessed 19 December 2017).

Solis, J., (2005). *New York Underground: The Anatomy of a City*. New York: Routledge.

Squires, N., (2017). 'Rome unveils 'museum' metro station packed with hundreds of ancient artefacts found during construction', 5th May 2017 *The Telegraph*. [Online] Available at: telegraph.co.uk/news/2017/05/05/rome-unveils-museum-metro-station-packed-hundreds-ancient-artifacts/?WT.mc_id=tmg_share_tw (Accessed 19 December 2017).

St. John, A., Frost, S., Barker, J., & Harris, D., (2016). 'Crossrail project: a deep-mined station on the Elizabeth line, London'. *Proceedings of the Institution of Civil Engineers*. [Online] Available at: learninglegacy.crossrail.co.uk/wp-content/uploads/2017/03/7A-028-A-Deep-Mined-Station-on-the-Elizabeth-line.pdf (Accesssed 25 March 2107).

Thienen-Visser, K., V, and Breunese, J. N., (2015). 'Induced seismicity of the Groningen gas field: History and recent developments'. T*he Leading Edge*. 34(6), pp664 – 671. Tulsa: Society of exploration Geophysicists.

Waterfield, B., (05 July 2013). 'Earthquakes from onshore gas drilling threaten a disaster, warn residents of Dutch city'. *The Telegraph*. [Online] Available at: telegraph.co.uk/news/worldnews/europe/netherlands/10162343/Earthquakes-from-onshore-gas-drilling-threaten-a-disaster-warn-residents-of-Dutch-city.html (Accessed 18 March 2017).

Planning in 3D

100 Resilient Cities, (2018). *Paris' Resilience Challenge*. [Online] Available at: 100resilientcities.org/cities/paris/ (Accesssed 11 January 2018).

Abu Baker, J., (2016). 'Orchard Malls not biting on grants for underground links'. *The Straits Times*. [Online] Available at: straitstimes.com/singapore/orchard-malls-not-biting-on-grants-for-underground-links (Accessed 14 May 2017).

Admiraal, H., (2015). 'Think Deep: Planning, development and use of underground space in cities'. *The Hague: International Society of City and Regional Planning*. [Online] Available at: isocarp.org/app/uploads/2015/05/FINAL_Think-Deep.pdf (Accessed 21 May 2017).

Admiraal, J.B.M., (2008) Building on underground space awareness. *Underground Infrastructure of Urban Areas*. London: CRC Press.

Allen, K., (2014). London goes underground: the city's subterranean building boom', *Financial Times* 14 March 2014, [Online] Available at: https://www.ft.com/content/c8b32740-a483-11e3-9cb0-00144feab7de (Accessed on 30 April 2017).

Araki, N., (2016). 'The PARK•ING Ginza. .*ArchDaily* (12 Jul 2016). [Online] Available at: www.archdaily.com/790709/the-parking-ginza-nobuo-araki-the-archetype/ (Accessed 21 May 2017).

Arcilla, P., (2015). 'JKMM's Helsinki Amos Anderson Art Museum to be Built Underground'. *ArchDaily* [Online] Available at: www.archdaily.com/625134/jkmm-s-helsinki-amos-anderson-art-museum-to-be-built-underground (Accessed 14 May 2017).

Balch, O., (2017). 'A world without waste: the rise of urban mining', *The Guardian* (25th October 2016). [Online] Available at: www.theguardian.com/sustainable-business/2016/oct/25/urban-mining-recyling-waste-buildings-offices-cities (Accessed 22 May 2017).

Barbara, A., (2017). 'The Challenges of Building Amsterdam's New Metro—the North-South Line'. *TEDxAmsterdam*. [Online] Available at: http://tedx.amsterdam/2015/09/the-challenges-of-building-amsterdams-new-metro-the-north-south-line/ (Accessed 21 May 2017).

Belanger, P., (2016). 'Altitudes of Urbanisation'. *Tunnelling and Underground Space Technology*. Volume 55, May 2016. Amsterdam: Elsevier.

Braess, D., Nagurney, A., & Wakolbinger, T., (2005) 'On a Paradox of Traffic Planning'. *Transportation Science*, Volume 39, 2005, pp446–450. [Online] Available at: pubsonline.informs.org/doi/abs/10.1287/trsc.1050.0127 (Accessed 22 May 2017).

Bureau of Urban Development Tokyo Metropolitan Government, (2017). *Outline of the City Planning*. [Online] Available at: www.toshiseibi.metro.tokyo.jp/eng/ (Accessed 20 May 2017).

Central Committee of the Communist Party of China (Compilation and Translation Bureau), (2015) *The 13th Five-Year Plan for Economic and Social Development of the People's Republic of China 2016 - 2020*. [Online] Available at: en.ndrc. gov.cn/newsrelease/201612/P020161207645765233498.pdf (Accessed 20 May 2017).

City of Espoo, Finland, (2017). Länsimetro [Online] Available at: www.lansimetro.fi/en/home/ (Accessed 19 December 2017).

City of Helsinki, Planning Department, (2013) *Helsinki City Plan Urban plan — the new Helsinki city plan Vision 2050*. [Online] Available at: www.hel.fi/hel2/ksv/julkaisut/yos_2013-23_en.pdf (Accessed 20 May 2017).

City of Helsinki, Planning Department, (2012). *Detailed Planning in Helsinki*. [Online] Available at: www.hel.fi/hel2/ksv/julkaisut/esitteet/esite_2012-3.pdf (Accessed 20 May 2017).

City of Helsinki, (2016) *Helsinki population continued strong growth in 2015*. [Online] Available at: www.hel.fi/uutiset/en/helsinki/population-growth (Accessed 14 May 2017).

City of New York, (2016). *Current and Estimated Populations*. [Online] Available at: www1.nyc.gov/site/planning/data-maps/nyc-population/current-future-populations.page (Accessed 2 July 2017).

City of Paris, (2017). *Reinventer Paris: The subterranean secrets of Paris*. [Online] Available at: http://www.reinventer.paris/en/home/ (Accesssed 7 January 2017).

Civil Engineering and Development Department Hong Kong SARG, (2017) *Pilot Study on Underground Space Development in Selected Strategic Urban Area*. [Online] Available at: www.urbanunderground.gov.hk/main.php (Accessed 2 July 2017).

Clement, A., & Thomas, G., (2001). *'Atlas du Paris souterrain: la doublure sombre de la ville lumière'*. Paris: Parigramme.

COST (European Cooperation in Science and Technology), (2016). *COST SUB-URBAN*. [Online] Available at: urbanunderground.community/Homepage/cost%20sub-urban.html (Accessed 11 June 2017).

Drainage Services Department Hong Kong, (2017). *Happy Valley Underground Stormwater Storage Scheme*. [Online] Available at: hvusss.eksx.com/index.php (Accessed 1 July 2017).

Drainage Services Department Hong Kong, (2017). *Relocation of Sea Tin Sewage Treatment Works to Caverns*. [Online] Available at: http://www.ststwincaverns.hk/index.php?lang=en (Accessed 02 July 2017).

Engel, M., (2014) 'The battle for Lord's cricket ground'. *Financial Times* [Online] Available at: www.ft.com/content/ba593db6-cad9-11e3-ba95-00144feabdc0 (Accessed 30 April 2017).

European Commission, (1999) *European Spatial Development Perspective: Toward Balanced and Sustainable development of the Territory of the European Union*. [Online] Available at: www.esponusespon.eu/dane/web_usespon_library_files/1228/esdp_european_spatial_development_perspective.pdf

(Accessed 30 April 2017).

Finn, R., (2017). 'The Great Race for Manhattan Air Rights'. *New York Times* (24th February 2013). [Online] Available at: http://www.nytimes.com/2013/02/24/realestate/the-great-race-for-manhattan-air-rights.html (Accessed 22 May 2017).

Gasser, M., (2003) 'Fenster und Leuchten', Factor Light. *Swiss Agency for Efficient Energy Use*, No. 4, 2003. Factor Light [Online] Available at: http://www.energie.gr.ch/merkblatter/faktorlicht04.pdf (Accesssed 12 January 2018).

Geotechnical Engineering Office of Hong Kong, (2009). *Enhanced Use of Underground Space in Hong Kong — Feasibility Study*. [Online] Available at: http://www.cedd.gov.hk/eng/underground_space/doc/Hong_Kong_Undergound_Space_Study-Executive_Summary.pdf (Accessed 21 May 2017).

Government of the Netherlands, (2017). *Spatial Planning in The Netherlands*. [Online] Available at: www.government.nl/topics/spatial-planning-and-infrastructure/contents/spatial-planning-in-the-netherlands (Accessed 21 May 2017).

Greater London Authority, (2009) *London's foundations: protecting the geodiversity of the capital*. [Online] Available at: www.londongeopartnership.org.uk/downloads/Londons%20Foundations%202009.pdf (Accessed 30 April 2017).

Greater London Authority, (2017) *London Datastore*. [Online] available at: https://data.london.gov.uk (Accessed 30 April 2017).

Greater London Authority, (2017) *The London Plan*. [Online] Available at: www.london.gov.uk/what-we-do/planning/london-plan/current-london-plan (Accessed 30 April 2017).

Greater London Authority, (2017) *Waste heat from the Tube will help warm hundreds of homes*. [Online] available at: www.london.gov.uk/press-releases-5910 (Accessed 30 April 2017).

Hawkins, A., (2017). 'Flying taxis or futuristic tunnels won't save us from the misery of traffic'. *The Verge*. [Online] Available at: www.theverge.com/2017/5/6/15518040/elon-musk-boring-company-uber-flying-car-public-transportation (Accessed 22 May 2017).

Hong Kong Special Administrative Region Government, Planning Department, (2016). *Land Supply Considerations and Approach*. [Online] Available at: www.hk2030plus.hk/document/Land%20Supply%20Considerations%20and%20Approach_Eng.pdf (Accessed 1 July 2017).

Hong Kong Special Administrative Region Government, Planning Department, (2016). *Planning and Urban Design for a Liveable High-Density City*. [Online] Available at: hk2030plus.hk/document/Planning%20and%20Urban%20Design%20for%20a%20Liveable%20High-Density%20City_Eng.pdf (Accessed 1 July 2017).

Hong Kong Special Administrative Region Government, Planning Department, (2017). *Hong Kong 2030+: Towards a Planning Vision and Strategy Transcending 2030*. [Online] Available at: www.hk2030plus.hk/ (Accessed 25 June 2017).

References

Hongo, J., (2014). 'Tokyo underground: taking property development to new depths'. *The Japan Times*. [Online] Available at: www.japantimes.co.jp/life/2014/04/12/lifestyle/tokyo-underground/#.WSCdYBPyuuU (Accessed 21 May 2017).

Hornby, L., (2017). 'Beijing's migrants no longer welcome as city caps population' *Financial Times* [Online] Available at: www.ft.com/content/822e982c-1b40-11e7-bcac-6d03d067f81f (Accessed 17 May 2017).

Huang, Y., 2004 'Urban Spatial Patterns and Infrastructure in Beijing' — *Land Lines October 2004* [Online]. Available at: www.lincolninst.edu/publications/articles/urban-spatial-patterns-infrastructure-beijing (Accessed 17 May 2017).

James, B. W., (2007). 'Expanding the gap: How the Rural Property System exacerbates China's Urban-rural Gap', *Columbia Journal of Asian Law*, 20:2: 451 (Accessed 20 May 2017).

Kruse, J. & Ellsworth, E., (2011). *Geologic city. 1st ed.* [New York]: Smudge Studio.

KPMG Hauzhen LLP, (2016). *The 13th Five-Year Plan – China's transformation and integration with the world Economy Opportunities for Chinese and foreign businesse*s [Online] Available at: assets.kpmg.com/content/dam/kpmg/cn/pdf/en/2016/10/13fyp-opportunities-analysis-for-chinese-and-foreign-businesses.pdf (Accessed 20 May 2017).

Langewiesche, W., (2017). 'New York Underground: A Centuries-Old Underworld of Caverns, Squatters, and Unmarked Doors', *Vanity Fair*. [Online] Available at: www.vanityfair.com/news/politics/2013/10/new-york-city-underground-subway-danger (Accessed 04 July 2017).

Leavenworth, S., (2016). 'Beijing has fallen: China's capital sinking by 11cm a year, satellite study warns', *The Guardian*. [Online] Available at: www.theguardian.com/world/2016/jun/24/beijing-has-fallen-chinas-capital-sinking-by-11cm-a-year-satellite-study-warns (Accessed 20 May 2017).

Li, H-Q., Parriaux, A., & Thalman, P., (2012). 'The Way to Plan a Sustainable "Deep City": *The Strategic Framework and Economic Model',* 13th ACUUS conference "Underground Space Development – Opportunities and Challenges (7 – 9 November 2012). [Online] Available at: ai2-s2-pdfs.s3.amazonaws.com/ef73/063ae9499cce9af5dc3334efe9a9ea2b4a8c.pdf (Accessed 31 December 2017).

Mansfield, I., (2017). *London's Lost Pneumatic Railways eBook.* [Online] Available at: www.amazon.co.uk/Londons-Lost-Pneumatic-Railways-Mansfield-ebook/dp/B00ABXMXDI/ref=sr_1_1?s=books&ie=UTF8&qid=1495445454&sr=1-1&keywords=pneumatic+railways (Accessed 22 May 2017).

Masuda, Y., Takahashi, N., & Ojima, T., (2004). *Utilization of Deep Underground Space in Tokyo — Urban Renewal with the City's New Backbone Lifeline.* [Online] Available at: global.ctbuh.org/resources/papers/download/1590-utilization-of-deep-underground-space-in-tokyo-urban-renewal-with-the-citys-new-backbone-lifeline.pdf (Accessed 20 May 2017).

Maurice, R., (2013). 'Zoning and urban development control'. European Network for Housing Research 2013 Conference: overcoming the crisis, Jun 2013, *Tarragone, Espagne*. [Online] Available at: halshs.archives-ouvertes.fr/halshs-00921226/file/13-05-30_paper_ENHR_R._Maurice.pdf (Accesssed 11 January 2018).

Metropole du Grand Paris, (2017). Grand Paris Project. [Online] Available at: http://www.grand-paris.jll.fr/en/grand-paris-project/overview/ (Accessed 11 January 2018).

Ministry of Infrastructure and the Environment, Government of the Netherlands, (2011). *Summary National Policy Strategy for Infrastructure and Spatial Planning Making the Netherlands competitive, accessible, liveable and safe.* [Online] Available at: file:///Users/lizreynolds/Downloads/summary-national-policy-strategy-for-infrastructure-and-spatial-planning.pdf (Accesssed 21 May 2017).

Ministry of Land, Infrastructure, Transport and Tourism, Japan (MILT), (2017). *An Overview of Spatial Policy in Asian and European Countries.* [Online] Available at: www.mlit.go.jp/kokudokeikaku/international/spw/general/france/index_e.html (Accesssed 11 January 2018).

Netherlands Court of Audit, (2017). *Spatial planning in the Netherlands.* [Online] Available at: www.youtube.com/watch?v=l2vC6-tecZg (Accessed 21 May 2017).

Nishioka, S., Y. Tannaka, et al, (2007). 'Deep Underground Usage for Effective Executing of City Facility Construction'. *11th ACUUS Conference*: "Underground Space: Expanding the Frontiers". Athens: Greece.

New York City, (2015). OneNYC. [Online] Available at: https://onenyc.cityofnewyork.us/wp-content/uploads/2019/10/OneNYC-2050-Full-Report-10.3.pdf (Accessed 2 July 2017)

NYC and Company, (2017). *NYC Travel & Tourism Visitation Statistics.* [Online] Available at: www.nycandcompany.org/research/nyc-statistics-page (Accessed 2 July 2017).

Paris Region, (2017). *Key Figures.* [Online] Available at: parisregion.eu/ (Accesssed 28 December 2017).

Reynolds, E., & Reynolds, P., (2015). 'Planning for Underground Spaces NY-Lon Underground'. *Think Deep: Planning, development and use of underground space in cities.* [Online] Available at: isocarp.org/app/uploads/2015/05/FINAL_Think-Deep.pdf (Accessed 19 December 2017).

Royal Borough of Kensington and Chelsea, (2016) *Basements Supplementary Planning Document.* [Online] Available at: www.rbkc.gov.uk/sites/default/files/atoms/files/01%20160414%20Final%20Basements%20SPD.pdf (Accesssed 29 April 2017).

Share, J., (2014). [Online] 'Geological Legacies of Paris Basin', *Written in Stone – Seen through my Lens.* Available at: written-in-stone-seen-through-my-lens.blogspot.co.uk/2014/06/geological-legacies-of-paris-basin-part.html (Accesssed 8 January 2018).

Singapore Department of Statistics, (2017). *Statistics*. [Online] Available at: http://www.singstat.gov.sg/statistics/latest-data#16 (Accesssed 29 April 2017).

Societé du Grand Paris, (2017). *Grand Paris Express*. [Online] Available at: www.societedugrandparis.fr/info/grand-paris-express-largest-transport-project-europe-1061 (Accesssed 9 January 2018).

Tatcher, O., (2017). 'Hong Kong must not rush into underground development' (05 February 2017) — *South China Morning Post*. [Online] Available at: www.scmp.com/comment/insight-opinion/article/2067868/hong-kong-should-not-rush-developing-underground-space-ease (Accessed 23 May 2017).

The Boring Company, (2017). *FAQ*. [Online] Available at: www.boringcompany.com/faq/ (Accessed 22 May 2017).

Tokyo Metropolitan Government, (2014). *Creating the Future: 0The Long-Term Vision for Tokyo*. [Online] Available at: www.metro.tokyo.jp/ENGLISH/ABOUT/VISION/index.htm (Accessed 21 May 2017).

Tokyo Metropolitan Government, (2017). *Tokyo's History, Geography, and Population*. [Online] Available at: www.metro.tokyo.jp/ENGLISH/ABOUT/HISTORY/history02.htm (Accessed 21 May 2017).

Urban Redevelopment Authority, (2012). Circular URA/PB/2012/12-CUDG: Central Area Underground Master PLan Revisions to the cash grant incentive scheme for underground pedestrian links. [Online] Available at: https://www.ura.gov.sg/-/media/User%20Defined/URA%20Online/circulars/2012/aug/dc12-12.pdf (Accessed on 19 December 2017).

Visser, R., (2008). 'Diagnosing Beijing 2020: Mapping the Ungovernable City', *Footprint*. [Online] Available at: journals.library.tudelft.nl/index.php/footprint/article/view/674 (Accessed 18 May 2017).

Wainwright, O., (2012). 'Billionaires' basements: the luxury bunkers making holes in London streets'. [Online] *The Guardian*. Available at: www.theguardian.com/artanddesign/2012/nov/09/billionaires-basements-london-houses-architecture (Accessed 22 May 2017).

Wainwright, O., (2016). Story of cities #4: Beijing and the earliest planning document in history (17 March 2016) - *The Guardian* [online]. Available at: www.theguardian.com/cities/2016/mar/17/story-cities-beijing-earliest-planning-document-history (Accessed 17 May 2017)

Wainwright, O., (2017). 'Billionaires' basements: the luxury bunkers making holes in London streets. [Online] *The Guardian*. Available at: https://www.theguardian.com/artanddesign/2012/nov/09/billionaires-basements-london-houses-architecture (Accessed 22 May 2017).

Wang, L.H., (2015). 'Underground and Cavern Space Development in Hong Kong', *Think Deep: Planning, development and use of underground space in cities*. [Online] Available at: isocarp.org/app/uploads/2015/05/FINAL_Think-Deep.pdf (Accessed 19 December 2017).

Yan Min, C., (2014). 'Jurong Rock Caverns officially opened after eight years of construction', *The Straits Times*. [Online] Available at: www.straitstimes.com/singapore/jurong-rock-caverns-officially-opened-after-eight-years-of-construction (Accessed 19 December 2017).

Adapting Underground Spaces

Crossrail, (2016). *Ground settlement — managing the effects of tunnelling*. [Online] Available at: www.crossrail.co.uk/construction/managing-the-effects-of-construction/ground-settlement-managing-the-effects-of-tunnelling (Accessed 6 July 2016).

Dickson, D., (2011). *The Vertical Farm*. New York: St. Marten's.

Digua Community, (2016). 'Digua Community', *Facebook*. [Online] Available at: www.facebook.com/diguacommunity/ (Accesssed 6 January 2018).

Dobraszczyk, P., Galviz, C. & Garrett, B.L., (2016). *Global Undergrounds: Exploring cities within*. London: Reaktion.

Feng, E., (2016). 'Breathing life into spaces well beyond 6 feet under Beijing's streets', *New York Times*. [Online] Available at: http://www.nytimes.com/2016/03/22/world/asia/beijing-bomb-shelters.html?_r=1 (Accessed 10 July 2016).

Harvey, D., (2009). *Social Justice and the City (Geographies of Justice and Social Transformation*. Georgia: University of Georgia Press.

Hickey, (2015). The Innovators: London air-raid shelters sprout a growing concern', *The Guardian*, 13 September 2015. [Online] Available at: https://www.theguardian.com/business/2015/sep/13/the-innovators-london-air-raid-shelters-sprout-a-growing-concern (Accesssed 6 January 2018).

Kong, P.-Y., Nowek, A., Beekmans, J., Gelmers, W., & de Boer, J., (2016) 'Beijng's underground bomb shelters get new life as community centers', *Pop Up City*. [Online] Available at: http://popupcity.net/beijngs-underground-bomb-shelters-get-new-life-as-community-centers/ (Accessed: 9 July 2016).

Rifkin, J., (2013). *The Third Industrial Revolution*. Basingstoke: Palgrave Macmillan.

Singer, M., (2011). *Dark Days*. London: Dog Woof Films.

Soja, E.W., (2000) *Postmetropolis: Critical Studies of Cities and Regions*. Chichester: Wiley-Blackwell.

Staff, N., (2014) 'A universe beneath our feet': Life in Beijing's Underground, *National Public Radio*. [Online] Available at: http://www.npr.org/2014/12/07/368760646/a-universe-beneath-our-feet-life-in-beijings-underground (Accessed 10 July 2016).

Transport for London, (2004). *TfL secures planning permission to bring former WWII deep-level shelter to life*. [Online] Available at: tfl.gov.uk/info-for/media/press-releases/2015/december/tfl-secures-planning-permission-to-bring-former-wwii-deep-level-shelter-to-life (Accessed: 6 July 2016).

Transport for London, (2016). *The future of the Rotunda at Clapham*. [Online] Available at: consultations.tfl.gov.uk/general/rotunda-clapham/user_uploads/the-rotunda-at-clapham.pdf (Accesssed 7 January 2018).

Von Meijenfeldt, E., (2003). *Below Ground Level: Creating New Spaces for Contemporary Architecture*. Basel: Birkhauser Verlag AG.

Architectural responses to the Underground

Crossrail, (2016). *Ground settlement — managing the effects of tunnelling*. [Online] Available at: www.crossrail.co.uk/construction/managing-the-effects-of-construction/ground-settlement-managing-the-effects-of-tunnelling (Accessed: 6 July 2016).

Arne Fender Katsalidis, (2016). Museum of Old and New Art (MONA) [Online] Available at: http://www.afkstudios.com/project/museum-for-old-and-new-art-mona/culture (Accessed: 10 July 2016).

Australian Government Department of the Environment and Energy, (2016). *Moorilla Estate Residences, 655 Main Rd, Berriedale, TAS, Australia*. [Online] Available at: www.environment.gov.au/cgi-bin/ahdb/search.pl?mode=place_detail;search=list_code%3DRNE%3Bkeyword%3Dmoorilla%3Bkeyword_PD%3Don%3Bkeyword_SS%3Don%3Bkeyword_ (Accessed 10 July 2017).

Franklin, A. (2014). *The Making of MONA*. Pengiun Books Australia: Melbourne.

Stevens, P., (2015). 'Bjarke ingels expands gammel hellerup school beneath a lifted football field', *Designboom*. [Online] Available at: https://www.designboom.com/architecture/bjarke-ingels-group-big-gammel-hellerup-gymnasium-expansion-copenhagen-05-12-2015/ (Accessed 10 July 2016).

Tourism Tasmania, (2016). MONA Visitor Profile September 2016. [Online] Available at: http://www.tourismtasmania.com.au/__data/assets/pdf_file/0006/44691/MONA-Visitor-Profile-YE-June-2016.pdf (Accessed 12 November 2016)

Creating Quality Underground Spaces

Assemble, (2017). *Folly for a Flyover*. [Online] Available at: assemblestudio.co.uk/?page_id=5 (Accesssed 16 July 2017).

Berg, N., (2011). *Classic Documentary on Public Space Now Available* [Online] Available at: www.citylab.com/design/2011/10/social-life-public-space/237/ (Accesssed 27 July 2017).

Black, A., Luna, P., Lund, O., & Walker, S., (2017)., *Information Design: Research and Practice*. London: Routledge.

British Standards Institute, (2014). Guidance on sound insulation and noise reduction for buildings. [Online] Available at: http://bailey.persona-pi.com/Public-Inquiries/M4-Newport/C%20-%20Core%20Documents/14.%20Noise%20and%20Vibration/14.2.14.pdf (Accesssed 28 July 2017).

Budds, D., (2016). *How One Florida City is Reinventing Itself with UX Design*. [Online] Available at: www.fastcodesign.com/3065107/how-one-florida-city-is-reinventing-itself-with-ux-design (Accesssed 27 July 17).

Burton, G., Korda, S., & Qualmann, C., (2010). 'Fear on the Bridge', *Pedley Street RIP*. [Online] Available at: pedleystreetrip.blogspot.co.uk/2010/07/fear-on-bridge.html (Accessed 15 July 2017).

City of Toronto, (2018). *PATH — Toronto's Downtown Pedestrian Walkway*. [Online] Available at: www.toronto.ca/explore-enjoy/visitor-services/path-torontos-downtown-pedestrian-walkway/ (Accesssed 30 July 2017).

Cree, (2013). *Pedestrian Upgrade Brooklyn Bridge* [Online] Available at: www.cree.com/lighting (Accesssed 17 July 2017).

Crossrail, (2015). *Crossrail's final shipment of earth arrives at Wallasea island*. [Online] Available at: www.crossrail.co.uk/news/articles/crossrails-final-shipment-of-earth-arrives-at-wallasea-island (Accessed 12 July 2016).

Cullen, G., (1961) *Townscape*. London: The Architectural Press.

Delaney. P. E., (1983). *Sandhogs A History of the Tunnel Workers of New York*. New York: Clark & Fritts.

De Muynck, B., (2008). 'Ewha Campus Complex, Seoul, by Dominique Perrault' *Icon*. [Online] Available at: www.iconeye.com/404/item/3543-ewha-campus-complex-seoul (Accesssed 31 July 2017).

Department for Culture Media and Sport, (2015). The Farrell Review. [Online] Available at: www.farrellreview.co.uk/ (Accesssed 27 July 2017).

Design Trust for Public Space, (2015). *Under the Elevated*. New York: Design Trust for Public Space.

Elledge, J., (2017). 'London's Tube has been running so long it's literally raising the temperature of the earth around it'.

Citymetric. [Online] Available at: www.citymetric.com/transport/londons-tube-has-been-running-so-long-its-literally-raising-temperature-earth-around-it (Accesssed 31 July 2017).

Fawcett-Tang, R., (2008). *Mapping graphic navigational systems*. Rotovision SA: Switzerland.

Gardiner, J., (2013). *Case Studies of basement excavation in relation to programme and vehicle movements*. London: Alan Baxter and Associates LLP.

Garnett, M., Bell, I., Turpin, N., Marino, L., Riggs, T., Cadman, R., Johnson, B., Ruane, D., Thomas, S., & Newkey-Burden, T., (2015) *Station Design Idiom*. London: Transport for London.

Gasser, M., (2003) 'Fenster und Leuchten', Factor Light. Swiss Agency for Efficient Energy Use, No. 4, 2003. Factor Light [Online] Available at: http://www.energie.gr.ch/merkblatter/faktorlicht04.pdf (Accessed 12 January 2018).

GLA, (2017). *London Datastore*. [Online] Available at: data.london.gov.uk/ (Accesssed 27 July 2017).
Hashiguchi, S., (2017). 'Kogane Studio', *Shift City Guide*. [Online] Available at: www.shift.jp.org/guide/yokohama/others/kogane-studio.html (Accessed 16 July 2017).

Hechaime, S., (2014). *Urban Factorisation Report*. [Online] Available at: www.definingfactors.com/wp-content/uploads/2014/10/factors-_-urban-factorisation-lab-findings-report.pdf (Accessed 29 July 2017).

Henley, S. & Barr, S., (2009). *The architecture of parking*. 1st ed. London: Thames & Hudson.

Hongo, J, (2014). 'Tokyo underground: taking property development to new depths'. *The Japan Times*. [Online] Available at: www.japantimes.co.jp/life/2014/04/12/lifestyle/tokyo-underground/#.WYCJptPyuuV (Accesssed 31 July 2017).

IDEO (2015) *The Field Guide to Human-Centered Design* [Online] Available at: www.designkit.org/human-centered-design ISBN: 978-0-9914063-1-9 (Accesssed 27 July 2017).

Light Lab., (2014). *Spotlight Kings Cross Tunnel Light Wall Bespoke Lighting*. [Online] Available at: www.thelightlab.com/new-project-focus-kings-cross-tunnel-light-wall/ (Accessed 16 July 2017).

Liotta, S., (2013). *Architecture Reincarnated*. [Online] Available at: http://www.domusweb.it/en/architecture/2013/06/26/architecture_reincarnated.html (Accessed 16 July 2017).

Lovell, S. (2011). *As Little Design as Possible*. 1st ed. London: Phaidon.

Lowline, (2018). How can we build more green space in our cities? [Online] Available at: http://thelowline.org/ (Accessed on 7 January 2018).

Meijenfeldt, E., V., (2003) *Below Ground Level: Creating New Spaces for Contemporary Architecture*. Berlin: Birkhauser Verlag AG.

Metropolitan Museum of Art, (2016). *The Future of Mapping and Wayfinding at The Met*. [Online] Available at: www.metmuseum.org/blogs/digital-underground/2016/future-of-mapping-and-wayfinding (Accesssed 31 July 2017).

O'Neill, P., (2012). 'Why New York has the most valuable muck in the world'. *City Atlas* [Online] Available at: newyork.thecityatlas.org/lifestyle/why-new-york-has-the-most-valuable-muck-in-the-world/ (Accessed 12 July 2016).

Otterness, T., (2017). *Life Underground —Artworks —Tom Otterness*. [Online] Available at: www.tomostudio.com/artworks/life-underground (Accessed 16 July 2017).

Project for Public Spaces, (2010). *William H Whyte*. [Online] Available at: www.pps.org/reference/wwhyte/ (Accesssed 27 July 2017).

Renfroe, N, A., & Smith, J.L., (2014). *Threat / Vulnerability Assessments and Risk Analysis*. Washington, DC: National Institute of Building Sciences.

Rogers, E., (2003). 'Metropolitan Library'. *The New York Times*. [Online] Available at: www.nytimes.com/2003/05/12/nyregion/metropolitan-diary-654191.html (Accesssed 31 December 2017).

Steer Davies Gleave, (2016). *Toronto PATH*. [Online] Available at: dfm.steerdaviesgleave.com/home/path (Accesssed 30 July 2017).

Strategy, J., (2016). *Tokyo's Hippest New Select Shop is a Basement Parking Garage. Spoon & Tamago*. [Online] Available at: www.spoon-tamago.com/2016/03/29/tokyo-hiroshi-fujiwara-parking-garage/ (Accessed 16 July 2017).

Transport for London, (2014). *Improving the health of Londoners: transport action plan*. [Online] Available at: content.tfl.gov.uk/improving-the-health-of-londoners-transport-action-plan.pdf (Accessed 29 July 2017).

Transport for London, (2015). *London Underground Station Design Idiom*. [Online] Available at: content.tfl.gov.uk/station-design-idiom-2.pdf (Accesssed 29 July 2017).

Trust Housing Association, (2011). *Colour and Wayfinding*. [Online] Available at: www.trustha.org.uk/media/uploads/nlc/01_ColourWayfinding_15%2011.pdf (Accesssed 31 July 2017).

University of West England, (2015). *Noise Impacts on Health*. [Online] Available at: http://ec.europa.eu/environment/integration/research/newsalert/pdf/47si.pdf (Accesssed 31 July 2017).

US Green Building Council, (2014). LEED V4. [Online] Available at: www.usgbc.org/leed-v4-old-new (Accesssed 29 July 2017).

Walker, P., (2013). 'Construction lorries disproportionately responsible for cyclist deaths'. *The Guardian*. [Online] Available at: www.theguardian.com/lifeandstyle/2013/feb/01/construction-lorries-cyclist-deaths-report (Accessed 31 December 2017).

Wert, R., (2010). *'How to See New York's Secret City Hall Subway Stop', Jalopnik*. [Online] Available at: jalopnik.com/5684329/how-to-see-new-yorks-secret-city-hall-subway-stop (Accesssed 16 July 2017).

Whyte, W., H., (1980). *The Social Life of Small Urban Spaces*. New York: Project for Public Spaces Inc.

Wilmott & Associates, (2017). *Lyon Parc Auto*. [Online] Available at: www.wilmotte.com/en/project/273/Huit-Parkings-avec-interventions-dartistes-Lyon-Parc-Auto (Accessed 16 July 2017).

Yokoi, K., Yabuki, N., Fukuda, T., Michikawa, T., & Motamedi, A., (2015) *Wayfinding Assistance System for Underground Facilities Using Augmented Reality*. [Online] Available at: www.int-arch-photogramm-remote-sens-spatial-inf-sci.net/XL-4-W5/37/2015/isprsarchives-XL-4-W5-37-2015.pdf (Accesssed 30 July 2017).

Dedication
The Journalist, Urbanist and citizen advocate Jane Jacobs wrote many wise words, but perhaps the sweetest was *'at last I have finished my book!'* It is with love and thanks, that I dedicate this book to my husband and family.

Thanks
Sincere thanks to the International Society of City and
Regional Planners; International Tunnelling and
Underground Space Association; Urban Design Group;
and Academy of Urbanism — all of which operate with a
commitment to sharing knowledge on our built and natural
urban environments.

Thank you to all of the people who took time out of
their busy schedules to contribute to this book — it is an
incredibly inspiring mix of professionals, who are actively
working to make cities better places. To the researchers,
writers, illustrators and photographers who generously
shared their work, I thank you all for taking the time to
speak with me about your projects, and for being willing
to share your experiences with a wider audience.

A huge thank you to my patient publisher Routledge,
and also to BOB Design who through skilful visual
communication, have bought a complex subject to life.

Index

For Product Safety Concerns and Information please contact our EU
representative GPSR@taylorandfrancis.com
Taylor & Francis Verlag GmbH, Kaufingerstraße 24, 80331 München, Germany

www.ingramcontent.com/pod-product-compliance
Lightning Source LLC
Chambersburg PA
CBHW080131270326
41926CB00021B/4434